IT'S ALL IN THE
TIMING

PLAN, COOK, AND SERVE
GREAT MEALS WITH
CONFIDENCE

GAIL MONAGHAN

SURREY
BOOKS

AN AGATE IMPRINT

CHICAGO

Printed in China

Photographs on pages viii, 4, 7, 17, 41, 47, 50, 60, 65, 78, 99, 120, 131, 165, 168, 173, 186, 189, 203, 207, 216, 250, and 269 by Julia Becker.

Photographs on pages iv, 8, 54, 102, 160, 212, and 312 by Gary Duff.

Photograph on page 199 from iStock.com/rez-art.

Photograph on page 233 from iStock.com/dem10.

It's All in the Timing

ISBN-13: 978-1-57284-199-4

ISBN-10: 1-57284-199-0

First printing: November, 2016

Library of Congress Cataloging-in-Publication Data has been applied for.

10 9 8 7 6 5 4 3 2 1   16 17 18 19 20

Surrey is an imprint of Agate Publishing.
Agate books are available in bulk at discount prices.
agatepublishing.com

This book is dedicated to my many students,
whose enthusiasm, curiosity, and passion have
inspired these pages.

CONTENTS

Introduction, p. 1

The Flexibility of Making Ahead, p. 3

How to Use This Book, p. 5

Chapter 1: Dinner in a Flash, p. 8

45 Minutes or Less, p. 12

Green Vegetable Ragoût

Sizzling Cod Pan-Roast with Tomato–Caper Salsa

Potato, Veggie, and Garlic Smash

Boozy Bananas Foster

Fast French, p. 22

Fricassee of Mixed Mushrooms and Fresh Herbs

Oven-Finished Rib-Eye Steaks with Béarnaise Mayonnaise

Quick Roast of Potatoes and Red Onions

Mini Molten Chocolate Cakes

Mexican Fiesta, p. 32

Guacamole Salad

Store-Bought Tortilla Chips or Warm Tortillas

Pan-Seared Chipotle-Citrus Turkey Paillards with Adobo Mayonnaise

Mango and Plum Salsa with Cilantro and Lime

Rice Casserole with Cheese and Green Chilies

Rich and Easy Mexican Chocolate Mousse

Summer Refresher, p. 42

Cold Yogurt Soup with Fresh Herbs, Cucumber, Cumin, Feta, and Pink Peppercorns

Seared Scallops with Cilantro–Mint Pesto

Fresh Corn Salad with Sun-Dried Tomatoes and Fresh Herbs

Oversized Cheddar and Chive Biscuits

Key Lime Pie

Chapter 2: Class Favorites, p. 54

French Country Dinner, p. 58

Salad of Mixed Baby Greens with Pears and Roquefort

Roast Chicken with 40 Cloves of Garlic

Country Toasts

Pan-Roast of Root Vegetables and Bell Peppers

Caramelized Apple Galette with Rum-Raisin Ice Cream

Flavors of Morocco, p. 70

Tomato–Cumin Soup

Butterflied Moroccan Spice-Crusted Leg of Lamb

Black Lentil and Moroccan Preserved Lemon Salad with Roasted Beets and Carrots

Raspberry–Nectarine Streusel Tart with Vanilla Ice Cream

California Dreamin', p. 80

My Favorite Caesar Salad

Cioppino with Crusty Toasts and Garlic Mayonnaise

Coffee Ice Cream Baked Alaska

Asian Sensations, p. 90

Vietnamese Summer Rolls with Sweet and Spicy Chili Dipping Sauce

Sweet 'n' Hot Malaysian Chicken

Asian Salsa Salad

Wild Rice Salad with Ginger Vinaigrette

Frozen Lemon Meringue Bombe

Chapter 3: Entertaining by the Light of Day, p. 102

Picnic Table, p. 108

Grilled Seafood and Chorizo Salad with Lemon–Shallot Vinaigrette

Pan-Fried Mixed Pepper Polenta

Almond Marzipan Cake with Mixed Berries

Contents

Lunch with Friends, p. 116

Caramelized Onion and Goat Cheese Crostata

Warm Green Bean and Bacon Salad with Sherry Vinegar Vinaigrette

Store-Bought Baguettes or Crusty Peasant Bread

Store-Bought Ice Cream with Crumbled Store-Bought *Amaretti* and Bitter Chocolate Sauce

Rustic Brunch, p. 124

Roasted Cauliflower and Watercress Salad with Walnuts and Gruyère

Homemade Gravlax with Sweet Mustard–Dill Sauce

Irish Brown Bread

Golden Coconut–Chocolate Chunk Brownies

Brunch, Italian Style, p. 134

Heirloom Tomato Salad with Fresh Herbs and Marjoram–Balsamic Vinaigrette

Baked Pasta with Asparagus, Green Peas, and Lemon

Store-Bought French or Italian Bread

Chocolate–Ginger Biscotti

La Dolce Vita Reprise, p. 140

Arugula Salad with Green Apples and Marcona Almonds

Mixed Mushroom Risotto

Venetian Polenta Cake with Dried Fruit and Cognac

Early Autumn Brunch, p. 146

Fresh Melon and Fig Platter with Prosciutto and Fresh Lime

Roast Potato and Feta Frittata with Scallions and Dill

Creamy Green Polenta

Miniature Cream Scones with Crème Fraîche and Jam

Soup 'n' Sandwich, p. 154

Cold Yogurt Soup with Fresh Herbs, Cucumber, Cumin, Feta, and Pink Peppercorns

Pan-Fried Soft-Shell Crab Sandwiches with Bacon and Green Goddess Dressing

Gingered Cabbage and Tomato Slaw

Store-Bought or Homemade Cookies and/or Biscotti

Chapter 4: Dinner for 8, p. 160

Candlelight Soirée, p. 166

Wilted Spinach Salad with Dates and Crispy Bacon

Pan-Seared Duck Magrets with Raspberry–Port Sauce

Mixed Cheese, Garlic, and Fresh Herb Soufflé

Mushy Peas

Fané

Shanghai Nights: East Meets West, p. 178

Shrimp and Lemongrass Bisque with a Confetti of Stir-Fried Vegetables

Shanghai Beef Short Ribs

Wasabi Rémoulade with Cucumber and Radish (optional)

Sweet 'n' Spicy Cabbage Salad

Steamed or Boiled White or Brown Rice

Ginger-Caramelized Pears with Vanilla Crème Fraîche

Genteel Grilling, p. 190

Grilled Asparagus Mimosa

Grilled Whiskey-Marinated Salmon with Ginger–Garlic Mayonnaise

Red Onion Confit

Doubly Corn Pudding

Mixed Berry Pavlova

Autumn Flavors, p. 200

Arugula Salad with Green Apples and Marcona Almonds

Pan-Roasted Pork Loin with Honeyed Figs and Caramelized Fennel

Delmonico Potatoes Gratin

Caramelized Plum and Rosemary Polenta Pound Cake

Chapter 5: Holidays, p. 212

Easter or Passover, p. 218

Green Pea, Lettuce, and Celery Soup

Mustard-Coated Leg of Lamb

Asparagus with Lemon–Shallot Vinaigrette

Scalloped Potatoes with Onions, Tomatoes, Anchovies, and Fresh Herbs

For Passover: Individual Chocolate–Espresso Soufflés

For Easter: Coconut Layer Cake

Thanksgiving, p. 234

Roast Turkey with Pan Gravy

Cornbread Stuffing with Wilted Greens, Chorizo, and Roasted Garlic

Cranberry–Tangerine Relish

Grated Sweet Potato–Ginger Gratin

Mushy Peas

Mixed Green Salad

Pumpkin Crème Caramel

Candied Pecan Tart

Christmas, p. 252

Mixed Lettuce Salad with Pears, Tarragon, and Pomegranate–Hazelnut Vinaigrette

Prime Rib Roast with Pan Juices and Horseradish Cream Sauce

Fresh-Herbed Popovers

Creamed Spinach Gratin

Caramelized Cauliflower with Crispy Capers

Wheel of Stilton and a Bowl of Fresh Pears with a Selection of Breads and Crackers (optional)

Devil's Food Layer Cake with Double Fudge Frosting

Vanilla Ice Cream Mold

Chapter 6: Assets, p. 266

Kitchen Staples, p. 268

Kitchen Extras, p. 270

Make-Ahead Recipes, p. 272

Critical Condiments & Marinades, p. 273

My Pepper Mix

Garlic Oil

Fresh Herb Butter

Basic Mayonnaise

Fresh Mango and Mint Salsa

Moroccan Preserved Lemons

Basic Marinade for Lamb, Chicken, and Steak

Asian Marinade for Chicken Pieces or Steak

Basic Marinade for Shrimp, Scallops, and Fish

Delicious Dressings, p. 279

The Essential Vinaigrette

Walnut, Hazelnut, or Pecan Vinaigrette

Truffle Vinaigrette

Lemon–Shallot Vinaigrette

Savory Sauce Essentials, p. 282

Beurre Blanc

Quick Tomato Sauce

My Favorite Pesto

My Favorite BBQ Sauce

Simple Stocks, p. 285

Very Basic Chicken Stock

Noteworthy Nibbles, p. 289

Gourmet Trail Mix

Parmesan–Rosemary Coins

Curry Coins

Truffled Almonds

Marinated Olives

Something Sweet, p. 293

Vanilla Sugar

Sweet Pie Crust

Meringue Shell

Basic Shortbread with Variations

Chocolate–Chocolate Shortbread

Peppermint Bark

Chocolate–Ginger Biscotti

Tiny Chocolate Chip Cookies

Sour Cream Coffee Cake

Nut Praline

Bitter Chocolate Sauce

Raspberry Sauce

Caramel Sauce

Lemon Curd

Acknowledgements, p. 305

Index, p. 306

About the Author, p. 312

INTRODUCTION

find the apt adage, "Time and the tides wait for no man," increasingly relevant as birthdays pass. And negotiating time and its passage is at least as important in the kitchen as in other aspects of daily life. "When should I do that?" and "How far in advance can I make it?" are the questions students most frequently ask in my cooking classes.

Culinary school taught me invaluable lessons, but after I graduated and found myself alone in the kitchen, I was still incapable of smoothly orchestrating a dinner for company. Attempt after attempt left me feeling awkward, frustrated, and embarrassed. Despite the multitude of newly acquired techniques and foolproof recipes at my fingertips, serving dinner at eight remained a fantasy. I was still not up to the "simple task" of getting the various components of a meal on the table simultaneously—and certainly not appropriately hot, warm, or cold. Rib roasts overcooked while garlic custards refused to set; a first-course soufflé was on the table—and beginning to fall—while guests were stuck in traffic. Relatives had finished the hors d'oeuvres and were increasingly tipsy, but the thermometer in the Thanksgiving turkey continued to register raw. Sound familiar?

Clearly, there was a lot that cooking school had not taught me. I realized that for the home cook, seamless meal preparation largely depends on properly fitting together the chronological puzzle pieces of making dinner. If it were possible to produce one recipe at a time—one after the next and each straight through from beginning to end—mealtime would not invite kitchen chaos. But sadly, there aren't enough hours in the day. Even if there were, most menus—certainly the hot ones—require dishes to be prepared concurrently rather than consecutively.

I decided to hit the books. Nowhere, however, could I find what I sought: reliable and comprehensive information on culinary timing. Finally acknowledging there was no one to teach me but me, I began a many-years-long period of learning through experimentation.

Today, I'm a cooking teacher with that period of my life far behind me, and I see far too many people in the same boat I was in back then. People want to make healthy, satisfying food at home but are unable to fit yet another activity into already jam-packed schedules. Thus, keeping the goal of smooth, stress-free meal preparation front and center just as I do each time I teach a class, I've written *It's All in the Timing* to share the culinary credos and tips I've discovered over the years, along with my very best recipes. This is the book I wish I'd had way back when. It provides answers to my students' and my *Wall Street Journal* readers' most common questions and conveys information they complain they can't find anywhere else.

We've all been cautioned to read a recipe through before beginning it, but no one ever explains the necessity and "how-to" of getting a grip on the multiple recipes of an entire meal before lifting a finger. Each menu in this book begins with a detailed Order of Preparation chart laying out the entire meal step-by-step from beginning to end.

This culinary sequencing is exactly what is called for to ensure relaxed time in the kitchen followed by easy, enjoyable meals, whether you're entertaining or just feeding the family. By adhering to my plan-ahead—and often even make-ahead—philosophy and following my timing charts, you'll find yourself anticipating your next home-cooked meal with pleasure rather than dread.

In my 20s, I entertained on a shoestring. Once married and a mother, I prepared family suppers as well as more elaborate dinner parties for friends. Now that I'm single again, there are the lunches, brunches, and dinners that go along with that. Having done it all, I want to share the lessons my culinary journey has taught me, including ways to troubleshoot, anticipate and avoid pitfalls, and correct the unforeseen mistakes that will still inevitably arise. By demystifying meal-making, *It's All in the Timing* aims to dispel the overwhelming intimidation so often felt when entering the kitchen.

This cookbook runs the gamut from basic eating to elaborate entertaining. Within these pages, you'll find menus for short-order meals;

my cooking students' all-time favorites; brunches, lunches, and picnics; serious dinner parties; and holiday feasts. Each menu is composed of user-friendly, well-crafted recipes culled from my decades of teaching and entertaining, including the most popular dishes from my classes and *Wall Street Journal* articles. All pack in maximum flavor and pizzazz with minimal effort. This is not restaurant cooking but rather tasty, stylish food that anyone can easily prepare at home.

Just like my students, I cook in a home kitchen without an entourage of sous-chefs. I, too, am prone to misreading a recipe, forgetting to set the timer, letting the soup boil over, and needing a quick substitute when I run out of milk. I truly believe that kitchen perfection is impossible and that aiming for it only invites failure. This message reassures and empowers my students. It's essential to accept the fact that mistakes happen, and it's even more important to not let that knowledge scare you. Most mistakes can be reversed. I'll show you how to correct them and, even more important, how to learn from them.

The Flexibility of Making Ahead

The key to creating a meal in an orderly fashion is knowing what can be done in advance and—equally important—how far in advance. Through trial and error, I've ascertained what can be prepared ahead and what cannot. Initially, "ahead" for me meant earlier in the day, but I experimented and discovered dishes that could be made several days—or even weeks—in advance. How lucky we are to live in the 21st century when staples can be prepared and then tucked away in the freezer, sometimes for as long as a year.

As I mastered the art of making the disparate parts of dinner in advance, it became clear that less last-minute fuss resulted in less chaos and calamity and thus far more quality time at the table with guests. As my sequencing skills improved, so did my levels of self-assurance and comfort and the stress-free enjoyment of my own parties. Belatedly, I

Please feel free to tweak the recipes and menus in this book. Giving you the confidence and ability to make them your own is my ultimate goal. For example, if you're running late and your kids are starving, speed things along by omitting a first course, a dessert, or both. Fresh berries, fruit and cheese, a simple fruit salad, or purchased cookies or chocolates—though basic—are appropriate desserts when entertaining. In autumn—and only marginally more work—I like to pass a platter of fresh figs, walnuts halves, and red or champagne grapes. And I sometimes tuck in almond macaroons, or *amaretti*, here and there for those who are never truly satisfied without an end-of-meal sugar hit.

Chopping your veggies ahead can save last minute hassle.

understood that no guest can truly relax if the host is sweating, fretting, and freaking out in the kitchen.

When confronted with more elaborate entertaining or holiday meals, prescheduling, once again, saves the day. A large supply of at-the-ready tricks and treats makes me feel confidently forearmed, and I like to have as many freezer and fridge make-aheads as possible on hand. I've certainly cooked too many major meals on the spot and under pressure, but given a choice, my preferred scenario is a relaxed, bits-and-pieces approach. When I have 15 minutes to spare between meetings, I make salad dressing or crème anglaise. Ditto fresh mayonnaise and chocolate sauce. There's welcome security knowing these goodies are waiting in the fridge. I also thrill to the concept of ice cream bombes in the freezer, meringues in the pantry, and both sweet and savory pie crusts already rolled out and waiting for me to turn them into pies, tarts, and crostatas.

Chapter 6, the Assets chapter, contains many of these life-saving must-have and useful-to-have recipes. In addition there are instructions for complete dishes that can be made weeks or months in advance and kept frozen. Stocking your pantry, fridge, and freezer with basics provides yet another level of control and confidence in the kitchen.

Whether you spend a few weekend hours per month making and storing these staples, or whether—as I tend to do—you make them when time permits, they're godsends to have at your fingertips. With these basics at the ready and a bit of practice, you'll soon find yourself turning out near-flawless meals. Like magic, they'll emerge from your kitchen while you sit back and actually have fun at your own party.

How to Use This Book

In addition to the recipes, each menu includes an Order of Preparation chart that provides a brief timeline for the entire meal. All of the meal's steps are listed in the chart, with icons indicating how far in advance of the start of the meal to complete them. To help you stay on track, these same icons are also included in the full recipes that follow.

There are many ways to approach preparing a meal and many workable timetables. For this book, however, each menu is paired with a specific chart that lays out a single, suggested way to proceed. For those—possibly most—of you who are trying to cook and host a multicourse meal for the first time, I suggest adhering initially to Order of Preparation timing as written. You'll find that the charts offer enough flexibility to cook at a leisurely pace, if you prefer, or even to speed up the process.

Of course, there are also specific recipes or elements of those recipes that can be prepared much farther in advance than my charts

ICONS

Look for timing icons like these throughout the book to help you stay on track from start to finish.

1 DAY

3 HOURS

15 MINS

SERVE

suggest. I personally like to make as much as possible as far ahead of time as possible. Because of this, I've included menu-specific make-ahead advice in the Get a Head Start boxes, located near the Order of Preparation charts. Other tips, tricks, and ideas are highlighted throughout the book, and I encourage you to take advantage of all of them with the goal of making your hours in the kitchen as relaxing as possible. I hope this book provides guidance to both those who crave specific direction and those who, like me, prefer looser rules but still want a guarantee that things will work out.

That being said, here are a few basic make-ahead principles to help you navigate the menus:

- You can prewash most salad greens up to five days in advance. Simply wrap the washed and dried greens in paper towels or tea towels, place in open plastic bags, and refrigerate.
- You can almost always chop fresh herbs earlier in the day, place them in a lidded container covered with damp paper towel, and refrigerate until ready to use.
- Hearty produce, such as bell peppers, parsnips, carrots, and turnips, can often be prepped the day before you start a dish. Wash, trim, cut, wrap, and store them in the refrigerator.
- Not every item can be prepped in advance. For example, chopped or minced garlic, onions, and shallots, as well as sliced endives, are at their best when prepped right before you need them.
- All recipes assume that you have thawed your meat and seafood products before starting.
- Most of my recipes suggest you let large meat items come to room temperature before cooking. If your meat is colder, that is fine—but keep in mind that it will affect the cooking time.
- Many of my recipes suggest that you cover and store various dishes or their components. It generally doesn't matter if you use aluminum foil, plastic wrap, or lidded containers to get the job done. However, for longer storage, especially in the freezer,

If not using a food processor, chopping onions by hand is easier than you think!

tempered-glass containers, metal containers, and foil are better than plastic—whether it's wrap, baggies, or containers. This is because all plastic is porous and will eventually allow freezer burn and over drying. Food may also pick up odors from its environment (or, in the case of garlic and onions, taint other food in your fridge or freezer).

- At room temperature, I tend to store items uncovered when they will be out for no more than a few hours. If you'd rather cover them, drape with tea towels or cover bowls and pots with plates—both are easy, green options. Do note that hot items should be cooled before covering. There are some rare exceptions to this, and I've pointed them out when they arise.

All of my suggestions are based on what has worked for me over the years. But cooks must use their own best judgment. With regard to proper storing, remember, your creations are only as fresh as your freshest ingredient! And common sense is your best friend. Use it.

DINNER IN A FLASH

DINNER IN A FLASH

MENUS

45 Minutes or Less
p. 12

Fast French
p. 22

Mexican Fiesta
p. 32

Summer Refresher
p. 42

Spending serious time in the kitchen is one of my absolute favorite activities. Whether orchestrating a major meal, canning and preserving summer's bounty, or stocking the freezer for a rainy day (or, more likely, for a busy one), I'm at my happiest passing extended hours behind the stove. More often than not, however, life intervenes, and I have 30 minutes, rather than 30 hours, to make dinner.

In my 20s, having worked late for the seventh night in a row, I'd usually throw up my hands and opt to eat out. Though not an entirely satisfactory solution to the age-old question of dinner, I muddled along in this vein for years—first solo and later with my former husband—until children arrived and put an end to such freewheeling behavior.

Staying in and fending for ourselves most evenings, we began with makeshift grazing—cereal, scrambled eggs, and thrown-together sandwiches. But this catch-as-catch-can eating, neither delicious nor particularly nutritious, grew old fast. As my husband's only culinary interest was the actual eating, it became glaringly apparent that the ball was in my court. I needed to find tasty meals I could make in 45 minutes max. Though initially challenging, these casual repasts soon became something I spent many a dull workday afternoon looking forward to preparing.

In the beginning, the ad hoc dinners were just for the two of us. But mired in the abyss of new parenthood with no time to socialize, my husband and I felt isolated. Cooking for an extended group *chez nous* could be a solution, and I happily envisioned our friends and their kids hanging out in the kitchen while I cooked. On a good day, some might even pitch in. But could I raise my culinary bar high enough to be comfortable serving these homespun meals to company?

It turned out to be easier than imagined. I began by taking advantage—especially in spring, summer, and early fall—of whichever seasonal vegetables both required minimal preparation and paired well with simple fish, meat, and poultry. The resulting meals came together in minutes. In winter, when market offerings were less enticing, I capitalized on make-ahead dishes that could be stored for days in the fridge or for months in the freezer.

The four menus in this chapter epitomize quick cooking at its best. All can be table ready in about 45 minutes because the recipes either come together in no time or can be made ahead so that mealtime remains hassle free.

And remember, these menus are templates. Mastering them will give you a leg up vis-à-vis short-order cooking in general, but please feel free to play with them—tweaking, adapting, and customizing to fit each situation. You'll be amazed what can be concocted in no time when you've got a few special somethings tucked away in the fridge, freezer, and pantry.

THE JOY OF OUTDOOR MARKETS

Saturday mornings I habitually check out the Union Square Greenmarket. It's such fun to turn the acquired bounty into a dinner for company that evening.

Whether it's Union Square around the corner from my Manhattan apartment, or Pike Place Market in Seattle, Il Campo de' Fiori in Rome, or La Boqueria in Barcelona, I'm magnetically drawn to their hustle, bustle, and sprawling array of irresistible edibles. This fascination extends back to the Sunday mornings of my childhood when my mother—with me in tow—would pop over to the legendary-even-then Los Angeles Farmer's Market at 3rd and Fairfax. To this day, the Market is a must-visit destination for tourists and serious foodies alike, all of whom flock to the historically landmarked sight for ethnic eateries and colorful stalls overflowing with specialty foods, local farm products, flowers, and bakery goods.

45 MINUTES OR LESS

DINNER FOR SIX

DISH	BEGIN PREP	PAGE
FIRST COURSE		
Green Vegetable Ragoût	1 day ahead	16
ENTREE		
Sizzling Cod Pan-Roast with Tomato–Caper Salsa	45 mins ahead	18
ON THE SIDE		
Potato, Veggie, and Garlic Smash	45 mins ahead	20
DESSERT		
Boozy Bananas Foster	after main course	21

’ve been making this short-order menu for years, and it continues to garner rave reviews. Simply prepared fish and abundant vegetables provide a meal as light, healthy, and colorful as it is delicious. In spring, summer, and early fall, you can complete the ragoût, fish, salsa, and veggie smash—and lay out the ingredients for dessert—up to four hours before eating. In winter, when temperatures drop, the menu is equally appropriate, but try to serve the food piping hot instead of room temperature.

If you're cooking last minute and working efficiently, the starter and main course should come together in about 45 minutes. Then count on 5 to 10 minutes of caramelizing, flaming, and assembling when time for dessert.

The gorgeous Green Vegetable Ragoût (p. 16) is tasty far beyond the sum of its simple parts. Asparagus, haricots verts, sugar snap peas, and frozen green peas are blanched and then tossed with nothing but truffle oil, salt, and pepper. The resulting dish is equally good hot, warm, or at room temperature—heaven-sent for the make-ahead cook.

The Sizzling Cod (p. 18) includes my super easy, go-to cooking method for thick fish fillets: just season, oil, and roast them on a preheated sheet pan in a very hot oven until they are sizzling, golden, and flaky.

Here, the cod is decked out with a heady, citrus-infused Tomato–Caper Salsa that I make virtually nonstop in late summer and early fall when tomatoes are at their best. Inspired by a pizza topping I first tasted on the tiny Italian island of Pantelleria, self-proclaimed caper capital of the world, I now also serve the salsa with chicken, pork cutlets, and shellfish. It's also great tossed with pasta or atop bruschetta.

Other large fish fillets can be cooked this same way and plugged into other menus. Try substituting another vegetable for the salsa. The ragoût from this menu, the Red Onion Confit (p. 196), and the Fricassee of Mixed Mushrooms (p. 27) all make fabulous toppings for roast fish.

Inspired by Barcelona street food, the versatile Potato, Veggie, and Garlic Smash (p. 20) serves double duty here as both vegetable and starch. Serve it hot and freshly made or later at room temperature. And feel free to change the proportion of potatoes to veggies or to replace the broccoli and spinach with garden bounty or fridge leftovers. Red chard and red bliss potatoes, for example, could provide a visual contrast to the green ragoût in this menu. But zucchini and corn, shaved Brussels sprouts and onion, carrot and beet, and arugula and tomato combinations all produce singular and scrumptious results. Chopped fresh herbs mixed in or strewn over last minute are tasty and attractive as well.

And save room for dessert—Boozy Bananas Foster (p. 21)! The only thing that improves these heavily caramelized, rum-flamed bananas is to serve them over rich vanilla bean ice cream, although you can gild the lily by adding toasted pound cake and dollops of whipped cream. And, if you dim the lights and dare to do the flaming tableside, the dish is an impressive presentation piece as well.

A super easy and foolproof way to cook thick fish fillets—such as cod, hake, halibut, and salmon—is to roast them in a hot oven on a preheated sheet pan. Place a sheet pan on the upper rack of the oven and preheat to 500°F. Rub both sides of the fillets with extra virgin olive oil and season with salt and pepper, and place them on the superheated pan. Roast 10 to 20 minutes, or until done. You don't even need to turn them over.

ORDER OF PREPARATION

START

1 DAY

1. Complete Steps 1 and 2 for the Ragoût (p. 16). Store as directed.

2 HOURS

1. Remove the Ragoût vegetables from the refrigerator and freezer (Step 3).

45 MINS

1. Complete Steps 1 through 4 for the Potato Smash (p. 20) and set aside.

2. Make the Tomato–Caper Salsa (p. 19) and set aside.

3. Place a sheet pan on a rack adjusted to the highest position, and preheat the oven to 500°F.

4. Complete Step 2 for the Cod (p. 18).

30 MINS

1. Complete Step 4 for the Ragoût.

2. Complete Steps 3 and 4 for the Cod.

15 MINS

1. Complete the Ragoût (Steps 5 through 7) and set aside.

SERVE

1. Serve the Ragoût.

AFTER THE FIRST COURSE

2. After eating the Ragoût, remove the ice cream from the freezer to allow it to soften.

3. Complete the Cod (Steps 5 and 6) and serve with the Potato Smash.

AFTER THE MAIN COURSE

4. After clearing the table, make the Bananas Foster (p. 21) and serve with the ice cream.

GET A HEAD START!

The **Ragoût**, **Cod**, and **Smash** can all be made up to 3 hours in advance and served at room temperature. However, top the fish with the salsa only when ready to serve.

Green Vegetable Ragoût

Yield: 6 side-dish or first-course servings

Approximately 1 pound haricots verts
Approximately 1 pound sugar snap peas
Approximately 1 pound asparagus
1 (10-ounce) package frozen green peas*

Pinch baking soda
2–4 tablespoons white or black truffle oil
Truffle salt or fine sea salt and freshly
    ground black pepper, to taste

1. Wash and trim the haricots verts, sugar snaps, and asparagus and then string the sugar snaps. Lay the asparagus on a cutting board with the tips lined up. Cut off and discard the tough bottoms of the stalks. Cut a 3-inch tip off each one, and set the tips aside. Cut the remaining stalks into 3-inch lengths and then vertically in halves or thirds, depending on thickness.

2. Wrap the prepped vegetables in damp paper towels, keeping the asparagus tips separate, and refrigerate in open plastic bags.

3. Remove the prepped vegetables and asparagus tips from the refrigerator and the frozen peas from the freezer.

4. Bring a very large pot of salted water to a boil over high heat.

5. Add the vegetables and baking soda to the boiling water. Cover and bring the water back to a boil. Uncover, lower the heat to medium–high and cook until the vegetables are almost al dente. Add the peas and asparagus tips and cook 1 more minute.

6. While the vegetables are cooking, put the truffle oil, salt, and pepper in a large serving bowl.

7. Drain the vegetables in a colander—shaking to remove all excess water—and add them to the serving bowl. Toss. Taste and adjust the seasoning as needed and set aside

8. Serve hot, warm, or at room temperature.

SERVE

I always have extra frozen peas on hand. Here, if needed, a second bag can be added to serve 2 to 3 more people.

Vegetables should not be cold when added to boiling water because once they're added, you want the water to return to the boil as quickly as possible and cold vegetables slow down this process. If you don't have time to bring vegetables to room temperature before boiling, place them in a bowl of hot water for a minute or so and then immediately drain and put the now warm vegetables into boiling water. However, don't do this ahead of time, as warming the vegetables in hot water starts their cooking.

If you would rather skip the first course, this ragoût is delicious eaten as a side dish along with the fish and the veggie smash.

This applause-worthy ragoût is equally good hot, warm, or at room temperature—heaven-sent for the make-ahead cook.

Sizzling Cod Pan-Roast with Tomato–Caper Salsa

Yield: 6 main-course servings

3 pounds large skinless cod fillets (hake, halibut, or other large whitefish fillets may be substituted)*

¼ cup extra virgin olive oil or Garlic Oil (p. 273)

Fine sea salt and freshly ground black pepper, to taste

1 recipe Tomato–Caper Salsa (recipe follows)

2–4 tablespoons julienned fresh basil, for garnish

45 MINS

1. With a rack adjusted to the highest position, preheat the oven to 500°F. Place a large sheet pan on the rack.**

2. Liberally paint both sides of the fish with the oil and season with the salt and pepper.

30 MINS

3. Remove the sheet pan from the oven and immediately lay the fish pieces on it, at least 2 inches apart, and return to the oven. The side that used to have skin on it is the side that should be touching the pan.

4. Bake 10 to 20 minutes, or until done. When the juices oozing from the fish begin to turn from clear to opaque, it is done. If in doubt, stick a fork into the fish to make sure that it is cooked through and perfectly flaky.

SERVE

AFTER THE FIRST COURSE

5. Slide the fish—with the help of a large metal spatula, if necessary—onto a large serving platter.

6. Pour the pan juices over the fish and then top with the Tomato–Caper Salsa followed by the julienned basil. Serve hot, warm, or at room temperature.

* When making dinner for 6, I ask the fishmonger to give me 2 (1½-pound) center-cut sections from 2 whole fillets.

** The sheet pan must be large enough for the fish fillets to be placed at least 2 inches apart so that they will bake, not steam. If scaling up the recipe, you may need more than one pan.

Tomato–Caper Salsa

Yield: approximately 8 cups

2 pints cherry tomatoes, halved or quartered

1 cup extra virgin olive oil

1 bulb fresh fennel, trimmed and thinly sliced

1 medium red onion, halved and sliced into paper-thin half rings

1 large clove garlic, finely minced

6 tablespoons freshly squeezed lemon juice

⅓ cup julienned fresh basil

¼ cup freshly squeezed orange juice

¼ cup capers, rinsed in cool water, drained, and patted dry

Freshly grated zest of 2 lemons

Freshly grated zest of 1 orange

Fine sea salt and freshly ground black pepper, to taste

If you hate chopping garlic, try putting the garlic for the salsa through a garlic press.

1. Stir all the salsa ingredients together in a large bowl. Set aside. (The salsa will keep at room temperature for up to 3 hours.)

This salsa is also delicious with other types of fish, shellfish, and grilled or roast chicken. And on top of toast, it makes a drop-dead bruschetta.

Potato, Veggie, and Garlic Smash

Yield: 6 side-dish servings

½ cup extra virgin olive oil

6 cloves garlic, minced

2 pounds Yukon gold potatoes, skin on, into large chunks

5 cloves garlic, peeled

2 tablespoons kosher salt

½ pound fresh broccoli florets and stems, washed, trimmed, and cut into small chunks

1 pound fresh spinach, washed and trimmed

Fine sea salt and freshly ground black pepper, to taste

1. Mix the olive oil with the minced garlic and set aside.

2. Put the potatoes and garlic cloves in a stockpot or large saucepan and cover with cool water by 2 inches. Add the kosher salt and bring to a boil over high heat.

3. Lower the heat to medium and simmer for 15 to 20 minutes, or until the potatoes and garlic are just tender. Raise the heat to high, bring back to a boil, and add the broccoli and spinach. Cook, partially covered, for 3 to 5 minutes, or until the vegetables are cooked through. Drain well in a large colander.

4. Transfer to a serving bowl and strain the garlic–oil mixture over the vegetables. Use a wooden spoon to stir and very roughly smash the vegetables. Some large chunks should still be visible. Taste and adjust the salt and pepper as needed. Set aside.

AFTER THE FIRST COURSE

5. Serve hot, warm, or room temperature.

Boozy Bananas Foster

Yield: 6 servings

6 tablespoons unsalted butter

6 hard-ripe bananas, peeled and sliced in half lengthwise

6 tablespoons dark brown sugar

Scant ¼ teaspoon ground cinnamon

6 tablespoons dark rum, such as Myers's

6 large scoops best-quality vanilla ice cream

SERVE

AFTER THE MAIN COURSE

1. Melt the butter in a large heavy skillet set over medium–high heat.

2. When the butter turns light brown, add the bananas in a single layer. Cook for about 2 minutes, or until the first side just begins to caramelize. Turn and brown the second side.

3. Sprinkle the bananas with the brown sugar and cinnamon. Toss gently and cook 1 to 3 minutes more, or until the sauce thickens. Don't let the mixture burn, but the stickier and more caramelized, the better. Turn off the heat and leave the skillet on the burner.

4. Warm the rum in a small saucepan over medium heat. Tilt the saucepan into the flame or turn the heat off and use a match to ignite the rum. Pour the flaming rum carefully over the bananas. Shake the skillet and toss gently until all the flames die out. (Be careful not to catch anything on fire!)

5. Pour the banana mixture into 6 dessert bowls over or under the vanilla ice cream and serve right away.

FAST
FRENCH

DINNER FOR SIX

DISH	BEGIN PREP	PAGE
FIRST COURSE		
Fricassee of Mixed Mushrooms and Fresh Herbs	1 day ahead	27
ENTRÉE		
Oven-Finished Rib-Eye Steaks with Béarnaise Mayonnaise	1 day ahead	28
ON THE SIDE		
Quick Roast of Potatoes and Red Onions	1 hour ahead	30
DESSERT		
Mini Molten Chocolate Cakes	1 day ahead	31

When you're stuck at the office and have guests arriving for dinner at 8:00, this easy, people-pleasing menu is a lifesaver. A richly flavored mushroom starter is followed by thick rib-eye steaks and a crispy potato and onion pan-roast that will satisfy even your most discriminating friends. And if it doesn't, the drop-dead finale—luscious little self-saucing chocolate cakes warm from the oven—certainly will.

On "big meat" occasions, my dilemma for years had been whether to go for a luscious prime rib roast or right-off-the-grill steaks. Eventually, I realized that a grilled or pan-seared slab of Rib-Eye (p. 28) finished in the oven offered the best of both worlds, and I've never looked back. Rosy-rare, heavily marbled steak, gloriously sheathed in a seriously seared crust, equals perfection.

If you don't have access to a real grill, I highly recommend a heavy-duty grill pan. When I bid farewell to my last apartment, I also bid farewell to my indoor Thermador grill and feared I'd never recover. My foodie aunt saved the day by sending me—what turned out to be—the perfect nonstick grill pan. However, if you want to make a great steak right now and have nothing but a heavy ovenproof skillet, miracles are still achievable. Just sear the meat on both sides and then pop the skillet into a 400°F oven to finish things off.

But *please*—no overcooking. Meat continues to cook as it rests. You can always cook a too-rare steak a bit more, but overdone meat is unsalvageable. If you are not confident in your ability to recognize perfectly cooked meat, I highly recommend purchasing an instant-read thermometer. Its inexpensive price tag is well worth saving even one expensive rib-eye from ruin.

Serve the Fricassee of Mixed Mushrooms (p. 27) hot, warm, or at room temperature. You can complete the recipe up to three hours ahead, unless you plan to serve it hot. For a hot starter, leave the mushrooms in their pan after cooking and reheat them over high heat while the rib-eye rests. Add salt, pepper, and a bit of olive oil if needed. Or you can prepare the mushrooms through Step 4 in advance, and when ready, finish the dish in less than 10 minutes.

I first encountered this simple sauté when staying with English friends at their 14th-century manor house in Devon. After foraging for chanterelles right outside the kitchen door, we went back inside and sautéed our bounty into lunch. The hunting and gathering experience was unforgettable fun and the fricassee a memorably aromatic bouquet. It's useful to note that a brief sauté dramatically deepens the flavor of even the most basic supermarket mushrooms. Ideally choose a mélange gleaned from chanterelles, oyster, lobster, porcini, morels, shiitakes, portobellos, and cremini. But don't despair if only a couple of these are available. After a garlic-and-fresh-herb enhancement, even white button mushrooms produce sumptuous results.

A basket of garlic toast is an appreciated—though optional—accompaniment. For a change of pace, serve the sauté atop a salad of mixed lettuces, and savor the vivid contrast between earthy, chewy mushrooms; crisp, clean greens; and tangy vinaigrette. This fricassee is also a brilliant topping for bruschetta, polenta, and pasta. And, as a side dish, it coaxes additional flavor from a roast chicken, leg of lamb, or juicy steak.

Béarnaise Mayonnaise (p. 29) is a no-cook answer to traditional Béarnaise sauce and elevates the meat and potatoes concept sky-high. Prepare it up to three days ahead, pop it in the fridge, and put it out of your mind until needed.

Here, the distinctive vinegar-shallot-tarragon triad is emulsified with olive and canola oils instead of with melted butter, resulting in a cold condiment that is equally rich and eggy but exponentially easier to prepare than the original. If making the reduction is too much work, omit it. No one will miss it as the resulting basic tarragon mayonnaise is still delicious.

For dessert, the Mini Molten Chocolate Cakes (p. 31) are divine. This Jean-Georges Vongerichten–inspired cross between a cake, a pudding, and a soufflé is a chocolate lover's dream. The decadent little desserts are baked until their outsides are set, while their insides are not. When cut, a rich sauce spills out and mingles seductively with the melty ice cream garnish. The best part? These little gems bake in 8 to 10 minutes. Keep extras ready to go in the freezer, and you can bake off second helpings on the spot.

Like the 45 Minutes or Less menu, this meal comes together in a snap. Here, however, last-minute speed relies on some advance preparation. Because you bake the cakes straight from the freezer when ready to eat them, you'll need to freeze them raw in their ramekins at least 3 hours and up to 6 months in advance. The rest of the meal is pretty straightforward, but it's even easier if you make the mayo a day ahead. If you also prepare the pan-roast and the fricassee in advance, there's virtually nothing to do at mealtime but grill the steak.

Tip!

Use the Béarnaise Mayonnaise recipe as a jumping off point for experimenting with other flavored mayos. Try replacing the tarragon with a different fresh herb, or for a heady punch, make a fresh ginger, soy sauce, or dried ancho or chipotle chili powder version. Flavored mayos are wildly versatile. Sublime on sandwiches, pizzas, bruschettas, and composed salads, they're also distinctive dress-ups for simple vegetable, meat, poultry, fish, and shellfish preparations, and constitute ideal dips for chips, shelled shrimp, crudités, and tiny potatoes.

Tip!

This menu can also be served buffet style. To do so, offer the mushrooms as a side dish along with the meat and potatoes, rather than as a first course.

ORDER OF PREPARATION

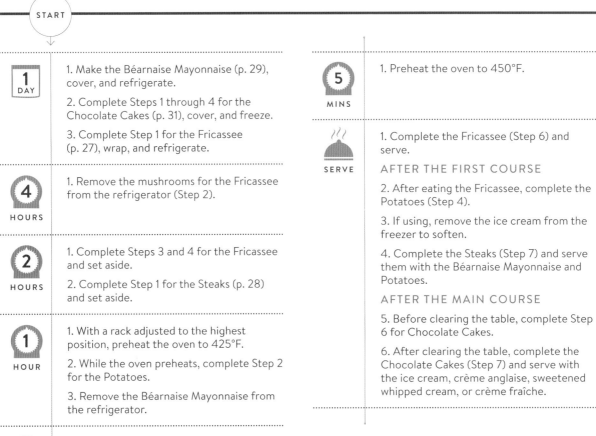

START

1 DAY
1. Make the Béarnaise Mayonnaise (p. 29), cover, and refrigerate.

2. Complete Steps 1 through 4 for the Chocolate Cakes (p. 31), cover, and freeze.

3. Complete Step 1 for the Fricassee (p. 27), wrap, and refrigerate.

4 HOURS
1. Remove the mushrooms for the Fricassee from the refrigerator (Step 2).

2 HOURS
1. Complete Steps 3 and 4 for the Fricassee and set aside.

2. Complete Step 1 for the Steaks (p. 28) and set aside.

1 HOUR
1. With a rack adjusted to the highest position, preheat the oven to 425°F.

2. While the oven preheats, complete Step 2 for the Potatoes.

3. Remove the Béarnaise Mayonnaise from the refrigerator.

45 MINS
1. Complete Step 3 for the Potatoes.

35 MINS
1. If using a grill for the Steaks, preheat it.

15 MINS
1. Complete Step 5 for the Fricassee.

2. If using a grill pan for the Steaks, set it over high heat.

3. When the grill or grill pan is hot, complete Steps 4 through 6 for the Steaks.

5 MINS
1. Preheat the oven to 450°F.

SERVE
1. Complete the Fricassee (Step 6) and serve.

AFTER THE FIRST COURSE

2. After eating the Fricassee, complete the Potatoes (Step 4).

3. If using, remove the ice cream from the freezer to soften.

4. Complete the Steaks (Step 7) and serve them with the Béarnaise Mayonnaise and Potatoes.

AFTER THE MAIN COURSE

5. Before clearing the table, complete Step 6 for Chocolate Cakes.

6. After clearing the table, complete the Chocolate Cakes (Step 7) and serve with the ice cream, crème anglaise, sweetened whipped cream, or crème fraîche.

GET A HEAD START!

The **Rib-Eye Steaks** can be finished up to 4 hours ahead and set aside to be eaten at room temperature.

The **Béarnaise Mayonnaise** can be made up and refrigerated up to 3 days ahead.

The **Quick Roast of Potatoes** can be made up to 5 hours in advance, set aside, and reheated in a 400°F to 500°F oven for 5 to 10 minutes when needed.

The **Chocolate Cakes** must be baked straight from the freezer so be sure to freeze them for at least 3 hours before baking. Well wrapped, they can be frozen for up to 6 months.

Fricassee of Mixed Mushrooms and Fresh Herbs

Yield: 6 first-course servings

3 pounds assorted fresh mushrooms: chanterelles, morels, shiitakes, cremini, oysters, lobster, hen-of-the-woods, porcini, portobellos, and/or white button mushrooms, depending on availability

¾ cup extra virgin olive oil

1 medium onion, chopped

4 cloves garlic, chopped

Fine sea salt and freshly ground black pepper, to taste

4 tablespoons walnut oil

1½ cups chopped mixed fresh herbs, including one or more of the following: parsley, chives, chervil, tarragon, and basil, divided

2 tablespoons white truffle oil or extra virgin olive oil, for drizzling

If there are oils that you use infrequently (truffle, sesame, nut oils, etc.), refrigerate them. Their shelf lives will be extended for months. Just remember most of them will need to come to room temperature before you can pour them.

 1. Trim the mushrooms and wipe them clean with a damp cloth. Cut the large ones into attractive sections and leave the small ones whole. Wrap in a damp kitchen towel, place in an open plastic bag, and refrigerate.

 2. Remove the mushrooms from the refrigerator.

 3. Place a large skillet over high heat and add the olive oil. When hot, add the mushrooms and cook, stirring frequently, for 6 to 10 minutes, or until quite tender.

4. Lower the heat to medium and add the onion and garlic. Cook, stirring frequently, for 3 to 4 minutes, or until the onion and garlic begin to color. Taste and adjust salt and pepper as needed. Remove from the heat and set aside in the skillet.

 5. Set the skillet back over medium heat. Add the walnut oil and cook, tossing frequently, for about 3 minutes, or until the mushrooms are hot. Remove from the heat, and toss in ¾ cup of the fresh herbs. Taste and adjust the seasoning as needed.

 6. Divide the mushrooms among 6 salad plates. Divide the remaining chopped herbs over the mushrooms and drizzle each portion with the white truffle or extra virgin olive oil. Alternatively, arrange on a serving platter and garnish with the herbs and oil.

7. Serve right away.

Oven-Finished Rib-Eye Steaks with Béarnaise Mayonnaise

Yield: 6 main-course servings

You can substitute any cut of well-marbled steak—T-bone, strip, porterhouse, or filet—for the rib-eye. Just make sure the steaks are at least 1½ inches thick. Tougher and less fatty cuts of steak, like flank, skirt, flat iron, round, and hanger, are best saved for recipes that call for a marinade.

If you use a nonstick grill pan (or any nonstick pan), be sure to set it over medium, rather than high, heat. Nonstick cookware should never be used over high heat not only because it can damage the nonstick coating, but also because it may release unhealthy toxins into your food.

3 (1½- to 2-inch thick) bone-in rib-eye steaks (about 1¼ pounds each; a total of 4–5 pounds)
Extra virgin olive oil, as needed

Kosher salt and freshly ground black pepper, as needed
1 recipe Béarnaise Mayonnaise (recipe follows), for serving

 2 HOURS

1. Generously rub the steaks all over with the olive oil, salt, and pepper. Set aside.

 35 MINS

2. If using a grill, preheat it.

 15 MINS

3. If using a grill pan, set it over high heat.

4. Place the steaks on the grill pan or on the hottest part of the grill. For medium rare, cook for about 4 to 6 minutes per side, or until grill marks appear and the steaks are lightly charred in spots. If using a grill and dripping fat causes a flare-up that doesn't subside in a few seconds, use tongs to slide the steaks away from the flame. Once flames die down, move the steaks back over the heat.

5. Stick an instant-read thermometer into the center of the steak; it should register 120°F for rare and 125°F for medium rare. Alternatively, make a small cut into the steak to see if it's done to your liking. If the steaks are nicely seared but not yet done, place them on a sheet pan in a 400°F oven until they are.

6. Transfer the steaks to a cutting board and let them rest for at least 8 minutes before slicing. The steaks will continue to cook as they rest.

 SERVE

AFTER THE FIRST COURSE

7. Cut the steaks—against the grain—into thick slices. Place slices on a serving platter or divide among 8 dinner plates. Serve hot, warm, or at room temperature with the Béarnaise Mayonnaise.

Béarnaise Mayonnaise

Yield: 1½–2 cups

For the Reduction

⅓ cup chopped shallot

¼ cup dried tarragon

¼ cup white wine vinegar

2 tablespoons white wine

⅛ teaspoon freshly ground black pepper

Large pinch of salt

For the Mayonnaise (all ingredients must be at room temperature)

1 egg

2 teaspoons white wine vinegar

2 tablespoons freshly squeezed lemon juice, or more to taste

1 large shallot, roughly chopped

½ teaspoon fine sea salt, or more to taste

¼ teaspoon freshly ground black pepper, or more to taste

¾ cup neutral vegetable oil, such as canola

½ cup extra virgin olive oil

½–¾ cup fresh tarragon leaves

When making any kind of mayonnaise, all of the ingredients **must** be at room temperature. Otherwise, the mixture may fail to emulsify or may break.

1. *Make the Reduction:* Combine all of the ingredients for the reduction in a small saucepan set over medium–high heat and bring to a boil. Boil for 2 to 5 minutes, or until almost dry. Remove from heat and set aside to cool completely.

2. *Finish the Mayonnaise:* Place the cooled reduction in the bowl of a food processor along with the room temperature egg, vinegar, lemon juice, shallot, salt, and pepper. Process until well blended.

3. Combine the 2 oils in a measuring cup. With the motor running, add the mixed oils in very slow drizzle. After about ¼ of the oil has been added, pour in the rest very slowly. If you add the oil too quickly, the mayonnaise may break.

4. Add the fresh tarragon and pulse a few times to combine. Taste and adjust the salt, pepper, and lemon juice as needed.

5. Use right away or store, covered, in the refrigerator for up to 3 days.

If your mayonnaise does break, transfer it to a pitcher. Crack a room temperature egg into the bowl of the food processor and start over: Pulse the egg a few times and then with the motor running, add the broken mayonnaise to the egg in a very slow stream just as you added the oil originally. Taste and adjust the seasoning as needed.

Quick Roast of Potatoes and Red Onions

Yield: 6 side-dish servings

5–6 large Yukon gold potatoes, scrubbed and cut into a rough 1-inch dice

3 large red onions, cut into a rough 1-inch dice

12 cloves garlic, peeled or unpeeled

⅓ cup extra virgin olive oil

2 teaspoons dried rosemary

2 teaspoons dried thyme

Fine sea salt and freshly ground black pepper, to taste

Almost all roast vegetable recipes can be made in advance and reheated when needed. If you have other things in the oven, you can roast vegetables at a temperature anywhere from 325°F to 500°F. Just adjust the cooking time accordingly. Alternatively most roast vegetable dishes—when roasted with oil—can be served at room temperature, a bit like a cooked salad.

1 HOUR

1. With a rack adjusted to the highest position, preheat the oven to 425°F.

2. While the oven preheats, toss the potatoes, onions, garlic, oil, rosemary, thyme, salt, and pepper in a shallow roasting pan or on a sheet pan large enough to hold everything in a single layer without crowding. Use 2 pans if necessary.

45 MINS

3. Roast, tossing occasionally, for 35 to 45 minutes, or until the vegetables are brown and crispy and the potatoes are tender. Set aside or leave on the door of an open turned off oven to stay warm.

SERVE

AFTER THE FIRST COURSE

4. Transfer to a serving bowl. Serve hot, warm, or at room temperature.

Mini Molten Chocolate Cakes

Yield: 6–8 servings

1 cup (2 sticks) unsalted butter, plus more for greasing the molds

½ pound best-quality bittersweet or semisweet chocolate, chopped into small pieces

4 large whole eggs, room temperature

4 large egg yolks, room temperature

½ cup granulated sugar

Large pinch fine sea salt

4 teaspoons all-purpose flour, plus more for preparing the molds

Ice cream, crème anglaise, sweetened whipped cream, or crème fraîche, for serving

1. Melt the butter and chocolate together in a double boiler or in a metal bowl set over a saucepan of simmering water. When almost melted, stir and remove from the heat to cool a bit and finish melting.

2. While the chocolate is melting, using a stand mixer fitted with the paddle attachment or an electric handheld mixer set on medium–high speed, beat the eggs, egg yolks, sugar, and salt together for about 5 minutes, or until pale, very light, and fluffy.

3. While the chocolate–butter mixture is still quite warm, add it to the egg mixture and beat on medium speed until well combined. Scrape down the sides of the bowl with a rubber spatula. Add the flour and beat on low speed until just combined.

4. Heavily butter and flour 8 (1-cup or 1½-cup) ramekins or custard cups. Divide the cake batter evenly among the molds. They will not be full. Cover and freeze at least 3 hours or until ready to bake.

5. Preheat the oven to 450°F.

AFTER THE MAIN COURSE

6. Remove the ramekins from the freezer, uncover, and place them on a sheet pan. Bake about 8 to 10 minutes, or until the edges are set but the centers remain moist and shiny.

7. Remove from the oven and immediately invert each cake onto a dessert plate. Serve right away with the ice cream, crème anglaise, sweetened whipped cream, or crème fraîche.

You can make your own crème fraîche (or sour cream) by stirring 2 cups of heavy cream together with 2 tablespoons of plain yogurt or buttermilk. Set aside at room temperature, stirring once or twice a day, until the desired thickness is reached. This could take anywhere from a few hours to 3 or 4 days. Refrigerate only when it is the consistency you want. You can scale up or down depending how much you need. The finished crème fraîche will keep for several weeks in the fridge.

MEXICAN FIESTA

DINNER FOR SIX

DISH	BEGIN PREP	PAGE
FIRST COURSE		
Guacamole Salad	4 hours ahead	36
Store-Bought Tortilla Chips or Warm Tortillas		
ENTRÉE		
Pan-Seared Chipotle-Citrus Turkey Paillards with Adobo Mayonnaise	1 day ahead	37
ON THE SIDE		
Mango and Plum Salsa with Cilantro and Lime	4 hours ahead	38
Rice Casserole with Cheese and Green Chilies	1 day ahead	39
DESSERT		
Rich and Easy Mexican Chocolate Mousse	1 day ahead	40

This menu showcases the things I love most about south-of-the-border food: spicy Guacamole Salad (p. 36), Mexican chilies, chunky salsa, and a cheese-laden rice casserole—plus heat, cilantro, and Mexican chocolate. It's all here in a flavorful menu virtually identical to one I created last year for a high-end tequila company. But each of last year's dishes included the iconic agave liquor. I omit it here, as I prefer to drink rather than eat my tequila. However, a spoonful or two of tequila added to the guacamole or fruit salsa is tasty and can help accelerate the onset of party mode.

Having made similar salsa, guacamole, and rice casserole recipes for decades, I recently felt it was time to update. With great success, I added plums to the mango salsa and pickled jalapeños to the rich avocado smash. At a friend's suggestion, I also put onion, garlic, and cilantro in a golden-crusted, melty-cheese Mexican rice casserole I'd been making since the 1980s. Back then, the dish contained five cups of sour cream (those were the days!) instead of Greek yogurt. No one has noticed the missing fat, but everyone loves the new inclusions.

With spices, citrus, and chilies, the Turkey Paillards (p. 37) extend the flavor range of this menu still further. Pounded thin, the turkey takes just minutes to grill or sauté. If you're iffy about the pounding, let the butcher do it for you. Or have him pound boneless, skinless chicken breasts or slices of pork loin instead.

The paillards' chipotle marinade is a crowd-pleaser; but if so inclined (and as part of a different menu), steep the paillards in an Asian soy or Italian lemon-garlic-rosemary mixture instead or experiment with your own favorite spice rubs and marinades. It's hard to go wrong with these versatile scaloppine.

The simplicity of unadulterated chocolate is a nice change of pace after a meal replete with complex flavors. This Chocolate Mousse (p. 40) hits the spot. It's easy to throw together and can be made ahead and refrigerated until time for dessert. Purists should leave well enough alone, but for those who want to "Mexicanize" it, add the optional cinnamon or espresso powder. Dollop with whipped cream and stand by for applause.

ORDER OF PREPARATION

START

1 DAY

1. Complete Steps 1 through 4 for the Turkey Paillards (p. 37) and store as directed.

2. Complete Steps 1 through 5 for the Rice Casserole (p. 39), cover, and refrigerate.

3. Complete Steps 1 through 5 for the Chocolate Mousse (p. 40), cover, and refrigerate.

4 HOURS

1. Complete Step 1 for the Mango and Plum Salsa (p. 38), cover, and set aside.

2. Complete Steps 1 through 4 for the Guacamole (p. 36) and store as directed.

3. Remove the Rice Casserole from the refrigerator (Step 6).

1 HOUR

1. Preheat the oven to 350°F.

30 MINS

1. Complete Step 8 for the Rice Casserole.

2. If grilling or broiling the Paillards, preheat the grill or broiler.

3. Remove the adobo mayonnaise for the Paillards from the refrigerator (Step 6).

10 MINS

1. If using a grill pan for the Paillards, set it over high heat.

2. Complete Step 8 for the Paillards.

3. If using, wrap the tortillas in aluminum foil and warm them in the still-warm oven.

SERVE

1. Complete the Guacamole (Step 5) and serve with the tortilla chips or warmed tortillas.

AFTER THE FIRST COURSE

2. After eating the Guacamole, complete the Salsa (Step 2) and the Rice Casserole (Step 9).

3. Complete the Paillards (Step 9) and serve with the adobo mayonnaise, Salsa, and Rice Casserole.

AFTER THE MAIN COURSE

4. After clearing the table, complete the Chocolate Mousse (Steps 6 and 7) and serve with the whipped cream.

GET A HEAD START!

Complete the **Paillards** through Step 4 and refrigerate up to 3 days in advance.

The **Chocolate Mousse** can be made through Step 5 up to 3 days in advance and refrigerated. Make the whipped cream garnish just before serving.

Guacamole Salad

Yield: 6–8 side-dish servings

1 tablespoon ground cumin,
⅛ teaspoon cayenne pepper
Pinch granulated sugar
Kosher salt and freshly ground black pepper, to taste
6 hard-ripe Hass avocados
Freshly grated zest and freshly squeezed juice of 2 limes

1 cup quartered cherry tomatoes
½ cup minced red onion
⅓ cup coarsely chopped fresh cilantro
3 tablespoons extra virgin olive oil
2 tablespoons minced pickled jalapeños (optional)
Store-bought tortilla chips or warmed fresh tortillas, for serving

4 HOURS

1. Stir together the cumin, cayenne, sugar, salt, and pepper and set aside.

2. Cut each avocado in half lengthwise and remove and reserve the pits. Use a large spoon to scoop out each half in a single piece. Lay the pieces, cut side down, on a cutting board. Cut crosswise into ½-inch slices and transfer to a large bowl.

3. Gently toss the avocado slices with the lime zest and juice. Fold in the tomatoes, onion, and cilantro, followed by the pickled jalapeños, if using, and the oil and spice mix.

4. Taste and adjust the seasoning as needed. Stick the seeds down into the guacamole, cover the surface flat with plastic wrap (see wrapping details in the Tip!), and refrigerate.

Guacamole made ahead of time runs the risk of discoloring. Prevent this by pushing the avocado pits into the bowl of finished guacamole and smoothing a piece of plastic wrap over and touching the surface to keep all air out. Refrigerate for up to 6 hours. Remove the pits before serving.

SERVE

5. Remove the pits and serve the guacamole with the store-bought tortilla chips or warmed tortillas.

Pan-Seared Chipotle-Citrus Turkey Paillards with Adobo Mayonnaise

Yield: 6 main-course servings

2 (7-ounce) cans chipotle chilies in adobo

1 large white onion, cut into chunks

4 cloves garlic

3 tablespoons whole cumin seed

1 tablespoon New Mexican chili powder

½ cup extra virgin olive oil

Freshly grated zest and freshly squeezed juice of 1 lime

1 bunch fresh cilantro, chopped, divided

Fine sea salt and freshly ground black pepper to taste.

1½ cups Hellman's or Basic Mayonnaise (p. 275)

6 (5- to 6-ounce) slices turkey breast, pounded into very thin paillards

1. To make the marinade, purée the chilies in adobo, onion, garlic, cumin seed, and chili powder in a blender or food processor until smooth. With the motor running, slowly pour in the olive oil.

2. Stir the lime zest and juice into the marinade. Add ½ the cilantro and season with the salt and pepper. Wrap the remaining cilantro in damp paper towels and store in an open plastic bag in the fridge.

3. To make the adobo mayonnaise, stir 1½ cups of the marinade together with the mayonnaise in a medium bowl. Place in a covered container and refrigerate until ready to use.

4. In a large bowl, toss the paillards together with the remaining marinade. Place everything in a large zip-lock bag or covered container and refrigerate for at least 2 hours.

5. If grilling or broiling, preheat the grill or broiler.

6. Remove the adobo mayonnaise from the refrigerator.

7. If using a grill pan, set it over high heat.

8. Wipe most of the marinade off the paillards and grill or broil for 2 to 3 minutes per side, or until just cooked through. Don't overcook.

AFTER THE FIRST COURSE

9. Transfer the paillards to a serving platter and top with dollops of the adobo mayonnaise and sprinkle with the remaining cilantro. Serve right away.

Certain whole spices, such as the cumin seed in this recipe, as well as whole coriander, anise, fennel, star anise among others, benefit from a light toasting before using—whether using whole or ground. Cool before grinding.

The adobo mayonnaise is also excellent with pork loin or chops or with roast or grilled chicken.

Mango and Plum Salsa with Cilantro and Lime

Yield: 6–8 side-dish servings

4 hard-ripe plums, halved, seeds removed, and cut into ½-inch dice

2 large hard-ripe mangoes, peeled and cut into ½-inch dice

1 jalapeño or serrano pepper, ribs and seeds removed, and finely minced

½ cup minced white onion

½ bunch fresh cilantro, coarsely chopped

½ packed cup julienned fresh mint

1 large clove garlic, minced

Freshly squeezed juice of 2 limes

Fine sea salt and freshly ground black pepper, to taste

4 HOURS

1. Toss all the ingredients together in a medium serving bowl. Cover and set aside for at least 1 hour.

SERVE

AFTER THE FIRST COURSE

2. Toss again, taste, and adjust seasoning as needed.

3. Serve at room temperature.

Of course, some types of peppers are hotter than others, but even peppers of the same type can vary dramatically vis-à-vis their heat. It's best to use them sparingly, taste the dish, and add more if needed. If you're particularly wary of making a salsa too hot, simply remove the seeds and cores, slice the peppers and toss the slices into the salsa. Toss and taste every 15 to 20 minutes until the salsa is the way you want it. Then, simply remove and discard the pieces of pepper. (But be sure to remove the same number you put in!)

Rice Casserole with Cheese and Green Chilies

Yield: 8 generous side-dish servings

5 cups sour cream or plain full-fat Greek yogurt, or a mixture

2 cups long-grained white rice, cooked according to package directions

⅓ cup minced white onion

⅓ packed cup chopped fresh cilantro

1 clove garlic, minced

Fine sea salt, freshly ground black pepper, and Tabasco sauce or a Mexican hot sauce, to taste

1 pound Jack, mild white cheddar, or a similar Mexican cheese, coarsely grated

2 (6-ounce) cans diced green chili peppers, drained

1. Mix together the sour cream or yogurt, cooked rice, onion, cilantro, and garlic in a large bowl. Add the salt, pepper, and Tabasco sauce to taste.

2. Fold all but 1¾ cups of the grated cheese into the rice mixture.

3. Arrange ⅓ of the rice and cheese mixture in the bottom of a medium casserole, soufflé dish, or large gratin dish.

4. Sprinkle ½ cup of the remaining cheese and ½ of the chilies over the top.

5. Add the second ⅓ of the rice mixture and top with another ½ cup of the cheese and the rest of the chilies. Top with the rest of the rice followed by the remaining cheese. Cover and refrigerate.

6. Remove the casserole from the refrigerator.

7. Preheat the oven to 350°F.

8. Uncover the casserole and bake for 30 to 40 minutes, or until piping hot and the cheese on top is melted and turning golden.

AFTER THE FIRST COURSE

9. Remove from the oven and serve hot or very warm.

Rich and Easy Mexican Chocolate Mousse

Yield: 8 generous servings

1 cup water

1 pound best-quality semisweet or bittersweet chocolate, roughly chopped

Pinch of fine sea salt

3 tablespoons instant espresso coffee granules or 1 teaspoon ground cinnamon (optional but very Mexican)

6 eggs yolks

1⅓ cups plus ½ cup heavy cream, very cold, divided

3 tablespoons cognac, dark rum, or Kahlúa

1 teaspoon granulated sugar

1. In the top of a double boiler or a metal bowl set over a saucepan of simmering water, combine the water, chocolate, salt, and espresso granules or cinnamon, if using. Heat, stirring frequently, until the chocolate has just melted. Remove from heat.

2. Whisk in the yolks, 1 at a time. Set aside to cool completely.

3. Using a stand mixer fitted with the whisk attachment or an electric handheld mixer set on medium–high speed, whip the 1⅓ cups of cream for 1 to 2 minutes, or until soft peaks form. Add liquor and whip for 15 more seconds. Don't overbeat.

4. Stir about ¼ of the whipped cream into the cooled chocolate mixture. Then gently fold in the rest.

5. Divide the mousse among to 8 to 10 individual dessert bowls or ramekins or spoon into one large serving bowl. Cover and refrigerate for at least 4 hours before serving.

When whipping cream—in this case for Chocolate Mousse—make sure the cream is very cold. It's even better if the bowl and beaters are cold as well. The warmer the cream is, the more likely it is to turn into butter when whipped.

SERVE

AFTER THE MAIN COURSE

6. Using a stand mixer fitted with the whisk attachment or an electric handheld mixer set on medium–high speed, whip the remaining ½ cup of the cream together with the sugar for 1 to 2 minutes, or until soft peaks form.

7. Serve the mousse cold with dollops of the whipped cream.

SUMMER REFRESHER

DINNER FOR SIX

DISH	BEGIN PREP	PAGE
FIRST COURSE		
Cold Yogurt Soup with Fresh Herbs, Cucumber, Cumin, Feta, and Pink Peppercorns	1 day ahead	46
ENTRÉE		
Seared Scallops with Cilantro–Mint Pesto	1 day ahead	48
ON THE SIDE		
Fresh Corn Salad with Sun-Dried Tomatoes and Fresh Herbs	1 day ahead	51
Oversized Cheddar and Chive Biscuits	1 day ahead	52
DESSERT		
Key Lime Pie	1 day ahead	53

Evoking balmy days and tropical breezes, this menu kicks off with Cold Yogurt Soup (p. 46). This refreshing starter is a warm weather staple in my kitchen. I got the recipe from a Persian friend whose extraordinary soup included raisins and saffron, but I like mine—with cilantro, mint, and lots of cumin— even better. The colorful garnishes, especially the pink peppercorns, make this go-to summer treat as gorgeous as it is mouthwatering. The feta and toasted cumin seductively reference the Middle East, but the dish as a whole is multi-national and more intriguingly enigmatic than the sum of its parts. I keep a pitcher in the fridge all summer long, as it's an instant revitalizer on even the very hottest days.

The briny sweetness of Seared Scallops (p. 48) is irresistible. Properly prepared—crispy-crusty on the outside and succulent within— these tender nuggets are delectable even without sauce. However, the adventurous should try dolloping them with Indian-inspired Cilantro– Mint Pesto (p. 49) or garnishing them with a drizzle of truffle oil and a sprinkling of fresh chives, the Tomato–Caper Salsa (p. 19), a flavored mayonnaise (p. 275), or beurre blanc (p. 282). The scallops are at their best hot, but warm or even at room temperature, they still pass muster.

Super-fresh corn—whether on or off the cob—is hard to beat. I eat it several times a week during high season, but to keep things interesting, I vary the preparation. This Fresh Corn Salad (p. 51) combines summer's best offerings: sugar-sweet corn and juicy, vine-ripe tomatoes. The former accentuates the sweetness of the scallops, while the acid in the tomatoes brings the other ingredients into perfect balance. Omit the sun-dried tomatoes if you must, but for me, they're the secret ingredient here, adding depth of flavor and a salty, chewy complexity.

While this versatile side dish is ideal alongside picnic fare, hot dogs, and burgers, its heady flavors also brilliantly enhance dinner table steak, chicken, fish, and shellfish.

Rich, flaky, and addictive oversized cheese biscuits consistently bring down the house. This sharp cheddar and chive version (p. 52) is adapted from a recipe card I picked up years ago at BLT Steak in Manhattan. But other cheese and herb combinations are equally inviting. A Parmesan, fresh rosemary, and thyme version emerges molto Italiano, while Gruyère with fresh tarragon holds its own at the most elegant soirée. Or try a Jack cheese and cilantro combo with your next Mexican feast. They're all also great for breakfast-on-the-run and snack time.

Key Lime Pie (p. 53) seamlessly wraps up this hot-weather feast. The delectable Florida classic is simple enough to make all year long, and is as good consumed after months in the freezer as the day it was made. In summer, don't even think about thawing; when temperatures rise, it's addictively refreshing still frozen. Just remember that the whipped cream topping should be added last minute.

ORDER OF PREPARATION

START

1. Complete Step 1 for the Yogurt Soup (p. 46), cover, and refrigerate.

2. Make the Pesto (p. 49), cover, and refrigerate.

3. Preheat the oven to 350°F.

4. Complete Steps 2 through 6 of the Key Lime Pie (p. 53), cool, cover, and refrigerate or freeze.

5. Complete Steps 1 through 5 for the Cheddar Biscuits (p. 52), cover, and refrigerate.

6. Complete Step 1 for the Corn Salad (p. 51), cover, and refrigerate.

1. Remove the dressing for the Corn Salad from the refrigerator (Step 2).

1. Complete Step 1 for the Seared Scallops (p. 48), cover, and refrigerate.

2. Complete Step 3 for the Corn Salad and set aside.

1. Remove the Pesto from the refrigerator.

1. Preheat the oven to 425°F and complete Step 6 for the Biscuits.

1. Remove the Soup from the refrigerator (Step 2) and complete Step 3.

2. Complete Steps 2 and 3 for the Scallops.

SERVE

1. Complete Step 7 for the Biscuits.

2. Complete the Soup (Step 4) and serve.

AFTER THE FIRST COURSE

3. After eating the Soup, complete the Scallops (Step 4) and the Corn Salad (Step 4).

4. Serve the Scallops with the Pesto, Corn Salad, and Biscuits.

AFTER THE MAIN COURSE

5. After clearing the table, complete the Key Lime Pie (Steps 7 and 8) and serve.

GET A HEAD START!

The **Yogurt Soup** can be made and refrigerated up to 3 days ahead.

The dressing for the **Fresh Corn Salsa** can be made and refrigerated up to 3 days ahead.

The **Cheddar and Chive Biscuits** can be made and frozen—pre- or post-baking—for up to 3 months. If freezing, thaw before baking.

The **Key Lime Pie** crust can be baked up to 3 days ahead and stored at room temperature. Make the whole Key Lime Pie and freeze for up to 3 months. However, the whipped cream topping must be made and added within a few hours of serving. Keep refrigerated until ready to serve.

Cold Yogurt Soup with Fresh Herbs, Cucumber, Cumin, Feta, and Pink Peppercorns

Yield: 6 first-course servings

1 large (36-ounce) container nonfat Greek yogurt

1⅓–3 cups whole milk, for thinning as needed

1 small bunch fresh cilantro, finely chopped

⅓ cup julienned fresh mint

2 tablespoons extra virgin olive oil

1 large clove garlic, very finely minced

Fine sea salt and freshly ground black pepper, to taste

2 Kirby or Persian cucumbers, peeled if not organic and cut into very small dice, for garnish

1 small red onion, cut into small dice, for garnish

½ cup crumbled feta cheese, for garnish

1 tablespoon ground cumin, toasted, for garnish

2 tablespoons crushed pink peppercorns, for garnish

---

 1. Stir the first 7 ingredients together in a large bowl, starting with 1 cup of the milk and adding more as desired. Cover and refrigerate for at least 5 hours.

---

 2. Remove from the refrigerator.

3. Add more milk if the soup is thicker than desired. Thickness here is a matter of personal preference. I like my yogurt soup to be the consistency of melted ice cream (somewhat thicker than heavy cream, but still soupy). Taste and adjust the seasonings as needed.

---

 4. Divide evenly among 6 chilled (if possible) soup plates and top abundantly with the garnishes.

5. Serve right away.

Seared Scallops with Cilantro–Mint Pesto

Yield: 6 main-course servings

2½–3 pounds (about 30) large sea scallops

3 tablespoons unsalted butter

1 tablespoon extra virgin olive oil

Kosher salt and freshly ground black pepper, to taste

1 recipe Cilantro–Mint Pesto (recipe follows), room temperature, for serving

In order to **sear** properly, scallops must be completely dry. Always dry them well before cooking.

4 HOURS

1. Remove the small side muscle from each scallop, rinse with cold water, and drain. Cover and refrigerate until ready to use.

10 MINS

2. Put the butter and oil in 1 very large or 2 (12-inch to 14-inch) sauté pan(s) set over high heat. Dry the scallops well—scallops must be dry to sear properly. Season generously with the salt and pepper.

3. When the fat is almost smoking, place the scallops in the pan(s), making sure they are at least ¼ inch apart, and sear for about 1½ to 3 minutes on each side. When done, the scallops should be crusty and golden on the outside and remain translucent in the center. Remove from the heat.

SERVE

AFTER THE FIRST COURSE

4. Evenly divide the scallops among 6 warmed (if possible) dinner plates and drizzle with the Cilantro–Mint Pesto. Alternatively, place the scallops on a warmed (if possible) serving platter and drizzle with the pesto. In either case you can pass the pesto in a separate bowl, if you prefer.

5. Serve right away.

Cilantro–Mint Pesto

Yield: About 1½ cups

2 cups chopped fresh cilantro

1 cup fresh mint leaves

4 tablespoons freshly squeezed orange juice

4 tablespoons roughly chopped scallions (white and green parts)

2 cloves garlic

2 tablespoons freshly squeezed lime juice

4 teaspoons extra virgin olive oil

½ teaspoon fine sea salt, plus more to taste

To prevent potential discoloring, press a piece of plastic wrap flat onto the top of the pesto before covering with a lid and refrigerating.

1. Place all ingredients in the bowl of a food processor. Process until smooth.

2. Transfer to a covered container and refrigerate. Taste and adjust salt as needed before serving.

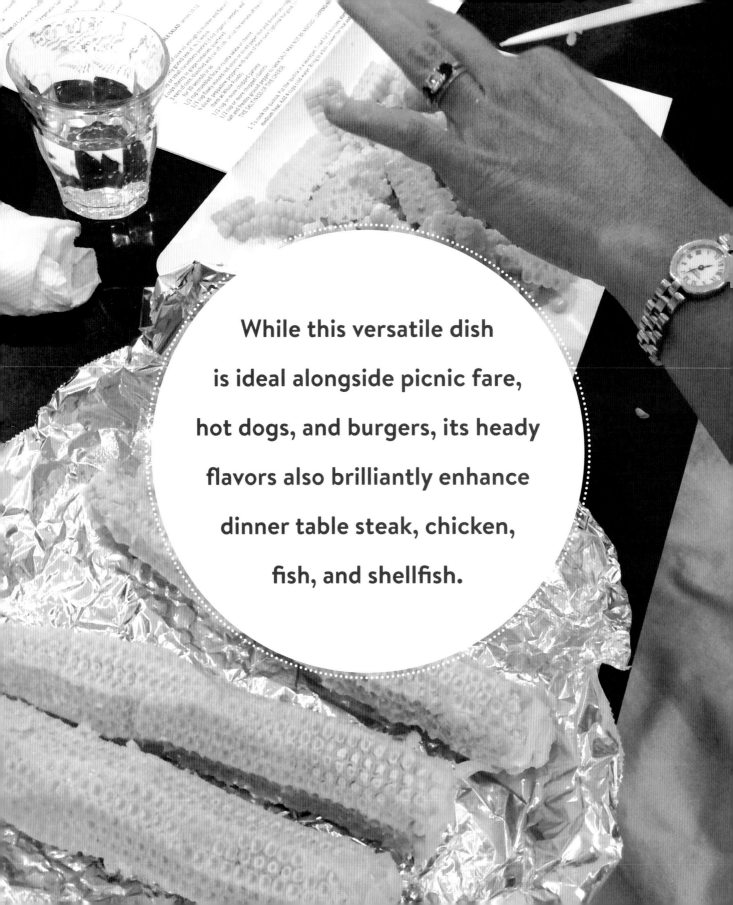

While this versatile dish is ideal alongside picnic fare, hot dogs, and burgers, its heady flavors also brilliantly enhance dinner table steak, chicken, fish, and shellfish.

Fresh Corn Salad with Sun-Dried Tomatoes and Fresh Herbs

Yield: 6–8 side-dish servings

½ cup extra virgin olive oil

½ cup balsamic vinegar

½ cup julienned fresh basil

4 large shallots, finely minced

6 tablespoons chopped fresh Italian parsley

6 tablespoons chopped fresh chives

2 cloves garlic, minced

Fine sea salt and freshly ground pepper, to taste

12 ears of corn, cooked and kernels cut off cob*

1 cup cherry tomatoes, quartered

⅓ cup oil-packed sun-dried tomatoes, drained, oil reserved, and finely chopped

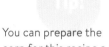

1. To start the dressing, place the first 8 ingredients in a lidded jar and shake vigorously to combine. Set aside for at least 1 hour to allow flavors to marry. Cover and refrigerate. (This dressing will keep in the refrigerator for up to 3 days).

You can prepare the corn for this recipe a day ahead, when you make the dressing.

2. Remove the dressing from the refrigerator.

3. Combine the corn and cherry and sundried tomatoes in a large bowl. Add 2 tablespoons of the reserved oil from the sundried tomatoes to the jar of dressing. Reshake the jar. Taste and adjust the seasoning as needed. Toss the salad with just enough of the dressing to moisten and flavor. Set aside.

AFTER THE FIRST COURSE

4. Taste and adjust the seasoning as needed. Serve.

Off season, you can substitute 6 to 7 cups of cooked frozen corn kernels for the cooked fresh corn. The salad won't be quite the same, but it will still be well worth making.

Oversized Cheddar and Chive Biscuits

Yield: 6 very large biscuits

1½ cups all-purpose flour

2 teaspoons baking powder

Scant 1 teaspoon fine sea salt

⅛ teaspoon cayenne pepper

6 tablespoons very cold unsalted butter, cut into small pieces

1 heaping cup grated sharp cheddar cheese

¾ cup heavy cream, very cold, plus more as needed

3 tablespoons chopped fresh chives

Instead of following Step 5, the dough for the biscuits can be patted out into 1 large, ¾-inch-thick circle, and then cut into 12 wedges; or rolled into logs about 2 inches in diameter and cut into 1-inch thick slices.

1. Using a stand mixer fitted with the paddle attachment or an electric handheld mixer set on low speed, combine the flour, baking powder, salt, and cayenne pepper.

2. Add the butter and mix on low speed for about 30 to 60 seconds, or until the butter pieces are the size of small peas.

3. Add the cheese, cream, and chives. Mix until the dough just begins to come together. Do not overmix. The dough should be relatively dry, but if it's really too dry to come together, add more cream, 1 to 2 teaspoons at a time, as needed.

4. Turn out onto a floured work surface and gently pat (do not roll with a rolling pin) the dough until it's about ½-inch thick. Fold the dough over 5 times and then gently press it into a rough rectangle about 1-inch thick.

5. Use a sharp knife to cut the dough into 6 squares. Alternatively, cut into 6 circles with a 3- or 4-inch round biscuit cutter. Place the raw biscuits at least 1 inch apart on a cookie sheet lined with parchment paper, cover, and refrigerate.

6. Preheat the oven to 425°F. Remove biscuits from the refrigerator.

7. Bake for 18 to 25 minutes, or until golden and cooked through. (If baked straight from the freezer, increase the baking time by at least 5 minutes.)

If you must **wait** longer than 15 minutes before serving, you can certainly serve the biscuits at room temperature. However, they're better warm. Simply pop them into a 350°F oven and reheat for about 5 minutes. The biscuits can be baked up to 6 hours before serving.

AFTER THE FIRST COURSE

8. Remove from the oven. Serve warm, within 15 minutes, if possible.

Key Lime Pie

Yield: 8 servings

For the Crust

11 double graham crackers (2¼-inch × 4¾-inch), broken into pieces

6 tablespoons unsalted butter, melted

2½ tablespoons granulated sugar

For the Filling

1 (14-ounce) can sweetened condensed milk

4 large egg yolks

½ cup plus 2 tablespoons freshly squeezed key lime juice or bottled Manhattan Key Lime Juice

For the Topping

¾ cup heavy cream, very cold

Freshly grated zest from 1 key lime, or if using bottled key lime juice, 1–2 teaspoons freshly grated lime zest.

1. Preheat the oven to 350°F.

2. *Start the Crust:* Place the graham cracker pieces, melted butter, and sugar in the bowl a food processor. Process until well combined.

3. Press the crust mixture evenly over the bottom of a 9-inch or 10-inch springform pan.

4. Bake for 10 minutes. Remove from the oven and set aside. Leave the oven on.

5. *Make the Filling:* Using a stand mixer fitted with the paddle attachment or an electric handheld mixer set on medium speed, beat the condensed milk and egg yolks until well combined. Add the key lime juice and continue beating until slightly thickened.

6. Pour the filling into the baked crust and bake for 15 minutes. Transfer to a wire rack to cool completely. The filling will set as it cools. Cover and refrigerate or freeze overnight. (The pie should be refrigerated for at least 8 hours or frozen for at least 4 hours.)

AFTER THE MAIN COURSE

7. *Make the Topping:* Using a stand mixer fitted with the whisk attachment or an electric handheld mixer set on medium–high speed, whip the cream for 2 to 3 minutes, until soft peaks form. Do not overwhip.

8. Spread the whipped cream over pie. Sprinkle with the lime zest and serve right away.

Bake the key lime pie at least 1 day in advance to make sure it's chilled and set in time for dinner.

CHAPTER 2
CLASS FAVORITES

CLASS FAVORITES

MENUS

French Country Dinner
p. 58

Flavors of Morocco
p. 70

California Dreamin'
p. 80

Asian Sensations
p. 90

've taught cooking for almost 20 years, and each class has revolved around a specific menu. Using or adapting recipes from friends, colleagues, the Internet, and hundreds of cookbooks, my students and I have well covered the gamut, the class table having been graced with everything from basic roast chicken to off-the-beaten-path Indian dosas, Tex-Mex tamale pies, and Vietnamese summer rolls.

Although some people claim that culinary success demands nothing more than the mastery of three good dishes, my students and I have in fact prepared hundreds of recipes together. I don't quite buy the "three good dishes" concept, but if you amend it to three good menus, I might agree. My very first cooking student came to me in a panic; her closest friends had embraced Julia Child and Marcella Hazan with a vengeance, and she felt she could no longer keep up. Deeply competitive by nature and increasingly insecure about her lack of kitchen prowess, Jill knew she'd need help to outshine her friends. She suggested trading me one of her highly collectible artworks for however many lessons were needed to get her cooking skills up to par. This offer was too good to turn down, and we got to work.

Jill was gung ho and amazingly focused, mastering three of the four menus below in an equivalent number of weeks. Then, out of nowhere, she announced she knew all she needed to know and was done with the lessons. I was initially flummoxed, but with a great painting of hers still on my wall, I definitely feel I came out ahead.

However, it seems Jill harbors no complaints. I ran into her recently; after all those years, she thanked me profusely for teaching her what she referred to as "*sine qua non* recipes and how to cook them." Clearly, a few good menus and the ability to put them together was all she'd needed.

This book abounds with menus like Jill's. The four in this chapter—each serving six—are tried-and-true class favorites featuring flavorful, relatively simple dishes that are guaranteed to both wow and satisfy friends, guests, and family alike. They contain no requisite make-aheads, and other than the desserts for the French Country and Asian Sensations menus (both of which do take a bit of advance prep), we make, serve, and consume these meals, start to finish, in a single three-hour class. You're about to do the same in your own kitchen.

Sometimes I'm inclined to cook in a more leisurely manner, and stretch meal preparation over several days. The Get a Head Start boxes for these menus discuss items that can be completed in advance. But the menus in this chapter—versus the more complicated ones in Chapters 4 and 5—can be easily be made straight through from beginning to end in an afternoon. Nonetheless, there are many ways to skin a cat (and to make dinner), and I'm hoping each of you will adjust the timing to fit your specific needs, schedule, and personality.

These four meals are varied and appetizing. And if you follow the step-by-step instructions, they're easy and verging on foolproof as well. And while I hope you cook from this entire book, if you do nothing but stick with Chapter 2, you'll have mastered Jill's three great (and very manageable) menus with one to spare.

FRENCH COUNTRY DINNER

DINNER FOR SIX

DISH	BEGIN PREP	PAGE
FIRST COURSE		
Salad of Mixed Baby Greens with Pears and Roquefort	10 mins ahead	63
ENTRÉE		
Roast Chicken with 40 Cloves of Garlic	5½ hours ahead	64
ON THE SIDE		
Country Toasts	3½ hours ahead	66
Pan-Roast of Root Vegetables and Bell Peppers	1 day ahead	67
DESSERT		
Caramelized Apple Galette with Rum-Raisin Ice Cream	2 days ahead	68

This menu takes me back to my very first years of teaching. The Salad of Mixed Baby Greens with Pears and Roquefort (p. 63) is a distinctive cold-weather starter that is simultaneously succulent, sweet, salty, and crunchy. The inspiration for this mélange of contrasting flavors and textures is a salad I ate frequently at Pino Luongo's Le Madri restaurant back in the 1980s, and it's the one against which I measure all others.

Adapted from a Richard Olney signature dish, the Roast Chicken with 40 Cloves of Garlic (p. 64) has been a class favorite for years. Enlivened with Pernod and a myriad of herbs and spices, the *cuisine de grandmère* concoction outdoes Grandma's wildest dreams. And because the casserole is covered until the last 20 minutes of cooking, optimum juiciness is guaranteed. When the lid is removed and the heat raised, the bird slips seamlessly from pale gold to crispy brown perfection.

Nonetheless, who could imagine that small children would embrace Pernod, or that anyone at all would go for 40 cloves of garlic? It turns out, however, that a few tablespoons of the anise-flavored liqueur impart a mellow opulence and that all those garlic cloves, once caramelized on

the outside while remaining sumptuously soft within, are food for the gods. Spread on thick slices of Country Toasts (p. 66), the garlic goes down as easily as creamery butter. Accompanied by a Pan-Roast of Root Vegetables (p. 67)—meltingly tender yams, shallots, and parsnips seasoned to perfection—this meal represents comfort food at its finest.

Last year, I replaced the menu's apple tart with an Apple Galette (p. 68). Rather than the shortbread crust I'd relied on in the past, the galette takes advantage of store-bought frozen puff pastry, making this dessert extra easy.

Slicing the apples paper-thin and baking the dessert in a very hot oven results in highly caramelized crust-cum-fruit that is at once both crispy and chewy. Best of all, fruit galettes are a perfect dessert any time of year. Use apples or pears in fall and winter and plums, nectarines, apricots, or peaches once the weather turns warm. Guests clamor for seconds, and leftovers are irresistible for both breakfast and snacking, so make extra.

PUFF PASTRY

Puff pastry is one of my favorite choices when entertaining. Everyone loves it, and recipes for hors d'oeuvres, main courses, and festive desserts can almost always be assembled ahead of time and baked off when needed.

But don't even think about preparing puff pastry from scratch. The endless time spent rolling, folding, and chilling makes no sense for today's home cook, especially since the readily available frozen version is a genius supermarket staple that delivers the benefits of homemade without the work.

For best results, buy an all-butter brand and let it thaw overnight in the fridge before using. In a pinch, 45 minutes at room temperature should suffice. Gently unfold the thawed-but-still-cool pastry and squeeze any tears or holes back together. To prevent sticking when rolling it out, keep the pastry cool and lightly flour the work surface and rolling pin. Better yet: roll the pastry between two large sheets of parchment paper and don't even bother to flour.

Keep in mind that the pastry must support toppings while still holding its shape, so don't roll it too thin— approximately ³⁄₁₆ of an inch is a good thickness. If the pastry warms up and becomes unworkably sticky at any point, return it to the fridge or freezer for a few minutes to firm up.

When you're done rolling, gently brush off any excess flour. You can then combine leftover scraps of puff pastry and roll them out to make cheese straws or palmiers. Or save them in the freezer to combine with other scraps to eventually make small pastries such as turnovers, potpies, and individual tarts. Recycled pastry won't puff up quite like the original, but that's less important when making smaller shapes.

Puff pastry tastes best freshly baked. Most recipes can be assembled and kept in the fridge for up to 24 hours to be baked off last minute. Or, to avoid last-minute hassle, little will be lost if you bake your creations a few hours ahead and reheat briefly before serving.

ORDER OF PREPARATION

START

3 DAYS

1. If required for your type of ice cream machine, place its bowl in the freezer to chill.

2 DAYS

1. Make the Rum-Raisin Ice Cream (p. 69) and freeze.

1 DAY

1. Complete Steps 1 and 2 for the Apple Galette (p. 68), cover, and refrigerate.

2. Make the Walnut Vinaigrette (p. 280) for the Salad of Mixed Baby Greens (p. 63), cover, and refrigerate.

3. Complete Step 1 for the Pan-Roast of Root Vegetables (p. 67), cover, and refrigerate.

5½ HOURS

1. With a rack adjusted to the highest position, preheat the oven to 400°F.

2. Complete the Apple Galette (Steps 4 through 7) and set aside.

3. Complete Steps 1 and 2 for the Roast Chicken (p. 64) and set aside.

4. Complete Step 2 for the Pan-Roast.

3½ HOURS

1. Raise the oven temperature to 450°F.

2. Complete Steps 8 and 9 for the Apple Galette.

3. Complete Step 4 for the Pan-Roast and set aside.

4. Complete Steps 1 and 2 for the Country Toasts (p. 66) and set aside.

2 HOURS

1. With a rack adjusted to the lower-third position, reduce the oven temperature to 350°F.

2. Remove the Walnut Vinaigrette from the refrigerator.

1½ HOURS

1. Complete Steps 4 and 5 for the Chicken.

30 MINS

1. Complete Step 6 for the Chicken.

10 MINS

1. Complete Step 7 for the Chicken and then reduce the oven temperature to 450°F and adjust racks to the highest and center positions.

2. Complete Steps 8 and 9 for the Chicken.

3. Complete Steps 1 and 2 for the Salad.

SERVE

1. Complete the Salad (Step 3) and serve.

AFTER THE FIRST COURSE

2. After eating the Salad, warm the Toasts on the top rack of the oven (Step 4) and reheat the Pan-Roast on the center rack (Step 6).

3. While items reheat, complete the Chicken (Steps 10 and 11) and remove the Ice Cream from the freezer to soften.

4. Once reheated, complete the Pan-Roast (Step 7).

5. If reheating the Galette, reduce the oven temperature to 350°F.

6. Serve the Roast Chicken with the garlic, pitcher of pan juices, Toasts, and Pan-Roast.

AFTER THE MAIN COURSE

7. After clearing the table, if reheating the Galette, complete Step 10.

8. Serve the Galette with the Ice Cream.

GET A HEAD START!

Like many **vinaigrettes**, the one paired with the **Salad of Mixed Baby Greens** can be made ahead and refrigerated for up to 2 weeks.

The **Roast Chicken** ingredients—other than the Pernod—can be assembled ahead and refrigerated up to 24 hours. Remove the casserole from the fridge and uncover 4 hours before roasting.

Slice the vegetables for the **Pan-Roast**, toss them in oil, and refrigerate, covered, for up to 3 days. If you'd rather make the entire recipe day-of, roast the vegetables a few hours before needed, set them aside, and when ready to serve, reheat in a 450°F oven for 5 minutes, or until piping hot.

Make and freeze the **Rum-Raisin Ice Cream** up to 2 weeks in advance.

Salad of Mixed Baby Greens with Pears and Roquefort

Yield: 6–8 first-course servings

3 bunches watercress, tough stems removed

3–4 heads Belgian endive, trimmed and sliced crosswise into ½-inch slices

1 large head frisée

¾ cup seedless red grapes, halved vertically

½ cup crumbled Roquefort or other blue cheese

½ cup thinly sliced (crosswise) celery

¼ cup toasted walnuts, coarsely chopped

2 tablespoons coarsely chopped fresh mint leaves

2 tablespoons coarsely chopped fresh Italian parsley

2 tablespoons finely sliced scallion rounds (white and green parts)

2 Bosc pears, ripe but still firm

1 recipe Walnut Vinaigrette (p. 280), room temperature

Fine sea salt and freshly ground black pepper, to taste

1. Place all the salad ingredients, except the pears, in a large salad bowl.

2. Core the pears. Slice them into ¼-inch-thick wedges and add them to the salad.

3. Toss with just enough of the Walnut Vinaigrette to moisten and flavor. Taste and add the salt and pepper as needed. Serve.

Roast Chicken with 40 Cloves of Garlic

Yield: 6 main-course servings

Roasted garlic is delicious. Just squeeze the cloves out of their peels and eat with the chicken and/or the toasts.

For the Seasoning

2 teaspoons dried thyme

1½ teaspoons fine sea salt

½ teaspoon freshly ground black pepper

For the Chicken

1 large onion, sliced

½ bulb fennel, trimmed and sliced

10 sprigs fresh Italian parsley

1 small bunch fresh tarragon, plus more, chopped, for garnish

1 (4½–5 pound) whole chicken, rinsed in cool water and dried

1 bay leaf

40 cloves garlic, whole and unpeeled

¼ cup extra virgin olive oil

¼ teaspoon fine sea salt

¼ teaspoon freshly ground black pepper

2 tablespoons of Pernod, Sambuca, or other anise-flavored liqueur

5½ HOURS

1. *Make the Seasoning:* Combine the thyme, salt, and pepper and set aside.

2. *Start the Chicken:* Place ½ each of the onion, fennel, parsley, and tarragon in the bottom of a lidded casserole just large enough to hold the chicken. Rub the chicken, inside and out, with the seasoning, place the bay leaf and the remaining ½ of the vegetables and herbs inside the chicken, and place it, breast side up, in the casserole. Set aside. (Refrigerate if not roasting within 4 hours.)

2 HOURS

3. With a rack adjusted to the lower-third position, preheat the oven to 350°F.

1½ HOURS

4. Combine the garlic, oil, salt, and pepper and pour the mixture over the chicken. Then pour the Pernod over the chicken.

5. Cover the casserole and roast for 1 hour.

30 MINS

6. Raise the oven temperature to 500°F and remove the casserole's lid. If, once you've removed the lid, you can fit the casserole on a higher rack, do so as the chicken will brown better. Continue roasting for 20 to 25 minutes, or until the chicken is golden and cooked through. Test for doneness by piercing the thickest part of the thigh with a fork or inserting an instant-read thermometer. The juices should run clear rather than pink and an instant-read thermometer inserted into the breast should register 158°F.

Resting is the critical final step in the cooking process of meat and poultry and absolutely requisite before slicing. During cooking, moisture moves outward. When removed from the oven, the juices need time to redistribute. If you slice immediately, juices will spill out and leave you with a dry bird. In addition, cooking actually continues for a few minutes outside the oven. This is why many recipes suggest you take poultry or a pork, lamb, or beef roast out of the oven while still slightly underdone. You can tent poultry or roasted meats with foil during the resting period, but I find it a wasted step—once carved, they are always lukewarm anyway.

10 MINS

7. Place the chicken on a carving board to rest for at least 15 minutes before carving.

8. While the chicken is resting, use a slotted spoon to transfer the cooked garlic to a small bowl. Set aside.

9. Strain the juices from the casserole into a heatproof pitcher. Refrigerate or freeze so that the fat will rise to the top more quickly.

SERVE

AFTER THE FIRST COURSE

10. Remove the pitcher from the refrigerator or freezer and use a spoon to remove as much of the fat as possible. Reheat the pan juices in a microwave or transfer them to a small saucepan and warm over medium heat.

11. Carve the chicken and arrange the slices on a serving platter. Pour about ¼ of the warmed pan juices over the chicken. Top with the cooked garlic and garnish with the chopped tarragon.

12. Serve the chicken hot or warm with the pitcher of remaining pan juices.

Country Toasts

Yield: 6–8 servings

6 tablespoons salted butter, room temperature

4 tablespoons minced fresh chives, parsley, basil, and/or chervil

1 long French baguette, cut into 3-inch or 4-inch sections, each halved horizontally

3½ HOURS

1. Combine the butter and herbs in a small bowl.

2. Place the baguette slices face up on a cookie sheet and spread them with the herb butter. Set aside.

10 MINS

3. With a rack adjusted to the highest position, preheat the oven to 450°F.

SERVE

AFTER THE FIRST COURSE

4. Toast for 5 minutes, or until golden. Watch carefully so they don't burn.

5. Transfer to a breadbasket and serve hot.

Pan-Roast of Root Vegetables and Bell Peppers

Yield: 6 side-dish servings

8 large shallots, halved

6 large parsnips, peeled and cut into sticks

4 large carrots, peeled and cut into 1-inch-long diagonals

4 medium yams, peeled and cut into large chunks

3 red bell peppers, cut vertically into ½-inch strips, seeds and white parts removed

1 medium celeriac (celery root), peeled and cut into ¼-inch half circles

½ cup extra virgin olive oil

1 teaspoon dried rosemary

½ teaspoon fine sea salt, plus more to taste

¼ teaspoon freshly ground black pepper, plus more to taste

3 tablespoons chopped fresh Italian parsley, basil, or chives

1. Combine the vegetables with the oil, rosemary, salt, and pepper in a large bowl and toss well. Cover and refrigerate.

2. Spread the vegetables in a single layer on 2 to 3 large sheet pans and set aside.

3. Preheat the oven to 450°F.

4. Roast the vegetables, tossing occasionally with a metal spatula, for 45 to 60 minutes, or until tender, golden, and more deeply colored in places. Rotate the pans in the oven a couple of times during cooking. When done, the vegetables will have shrunken considerably. Place them all on a single sheet pan and set aside.

5. With a rack adjusted to the center position, preheat the oven to 450°F.

AFTER THE FIRST COURSE

6. Reheat the vegetables on the center rack of the oven for 5 minutes, or until hot.

7. Transfer to a large serving bowl and toss with the fresh herbs. Taste and adjust the salt and pepper as needed. Serve hot or warm.

Caramelized Apple Galette with Rum-Raisin Ice Cream

Yield: 6–8 servings

1 (1-pound) package frozen all-butter puff pastry dough, thawed but still cool
8–10 large Granny Smith apples
¾ cup granulated sugar, divided

2 tablespoons unsalted butter, cold and cut into very small pieces
Rum-Raisin Ice Cream (recipe follows), whipped cream, or store-bought super-premium ice cream, for serving

1. Place the puff pastry dough on a lightly floured work surface. Using a floured rolling pin, roll it into a 12-inch × 14-inch rectangle. Alternatively (my preference), skip the flour and roll between 2 large pieces of parchment paper.

2. Trim the edges of the dough to get a neat and approximate 11-inch × 13-inch rectangle, and place on a cookie sheet lined with parchment paper. Cover and refrigerate for at least 1 hour or overnight.

3. With a rack adjusted to the highest position, preheat the oven to 400°F.

4. Peel, halve vertically, and core the apples. Cut them crosswise into ⅛-inch slices. Set aside. (If not using within 1 hour, cover and refrigerate.)

5. Remove the prepared pastry from the refrigerator. In a corner, starting ¾ of an inch from an edge of the rolled dough, place the apple slices in vertical rows, overlapping each other by two-thirds. Continue until you have neatly covered the dough with apples slices, leaving a ¾-inch border on all sides. Sprinkle the galette evenly with ¼ cup of the sugar. Dot the apple slices with the pieces of butter. (If not baking right away, cover and refrigerate.)

6. Bake for 30 minutes.

7. Sprinkle the remaining ½ cup of sugar evenly over the apples and continue baking for 30 to 60 minutes, or until the galette is golden and the fruit is tender. Don't worry if some of the juices burn. When done, transfer to a wire rack to cool.

8. Wait about 10 minutes and then, before the sugar hardens, use a metal spatula to loosen the crust from the parchment paper. Return the galette—now without the paper—to the rack. If the sugar

Coring the apple halves is a breeze if you use a melon baller to do it! This also works with pears.

If the crust is browning too quickly, reduce the temperature to 375°F and/or lower the oven rack. You can also prevent further browning by laying a piece of aluminum foil loosely over the tart for the remaining cooking time.

becomes too hard and the galette sticks, return to the warm oven for 5 minutes to soften the sugar and try again.

9. When the sugar is no longer sticky, transfer the galette to a serving platter. (Make sure it's ovenproof if you're planning to reheat the galette later—most ceramic platters are fine for this type of reheating.)

AFTER THE MAIN COURSE

10. If reheating, transfer the galette to a 350°F oven for about 5 minutes, or until warm.

11. Serve with the Rum-Raisin Ice Cream, whipped cream, or store-bought ice cream.

To give the finished product an attractive sheen, paint the puff pastry with an egg wash (1 egg lightly beaten with about 1 teaspoon of water, milk, or cream), but don't do this until just before baking or the pastry will get soggy.

Rum-Raisin Ice Cream

Yield: 1½ quarts or about 10 generous servings

1¼ cups black or golden raisins
3 tablespoons dark rum
2 cups whole milk
¾ cup granulated sugar

Pinch of fine sea salt
8 large eggs
2 cups heavy cream, very cold

2 DAYS

1. Place the raisins and rum in a small saucepan set over low heat until lukewarm. Remove from heat, cover, and set aside for 30 minutes, or until the raisins soften and absorb the rum.

2. In a large saucepan set over medium–high heat, bring the milk, sugar, and salt to a boil. Reduce the heat to low and simmer for 1 minute. Remove from the heat.

3. Meanwhile, using a stand mixer fitted with the paddle attachment or an electric handheld mixer set on high speed, beat the eggs for 5 minutes, or until thick and pale.

4. Reduce the speed to medium–low and very slowly pour the hot milk mixture into the beaten eggs. Strain the hot mixture into a metal bowl. Stir in the cold cream by hand. Set the ice cream base aside to cool. To speed up the cooling process, place the bowl in a larger bowl of ice water until cool. Refrigerate 4 to 6 hours, or until very cold.

5. Churn the ice cream base as per the manufacturer's directions. Add the rum-soaked raisins plus any remaining liquid once the ice cream is frozen, and churn for 20 more seconds or stir them in by hand.

6. Transfer to a covered container and freeze at least 4 hours and until ready to serve.

The rum-raisin mixture will keep at room temperature for up to 2 days or in the fridge for up to 1 month.

FLAVORS OF MOROCCO

DINNER FOR SIX

DISH	BEGIN PREP	PAGE
FIRST COURSE		
Tomato–Cumin Soup	2 days ahead	74
ENTRÉE		
Butterflied Moroccan Spice-Crusted Leg of Lamb	1 day ahead	75
ON THE SIDE		
Black Lentil and Moroccan Preserved Lemon Salad with Roasted Beets and Carrots	2 days ahead	76
DESSERT		
Raspberry–Nectarine Streusel Tart with Vanilla Ice Cream	1 day ahead	79

For me, this make-ahead lamb feast, replete with exotic spices, fresh aromatics, and preserved lemon, conjures up my several extraordinary visits to Morocco in the 1970s.

Featuring a cumin-y tomato soup starter, enticingly crusty lamb, and a spectacular streusel-berry-and-stone-fruit finale, the menu provides ideal dinner party fare from late spring through early fall, a period when room temperature food is particularly appealing and you can grill outside—and cook several hours in advance to boot. Though not imperative, I like to prepare everything but the lamb earlier in the week, preferably in the evening when I'm relaxed and the kitchen is cool. At mealtime, just ladle out the soup, reheated or not, garnish, and serve. Then offer the lamb and sides, finished and ready to go, as a room-temperature buffet.

The menu is also satisfying in late autumn and winter if you serve the food hot and replace the tart's nectarines and berries with an apple and rum-soaked raisin combo or with pears and candied ginger.

The centerpiece of this fantasy desert feast is the lamb with its sweet and spicy marinade adapted from a recipe I found years ago in the *New York Times* for use with salmon. (I now slather it on chicken as well.) The lamb version has been popular at my class and dinner-party tables for decades. Next-day sandwiches composed of thinly sliced leftover meat, red onion, tomato, and chopped cilantro—piled between slices of honey mustard–slathered multigrain toast or halved onion rolls—provide a scrumptious reprise.

The citrusy Black Lentil Salad (p. 76) tantalizingly sets off the rich lamb both at dinner and alongside those sandwiches! Strong flavors—lemon, garlic, scallions, and fresh herbs—explode on the palate just before the lush sweetness of the caramelized beets and carrots kicks in.

Just like those colorful vegetables, the Raspberry–Nectarine Tart (p. 79) dresses up any meal. And, with a miraculous food-processor crust that comes together in under a minute, it's particularly handy for those of you with pie-crust anxiety. A simple streusel (just sugar, flour, and butter) is effortlessly pressed into a springform pan, filled with fresh fruit, and topped with reserved streusel mid-baking. The result—crisply golden on top and bottom while meltingly fruity in between—represents the best of the season.

ORDER OF PREPARATION

 START

 2 DAYS

1. Make the Roasted Beets and Carrots (p. 77), cool, cover, and refrigerate.

2. Complete Steps 1 through 4 for the Tomato–Cumin Soup (p. 74), cool, cover, and refrigerate.

 1 DAY

1. Complete Steps 1 through 3 for the Leg of Lamb (p. 75), cover, and refrigerate.

2. Complete Steps 1 through 4 for the Raspberry–Nectarine Tart (p. 79) and store as directed.

 3 HOURS

1. Preheat the oven to 375°F.

2. Complete the Tart (Steps 6 and 7) and set aside.

3. Remove the Soup from the refrigerator and complete Step 5.

4. Remove the Lamb from the refrigerator (Step 4).

5. Remove the Roasted Beets and Carrots from the refrigerator.

 2 HOURS

1. Make the Lentil Salad (p. 76) and set aside.

 45 MINS

1. If grilling the Lamb, preheat the grill.

 30 MINS

1. If using a grill pan for the Lamb, set it over high heat.

2. Complete Steps 7 and 8 for the Lamb.

3. Complete Step 6 for the Soup.

 SERVE

1. Remove the ice cream from the freezer to soften.

2. If reheating the Tart, preheat the oven to 350°F.

3. Complete the Soup (Step 7) and serve.

AFTER THE FIRST COURSE

4. After eating the Soup, complete Lamb (Step 9) and serve with the Lentil Salad.

AFTER THE MAIN COURSE

5. After clearing the table, if reheating the Tart, complete Step 9.

6. Serve the Tart with the ice cream.

GET A HEAD START!

Like most soups, this **Tomato–Cumin** version deepens in flavor if made in advance. Refrigerate for up to 5 days or freeze for up to 6 months

Make the streusel crust and crumb topping for the **Raspberry–Nectarine Tart** and refrigerate for up to 2 weeks or freeze for at least 2 months.

Tomato–Cumin Soup

Yield: 6–8 generous first-course servings

¼ cup extra virgin olive oil
2 stalks celery with leaves, chopped
1 large yellow onion, chopped
¼ cup cumin seed, toasted
1 tablespoon coriander seed, toasted
2 teaspoons dried thyme
2 teaspoons ground paprika
1 bay leaf, crumbled
3 large cloves garlic, minced
2 tablespoons all-purpose flour
8 cups fresh or canned San Marzano chopped tomatoes

3 cups chicken stock
¼ cup Italian tomato paste
1 tablespoon red wine vinegar
1 tablespoon fine sea salt, or to taste
1 teaspoon light or dark brown sugar
Freshly ground black pepper, to taste
Few drops Tabasco sauce, or to taste
¼–½ cup heavy cream
½ cup sour cream or plain yogurt, for garnish
⅓ cup chopped fresh chives or cilantro, or a mixture of both, for garnish

2 DAYS

1. Warm the oil over medium heat in a very large saucepan, casserole, or stockpot. Add the celery, onion, cumin and coriander seeds, thyme, paprika, and bay leaf. Sauté, stirring occasionally, for about 20 minutes, or until the vegetables soften and the onions turn golden. Add the garlic and cook for 2 minutes. You may need to add a few tablespoons of water to prevent burning.

2. Reduce the heat to medium–low. Sprinkle the flour over the vegetables and cook, stirring frequently, for 6 minutes.

3. Stir in the tomatoes, stock, tomato paste, vinegar, salt, brown sugar, pepper, and Tabasco. Simmer, partially covered and stirring occasionally, for about 1¼ hours, or until the soup has reduced a bit and is very flavorful. Remove from the heat.

4. Purée the soup in the saucepan using an immersion blender or in batches in a blender once cooled to lukewarm. When completely cool, transfer to a covered container and refrigerate.

3 HOURS

5. Remove the soup from the refrigerator and transfer to a large saucepan.

30 MINS

6. Bring to a simmer, stirring frequently, over medium heat. Reduce the heat to low and add the cream. Continue to simmer until soup is piping hot. Do not boil. Taste and adjust seasoning as needed. Remove from heat and partially cover to keep hot.

SERVE

7. Ladle into 6 to 8 warmed (if possible) soup bowls. Garnish with the sour cream or yogurt and fresh herbs and serve.

Tip!

Homemade stock— whether vegetable, chicken, fish, or beef—is much better than the store-bought version and simpler to make than you might think (see p. 285). An added perk: Once stock is reduced to a concentrate, it takes up very little freezer space and keeps almost indefinitely. Like orange juice concentrate, just add water when ready to use. Or add a tablespoon or two of the reduction, undiluted, to sauces and soups for extra flavor.

Butterflied Moroccan Spice-Crusted Leg of Lamb

Yield: 6 main-course servings

2 tablespoons coriander seed

2 tablespoons cumin seed

2 tablespoons caraway seed

2 tablespoons cardamom pods

2 tablespoons anise seed

1 tablespoon curry powder

1 medium red onion, diced

3 cloves garlic

2 tablespoons honey

½ teaspoon freshly ground black pepper, plus more to taste

3 drops Tabasco sauce, or to taste

½ cup neutral vegetable oil, such as canola

2½–3 pounds boned and butterflied leg of lamb

¾ teaspoon fine sea salt, or more to taste

1. Put the first 5 ingredients in a medium saucepan and toast, stirring constantly, over medium heat for 1 to 2 minutes, or until just fragrant. Set aside to cool.

2. Using a food processor, coarsely grind the cooled spices. Add the curry podwer, onion, garlic, honey, pepper, Tabasco, and oil and process until combined.

3. Spread the marinade evenly over both sides of the lamb. Transfer to a covered container and refrigerate at least 8 hours or overnight.

4. Remove the lamb from the refrigerator.

5. If grilling, preheat the grill.

6. If using a grill pan, set it over high heat until hot.

7. Generously season the lamb with the salt and grill for 10 to 15 minutes per side, or until desired doneness is reached.

8. Transfer meat to a cutting board and let it rest for at least 10 minutes before carving.

AFTER THE FIRST COURSE

9. Carve the lamb against the grain into thin slices and serve from the cutting board or transfer to a serving platter. Serve hot, warm, or at room temperature.

Tip!

Butterflied leg of lamb is ideal for a crowd. Because the meat is not uniform in thickness, the various parts turn out rare, medium, and well done—something for everyone!

Tip!

Butterflied lamb varies dramatically in thickness so timing will vary as well. I like to remove the lamb from the grill (Step 7) when an instant-read thermometer inserted into the thickest part of the meat registers 125°F. The meat will continue to cook as it rests, so this will give you a range of medium rare to well done. If you prefer a more rare range, the thermometer should register 120°F.

Black Lentil and Moroccan Preserved Lemon Salad with Roasted Beets and Carrots

Yield: 6–8 side-dish servings

6 cups water

2½ cups black lentils, washed, drained, and picked over

1 tablespoon ground coriander

1 bay leaf

1½ teaspoons fine sea salt, plus more to taste

1 whole (8 wedges) Moroccan Preserved Lemon (p. 276 or store-bought), rinsed, dried, and finely diced

½ cup plus 3 tablespoons extra virgin olive oil, divided

½ cup julienned fresh mint

Freshly grated zest and freshly squeezed juice of 1 large lemon

3 cloves garlic, minced, or more to taste

3 whole scallions (white and green parts), sliced into paper-thin rounds

1 large shallot, minced

Freshly ground black pepper, to taste

1 recipe Roasted Beets and Carrots (recipe follows), room temperature

1 tablespoon balsamic vinegar

¼ cup chopped fresh chives, scallions, basil, and/or cilantro, for garnish

2 HOURS

1. Put the water, lentils, coriander, and bay leaf in a medium saucepan and bring to a boil over high heat.

2. Reduce the heat to low, simmer for 15 minutes, and then add the salt. Continue simmering for 5 to 15 minutes, or until the lentils are al dente (tender but still firm enough to hold their shape). Don't overcook. Remove and discard the bay leaf and drain.

3. While still warm, toss the lentils in a large bowl with the preserved lemon, ½ cup of the oil, the mint, the lemon zest and juice, the garlic, the scallions, and the shallot. Taste and adjust the salt and pepper as needed. Set aside for at least 20 minutes to allow the flavors to marry.

4. Mound the lentils in the center of a large serving platter. Toss the Roasted Carrots with 1 tablespoon of the oil and scatter them around the lentils. Toss the Roasted Beets with the remaining 2 tablespoons of oil and the balsamic vinegar and scatter in a circle around the carrots. Sprinkle the chopped herbs over everything. Set aside.

AFTER THE FIRST COURSE

SERVE

5. Serve at room temperature.

Roasted Beets and Carrots

Yield: 6–8 side-dish servings

6 large beets

2 pounds peeled baby carrots

2–3 tablespoons extra virgin olive oil

2 teaspoons granulated sugar

Fine sea salt and freshly ground black pepper, to taste

1. With a rack adjusted to the top position, preheat the oven to 350°F.

2. Wash the beets and, while still wet, place them in a single layer on a large piece of heavy-duty aluminum foil. Place another piece of foil on top. Fold and crimp the edges together to make a secure, airtight packet.

3. Place the packet on a sheet pan and bake for 2 hours, or until the beets feel soft when poked with your finger. Timing will vary depending on their size. Remove from the oven and set aside to cool completely in the foil packet.

4. While the beets are cooling, raise the oven temperature to 450°F.

5. Toss the carrots with the oil, sugar, salt, and pepper on a large sheet pan.

6. Bake, tossing once or twice, for 15 to 25 minutes or until soft, golden, and darkly caramelized in spots. Set aside to cool completely.

7. If not using within 4 hours, transfer the carrots to a covered container and refrigerate for up to 2 days.

8. Slip the skins off the cooled beets and cut them into a large dice. If not using within 2 hours, place them in a separate covered container and refrigerate for up to 2 days.

Raspberry–Nectarine Streusel Tart with Vanilla Ice Cream

Yield: 8 generous servings

For the Crust and Crumb Topping
2¼ cups sifted all-purpose flour
¾ cup plus 1 tablespoon granulated sugar, divided
¾ cup (1½ sticks) unsalted butter, room temperature
⅛ teaspoon fine sea salt

For the Filling
2 pounds nectarines, sliced into ½-inch wedges (approximately 5 cups)
1½ cups raspberries, fresh or frozen and thawed

½ cup granulated sugar
1 tablespoon freshly squeezed lemon juice
¼ teaspoon ground cinnamon
⅛ teaspoon freshly grated nutmeg
Pinch fine sea salt
Freshly grated zest of 1 lemon
3 tablespoons instant tapioca or all-purpose flour

For Serving
Store-bought super-premium vanilla ice cream

For a change of pace, replace the raspberries with an extra nectarine or use all plums or all peaches. In cooler months, use peeled and sliced apples or pears. When using apples, I add ¼ cup of rum-soaked raisins to the mix. If using pears, I toss in 3 tablespoons of chopped candied ginger and replace the cinnamon and nutmeg with ¼ teaspoon of ground ginger.

1 DAY

1. Preheat the oven to 375°F.

2. *Start the Crust and Crumb Topping:* Using a stand mixer fitted with the paddle attachment or an electric handheld mixer set on low speed, mix the flour, the ¾ cup of sugar, the butter, and the salt together until crumbly.

3. Press ⅔ of the mixture into the bottom of a 10-inch springform pan. Transfer the remaining crumbs to a covered container and refrigerate. (The crumbs and unbaked crust can be refrigerated for up to 2 weeks).

4. Bake the crust for 10 to 15 minutes, or until lightly colored. Set aside to cool and store at room temperature.

3 HOURS

5. Preheat the oven to 375°F.

6. *Start the Filling:* Combine all the filling ingredients, except the tapioca, in a large bowl. Just before baking, toss in the tapioca, mix well, and spoon the fruit mixture evenly over the partially baked crust.

7. Bake for 20 minutes. Sprinkle with the reserved crumb mixture followed by the reserved 1 tablespoon of sugar. Bake another 20 minutes, or until golden. Transfer to a wire rack to cool.

SERVE

8. If reheating, preheat the oven to 350°F.

AFTER THE MAIN COURSE

9. If reheating, bake for 5 minutes. Otherwise, serve at room temperature with the ice cream.

CALIFORNIA DREAMIN'

DINNER FOR SIX

DISH	BEGIN PREP	PAGE
FIRST COURSE		
My Favorite Caesar Salad	1 day ahead	84
ENTREE		
Cioppino with Crusty Toasts and Garlic Mayonnaise	3 days ahead	85
DESSERT		
Coffee Ice Cream Baked Alaska	3 days ahead	87

This flavor-forward menu takes me back to my California childhood. San Francisco—where we often spent family vacations—is famous for the Golden Gate Bridge and Fisherman's Wharf. And the Wharf is famous for the Ghirardelli chocolate factory and Cioppino (p. 85), one of a large number of robust seafood stews that have long flourished in ports around the world. This particular catch-of-the-day affair arrived in the Bay Area over a century ago along with Genoese fisherman immigrating to the United States and includes a wide a variety of Pacific seafood cooked in a garlicky tomato broth. But this soup readily welcomes substitutions and additions, so go ahead and experiment with your fishmonger's local catch with impunity. For greater panache—and as they do in Nice, Cannes, and St. Tropez—I use roasted rather than raw tomatoes and add saffron, orange zest, and Pernod to the mix. And at the table, I pass baskets of Crusty Toasts.

Use best-quality, super-fresh ingredients here, and you can't go wrong. My only other suggestion is to offer crab forks and shellfish crackers. Although they weren't available on the rough-and-tumble fishing boats a hundred years ago, they do come in handy for the 21st-century diner. And bibs, napkins, and bowls for discarding the shells don't hurt either.

The Wharf also offers fabulous Caesar Salads (p. 84). The clean taste of crunchy romaine—enhanced with a piquant mix of anchovies, lemons, just-cooked eggs, Parmesan, and cracked pepper—primes the palate for the complex fish ragoût to follow. However, if you want something simpler, opt for melon and figs with prosciutto or a simple platter of charcuterie and/or crudités instead.

I usually finish this menu with Baked Alaska (p. 87). Created in the 1860s by legendary chef Charles Ranhofer at Manhattan's equally legendary Delmonico's restaurant to celebrate the United States' purchase of Alaska from Russia, the impressive dessert was ubiquitous on fancy restaurant menus for more than a century. The miraculous contrast between cold, silky ice cream within and hot, chewy meringue without is achieved by insulating the ice cream with both sponge cake and meringue before toasting the meringue in a hot oven.

Though not a Wharf specialty, I associate Baked Alaska with San Francisco because my mother made it regularly during the years we vacationed there. She prepared other desserts as well but saved this special concoction for her grandest soirées. Rather than using traditional vanilla, she purchased lemon custard ice cream from the world's very first Baskin-Robbins 31 Flavors, in Beverly Hills less than a mile from our home. These days, I favor coffee ice cream, and I douse the cake layer with dark rum. But any ice cream or sorbet is fine (or layer up several) and liquor is optional. An added bonus: the entire dessert—except for the final few minutes of whipping the egg whites and browning the meringue—can be made in advance and frozen for weeks.

ORDER OF PREPARATION

START

3 DAYS

1. Complete Steps 1 through 9 for the Cioppino (p. 85), cool, cover, and refrigerate.

2. If using, make the Cake Layer (p. 89) for the Baked Alaska (p. 87), cool, wrap, and freeze.

2 DAYS

1. Complete Steps 1 through 4 for the Baked Alaska, wrap, and freeze.

2. Make the Garlic Oil (p. 273) for the Caesar Salad (p. 84).

1 DAY

1. Complete Steps 1 through 3 for the Salad and store as directed.

2. Make the Garlic Mayonnaise (p. 275) for the Crusty Toasts, cover, and refrigerate.

2 HOURS

1. Remove the anchovy mixture for the Salad from the refrigerator (Step 4).

2. Toast the bread for the Cioppino.

3. Complete Step 5 for the Salad.

1 HOUR

1. Remove the broth and seafood for the Cioppino from the refrigerator (Step 10).

20 MINS

1. Complete Steps 11 and 12 for Cioppino.

5 MINS

1. Complete Steps 6 and 7 for the Salad.

SERVE

1. Complete the Salad (Step 8) and serve.

AFTER THE FIRST COURSE

2. After eating the Salad, preheat the oven to 500°F.

3. Complete the Cioppino (Step 13) and serve with the toasts and Garlic Mayonnaise.

AFTER THE MAIN COURSE

4. After clearing the table, complete the Baked Alaska (Steps 6 through 10) and serve.

GET A HEAD START!

The broth for the **Cioppino** can be made ahead and frozen for up to 3 months.

The **Cake Layer** for the **Baked Alaska** can be made, wrapped well in foil, and refrigerated for up to 2 days or frozen for up to 3 months. You can get an additional head start by unmolding the ice cream onto the Cake Layer and freezing the combination, wrapped well in foil, for up to 1 month.

My Favorite Caesar Salad

Yield: 6–8 first-course servings

¾ cup Garlic Oil (p. 273), divided

8 slices stale French or Italian bread, crusts removed and cut into ½-inch cubes

12 oil-packed anchovy fillets, minced, or more to taste

1 scant teaspoon freshly ground black pepper

½ teaspoon granulated sugar

Pinch of cayenne pepper

Tabasco sauce, to taste

2 large heads romaine lettuce, outer leaves removed.

3 large eggs, room temperature

1 tablespoon freshly squeezed lemon juice

1 cup freshly grated Italian Parmesan cheese

Fine sea salt, to taste if needed

1. Heat ¼ cup of the Garlic Oil in a large skillet over medium–high heat. Add the bread cubes and fry, tossing constantly, for 3 to 5 minutes, until golden. Transfer to a plate lined with paper towels and cool completely. Place in a covered container and store at room temperature.

2. Add the anchovies, black pepper, sugar, cayenne pepper, and Tabasco sauce to the remaining ½ cup of Garlic Oil. Cover and refrigerate the anchovy mixture.

3. Cut each head of romaine crosswise into ½-inch slices and then wash and dry in a salad spinner. Wrap in a kitchen towel or paper towels, place in open plastic bags, and refrigerate.

4. Remove the anchovy mixture from the refrigerator.

5. Bring a medium saucespan of water to boil over high heat. Add the eggs and boil for 1 minute. Immediately transfer to a large bowl of cold water to stop the cooking process.

6. Toss the romaine with the anchovy mixture in a large salad bowl.

7. Scrape the eggs out of their shells and onto the romaine. Squeeze the lemon juice over the salad and toss well.

8. Add the Parmesan and croutons and toss again. Taste and adjust the salt if needed. You may not need any, as anchovies are salty. Serve right away.

Cioppino with Crusty Toasts and Garlic Mayonnaise

Yield: 6 generous main-course servings

For the Roasted Tomatoes

4 large tomatoes, cut into ½-inch slices

3 tablespoons extra virgin olive oil

Fine sea salt and freshly ground black pepper, to taste

For the Broth

¼ cup extra virgin olive oil

1 cup finely chopped onion

¾ cup thinly sliced celery

¾ cup finely chopped fennel bulb

¾ cup finely chopped and peeled carrots

8 cups rich fish stock, plus more as needed

4 cloves garlic, minced

¼ cup Pernod or other anise-flavored liqueur

1 teaspoon fine sea salt, plus more to taste

1 teaspoon saffron threads

Freshly grated zest of 1 orange

Freshly ground black pepper, to taste

For the Cioppino

30 cherrystone clams, rinsed in cool water

30 mussels, well scrubbed and beards removed, if necessary

30 medium shell-on shrimp

1½ pounds monkfish, cut into 1-inch squares

1½ pounds squid, cleaned and cut into ¼-inch rings

⅓ cup chopped fresh Italian parsley

⅓ cup chopped or julienned fresh basil

½ cup chopped fresh fennel fronds (if available)

1 recipe Garlic Mayonnaise (p. 275), for serving

1 large loaf crusty peasant or French bread, sliced and toasted, for serving

3 DAYS

1. Preheat the oven to 425°F.

2. *Start the Roasted Tomatoes:* Lay the tomato slices on a greased sheet pan and drizzle with the oil. Season with the salt and pepper.

3. Roast for 30 to 45 minutes, or until the tomatoes are caramelized and slightly blackened in spots. Set aside to cool completely.

4. Cut the roasted tomatoes into medium dice. Set aside.

5. *Start the Broth:* Heat the oil with the onion, celery, fennel, and carrots in a large casserole or stockpot over medium heat. Cook, stirring frequently, for 10 minutes. If the mixture becomes too dry or begins to burn, add a bit of the fish stock or water.

6. Add the garlic and cook for 10 to 15 minutes, or until the vegetables are soft and beginning to caramelize.

CONTINUED

Cioppino with Crusty Toasts and Garlic Mayonnaise

CONTINUED

7. Warm the Pernod in a small saucepan over medium heat. Remove both pans from the heat and add the warm Pernod to the vegetables. Flame, stirring, until the flames have completely subsided. Be careful.

8. Return the casserole or stockpot to medium heat and add the 8 cups of fish stock and the salt, saffron, zest, pepper, and roasted tomatoes. Bring to a simmer (*do not boil*). Stir well, reduce the heat to low, and cook for 5 minutes to combine the flavors.

9. Cool completely. Transfer to a covered container and refrigerate.

10. Remove the broth and seafood from the refrigerator.

11. *Assemble the Cioppino:* Return the broth to the casserole or stockpot, partially cover, and bring to a simmer over medium heat. Again, do *not* boil. Add the clams and mussels, cover, and cook for 2 minutes. Add the shrimp and monkfish, cover again, and cook for 2 more minutes. Add the squid and cook for 1 minute or so. Do not overcook, but make sure the clams and mussels are open and the shrimp, fish, and squid are done (taste them if necessary). Remove from the heat.

12. Stir in the parsley, basil, and fennel fronds. Taste and adjust the salt and pepper as needed.

AFTER THE FIRST COURSE

13. Divide the Cioppino among 6 warmed (if possible) bowls, being sure to give everyone some of everything. Serve hot. Pass the Garlic Mayonnaise and crusty toasts separately or place a piece of toast spread with a tablespoon of mayonnaise in the bottom of each bowl before adding the Cioppino. In that case, pass the remaining mayonnaise separately along with extra toasts.

Coffee Ice Cream Baked Alaska

Yield: 6–8 servings

2 pints super-premium coffee ice cream

1 round Cake Layer (recipe follows), or store-bought 10-inch single layer cake

2–3 tablespoons dark rum (optional)

4 large egg whites, room temperature

Large pinch fine sea salt

1 teaspoon cream of tartar

1 cup granulated sugar

1 teaspoon best-quality vanilla extract

2 tablespoons granulated sugar, for sprinkling

1. Remove the ice cream from the freezer to soften for about 20 minutes.

2. Pack the softened ice cream into a metal bowl 8 or 9 inches in diameter. Smooth the surface with a rubber spatula. Cover the bowl tightly with foil and freeze for at least 6 hours.

3. Place the Cake Layer on piece of aluminum foil. Drizzle with the rum, if using.

4. Fill a large bowl with very hot water. Remove the ice cream bowl from the freezer and dip it into the bowl of hot water. After 15 seconds, invert the bowl over the Cake Layer to unmold the ice cream, making sure the cake border is even all around. Wrap well with aluminum foil and freeze until ready to bake.

SERVE

AFTER THE FIRST COURSE

5. Preheat the oven to 500°F.

AFTER THE MAIN COURSE

6. Using a stand mixer fitted with the whisk attachment or an electric handheld set on low speed, beat the room temperature egg whites with the salt for 1 minute, or until frothy. Add the cream of tartar and increase the speed to medium–low. Mix—continuing to slowly increase the mixer speed to medium and then medium–high—until very soft peaks form.

7. With the motor running, add the sugar very, very slowly and, once all the sugar has been added, raise the speed to high, add the vanilla, and beat for 2 to 5 minutes more, or until the meringue is very stiff and glossy.

Coffee Ice Cream Baked Alaska

CONTINUED

8. Remove the prepared ice cream and cake from the freezer and place on a cookie sheet lined with parchment paper. Using a rubber spatula, decoratively swirl all the meringue over the cake and ice cream, running the meringue down to the platter or parchment paper. Make sure both the cake and ice cream are completely sealed in by the meringue.

9. Sprinkle the 2 tablespoons of sugar evenly over the meringue and bake for 2 to 5 minutes, or until lightly browned. Watch carefully. When ready, transfer to a platter. Present at the table.

10. Cut large wedges with a heavy knife and serve. If the ice cream is too hard to cut easily, wait 5 to 10 minutes and try again or dip the knife in very hot water before cutting each slice. Once sliced, serve right away.

WHIPPING EGG WHITES

Egg whites must be at room temperature and contain no trace of egg yolk if they are to mount properly. In addition, the bowl and the beaters must be clean and grease free. Use an electric handheld or stand mixer fitted with the whisk attachment, as it is difficult to achieve the requisite light-as-air consistency using a regular whisk. Yes, Escoffier and Carême did it, but if you're like me, you'll find it nearly impossible. Start on low and raise the speed as the egg whites mount. As you add the last of the sugar, raise to maximum speed.

After beating for 1 minute, I suggest adding a teaspoon or so of cream of tartar to help the egg whites hold their volume. The cream of tartar is not requisite but is highly recommended.

Folding whipped egg whites into something else (such as a cake batter, soufflé, or mousse) requires that you do not beat the whites past soft peaks. Be careful not to overbeat, as beating to stiff peaks will make the folding difficult. If the beaten whites break into little "icebergs" while folding you'll know you've overbeaten. It isn't the end of the world but beat less the next time.

When making a hard, dry meringue (for meringue shells, cookies, and kisses) or soft meringue toppings (for things like Baked Alaska, lemon meringue pie, and certain puddings)—and therefore not folding the beaten whites into anything else—you'll want very stiff, glossy peaks, and you'll need to beat the egg whites longer to achieve this.

Cake Layer

Yield: 1 (10-inch) cake layer about 1½ inches high

⅔ cup all-purpose flour, plus more for dusting the pan

⅔ teaspoon baking powder

⅛ teaspoon fine sea salt

5 tablespoons unsalted butter, plus more for greasing the pan, room temperature

⅔ cup granulated sugar

2 large eggs, room temperature

1½ teaspoons best-quality vanilla extract

1. With a rack adjusted to the upper-third position, preheat to 350°F. Butter and flour a 10-inch springform or cake pan and line it with parchment paper. Butter and flour the parchment paper.

2. Sift together the flour, baking powder, and salt. Set aside.

3. Using a stand mixer fitted with the paddle attachment or an electric handheld mixer set on medium–high speed, cream together the 5 tablespoons of butter and the sugar for about 5 minutes or until light and fluffy.

4. With the mixer running, add the eggs, 1 at a time, and then the vanilla. Beat well. With the mixer off, add the dry ingredients. Beat on low until just combined.

5. Transfer the batter to the prepared pan. Bake for 20 minutes, or until a toothpick inserted into the center comes out clean. Cool on a wire rack for 20 minutes.

6. Loosen the sides of the pan with a small knife and use a large spatula to lift the cake—along with the parchment paper—off the pan bottom. Return to the wire rack to cool completely.

7. Wrap the cake well in aluminum foil and refrigerate for up to 2 days or freeze for up to 3 months.

ASIAN SENSATIONS

DINNER FOR SIX

DISH	BEGIN PREP	PAGE
FIRST COURSE		
Vietnamese Summer Rolls with Sweet and Spicy Chili Dipping Sauce	1 day ahead	94
ENTRÉE		
Sweet 'n' Hot Malaysian Chicken	2 days ahead	96
ON THE SIDE		
Asian Salsa Salad	3 hours ahead	98
Wild Rice Salad with Ginger Vinaigrette	1 day ahead	100
DESSERT		
Frozen Lemon Meringue Bombe	2 days ahead	101

make this pan-Asian feast all year long. Whether eaten al fresco on the patio or indoors by the fire, this gutsy menu—a riot of flavors, colors, and textures—has serious star power. In cooler weather, serve the Malaysian Chicken (p. 96) hot instead of at room temperature and replace the Wild Rice Salad (p. 100) and the Frozen Lemon Bombe (p. 101) with piping hot Creamy Green Polenta (p. 151) and Ginger-Caramelized Pears (p. 188), respectively. Either way, the richly seasoned poultry is nicely balanced by a simple, starchy side.

Gourmet once described Vietnam's aptly named summer roll (*gỏi cuốn*) an "elegant . . . salad packed into an edible container." For these Summer Rolls (p. 94), paper-thin *bánh tráng* (rice paper sheets) are wrapped around a refreshingly light filling of vegetables, herbs, rice noodles, and a small amount of shrimp, pork, or chicken. Served cold or at room temperature, they are easily distinguished from spring or egg rolls, which are deep-fried and eaten hot.

This garden-fresh wrap is traditionally paired with an assertive Asian sauce, triggering a mélange of flavors and textures to explode in the mouth. I adore the Chili Dipping Sauce (p. 95), but peanut or hoisin-based sauces and *nuoc mam cham* all vie for a close second place.

Summer rolls are fun to make, and I often enlist guests to pitch in and prepare their own. Guests probably won't be helping with the chicken, though, as it requires six hours of marinating before baking. Though juiciest and most flavorful using all thighs, six halved chicken breasts or two (three-pound) chickens cut into eight pieces each will also do the trick.

I first tasted this Asian Salsa (p. 98) years ago as a guest on a private rail car. One evening en route to Santa Fe, the train's chef concocted this tropical side dish to accompany pan-grilled skate. He proudly shared his new recipe, and I use it to enliven all manner of fish, shellfish, and poultry; but I find its light, cool fruitiness best of all when paired with this spicy Malaysian Chicken.

Dessert is a frozen Lemon Bombe. It's my one recipe that actually went viral, although its invention was a complete accident. About to discard dinner-party leftovers, and in a "waste not, want not" mode, I mushed together the remains of a lemon Pavlova and absentmindedly stuck the concoction in the freezer. Days later, I sampled a spoonful, and found it provocatively sweet, tart, and tangy and way better than the sum of the parts. Citrus-loving friends and students alike claim it's second to none in the lemon dessert category. Of all the recipes in this book, this is the one I most strongly urge you to try.

GET A HEAD START!

The **Chili Dipping Sauce** can be made up to 4 days in advance and refrigerated.

The marinade for the **Malaysian Chicken** can be made up to 6 weeks in advance and refrigerated until needed.

In warmer weather, serve the **Chicken** at room temperature instead of hot or just complete the recipe through Step 9 up to 2 hours in advance and reheat in a 400°F oven for 5 to 10 minutes just before serving.

The vinaigrette for the **Wild Rice Salad**—like most vinaigrettes—can be made in advance and refrigerated for up to 2 weeks. Cook the rice, cool, cover, and refrigerate up to 1 day ahead

The **Meringue Shell** for the **Bombe**—well wrapped in foil—keeps for at least 4 months at room temperature.

Lemon Curd can be made in advance and refrigerated for up to 2 weeks or frozen for up to 1 year. Or assemble the entire dessert, cover with foil, and freeze for up to 4 days. Unmold just before serving.

ORDER OF PREPARATION

START

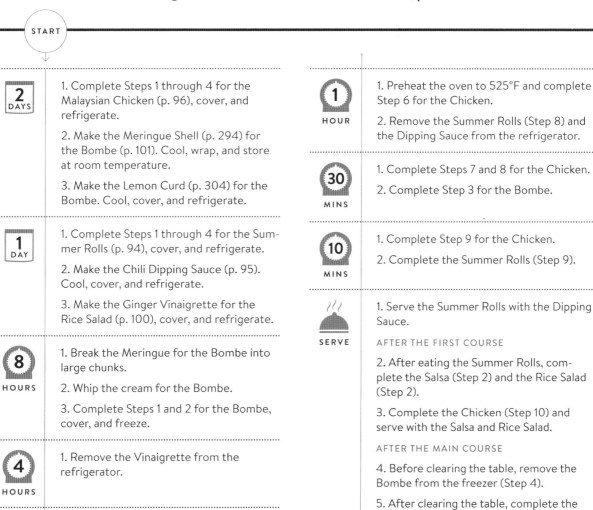

2 DAYS

1. Complete Steps 1 through 4 for the Malaysian Chicken (p. 96), cover, and refrigerate.

2. Make the Meringue Shell (p. 294) for the Bombe (p. 101). Cool, wrap, and store at room temperature.

3. Make the Lemon Curd (p. 304) for the Bombe. Cool, cover, and refrigerate.

1 DAY

1. Complete Steps 1 through 4 for the Summer Rolls (p. 94), cover, and refrigerate.

2. Make the Chili Dipping Sauce (p. 95). Cool, cover, and refrigerate.

3. Make the Ginger Vinaigrette for the Rice Salad (p. 100), cover, and refrigerate.

8 HOURS

1. Break the Meringue for the Bombe into large chunks.

2. Whip the cream for the Bombe.

3. Complete Steps 1 and 2 for the Bombe, cover, and freeze.

4 HOURS

1. Remove the Vinaigrette from the refrigerator.

3 HOURS

1. Complete Step 1 for the Rice Salad and set aside.

2. Remove the marinating Chicken from the refrigerator (Step 5).

3. Complete Steps 5 through 7 for the Summer Rolls, cover, and refrigerate.

4. Complete Step 1 for the Asian Salsa Salad (p. 98) and set aside.

1 HOUR

1. Preheat the oven to 525°F and complete Step 6 for the Chicken.

2. Remove the Summer Rolls (Step 8) and the Dipping Sauce from the refrigerator.

30 MINS

1. Complete Steps 7 and 8 for the Chicken.

2. Complete Step 3 for the Bombe.

10 MINS

1. Complete Step 9 for the Chicken.

2. Complete the Summer Rolls (Step 9).

SERVE

1. Serve the Summer Rolls with the Dipping Sauce.

AFTER THE FIRST COURSE

2. After eating the Summer Rolls, complete the Salsa (Step 2) and the Rice Salad (Step 2).

3. Complete the Chicken (Step 10) and serve with the Salsa and Rice Salad.

AFTER THE MAIN COURSE

4. Before clearing the table, remove the Bombe from the freezer (Step 4).

5. After clearing the table, complete the Bombe (Step 5) and serve.

Vietnamese Summer Rolls with Sweet and Spicy Chili Dipping Sauce

Yield: 16 rolls (8 first-course servings)

1 tablespoon neutral vegetable oil, such as canola

8 cloves garlic, minced

¾ pound cooked shelled shrimp, chicken, or roast pork, roughly chopped

4 ounces Asian vermicelli rice noodles

½ head Napa cabbage, finely shredded

4 medium carrots, peeled and shredded or coarsely grated

1 large bunch fresh cilantro, stems and roots reserved *

8 whole scallions (white and green parts), cut into paper-thin rounds

½ cup roughly chopped fresh mint leaves

1½ tablespoons ground coriander

Fine sea salt and freshly ground black pepper, to taste

16 sheets (22-cm round or square) rice paper (*bánh tráng*)

1 recipe Sweet and Spicy Chili Dipping Sauce (recipe follows), room temperature, for serving

---

1. Heat the oil and sauté the garlic in a medium skillet over medium heat, stirring frequently, for 5 minutes, or until golden. Remove from the heat, stir in the shrimp, and set aside.

2. Soak the vermicelli in a medium bowl of warm water for 15 minutes. Drain.

3. Meanwhile, bring a medium pot of water to a boil over high heat. Add the drained vermicelli and cook, stirring frequently to break up the clumps, for 2 to 3 minutes, or until just al dente. Drain the vermicelli and refresh under cold water. Drain again and set aside.

4. Toss together the garlic shrimp, vermicelli, cabbage, carrots, cilantro leaves, scallions, mint, and coriander in a large bowl. Taste and adjust the salt and pepper as needed. Cover and refrigerate.

---

5. Remove the filling from the refrigerator. To assemble the spring rolls, immerse one rice paper in a wide bowl or large skillet filled with very warm water. As the rice paper begins curling, immediately flip it over and continue flipping until it is just softened. This will take 30 to 60 seconds. Use both hands to lift it out of the water, being careful that it doesn't collapse on itself or tear, and spread it immediately on a damp kitchen towel.

---

* Reserve and refrigerate the cilantro stems and roots to make the Sweet and Spicy Chili Dipping Sauce. Be sure to wash them in several changes of cool water if necessary, as sometimes they are quite gritty.

6. Place 3 to 4 tablespoons of the filling mixture near the top of the wet rice paper sheet. Roll the top end tightly over the filling and then fold in the sides. Finish rolling until the "package" is closed and snug. The final product will look like a small burrito. Place the finished summer roll on a platter lined with a damp kitchen towel.

7. Repeat until all 16 summer rolls are prepared. If you have extra filling, make a few extra. Cover with another damp towel and refrigerate.

8. Remove the summer rolls from the refrigerator.

9. Cut each summer roll in ½ horizontally. Place 4 halves on each of 8 salad plates.

10. Serve right away with the Sweet and Spicy Chili Dipping Sauce. Ideally, divide the dipping sauce among 8 ramekins or very small bowls and place one on each plate next to the summer rolls.

Sweet and Spicy Chili Dipping Sauce

Yield: 1½ cups

1 tablespoon neutral vegetable oil, such as canola

Reserved cilantro stems and roots, well washed and chopped

2 cloves garlic, minced

¾ cup plus 1 tablespoon unseasoned rice wine vinegar or white wine vinegar

2 tablespoons Vietnamese fish sauce, or more to taste

1–2 tablespoons Asian chili garlic paste, or to taste

½ cup granulated sugar

2–3 tablespoons freshly squeezed lime juice, or more to taste

Fine sea salt and freshly ground black pepper, to taste

Using the full 2 tablespoons of chili garlic paste results in a very spicy sauce. If you prefer less heat, experiment with less.

1. Heat the oil and sauté the cilantro stems and roots and the garlic in a medium saucepan set over medium heat for about 5 minutes, or until very fragrant and the garlic begins to color.

2. Add the vinegar, fish sauce, chili paste, and sugar and simmer for 3 to 5 minutes, or until the sugar has dissolved. Remove from the heat and set aside to cool to room temperature.

3. Add 2 tablespoons of the lime juice. Taste and adjust the amount of fish sauce, lime juice, salt, and pepper if needed. Serve or transfer to a covered container and refrigerate for up to 4 days. Bring to room temperature before serving.

You can make the Chili Dipping Sauce closer to mealtime, but ideally allow at least 3 hours for the flavors to marry.

Sweet 'n' Hot Malaysian Chicken

Yield: 6–8 generous main-course servings

2 tablespoons coriander seed

1 tablespoon cumin seed

1 tablespoon fennel seed

1 cup *ketjap manis* (sweet Indonesian soy sauce)

¾ cup mirin or dry white wine

½ cup light or dark brown sugar

¼ cup fish sauce

1 (2-inch) piece fresh ginger, peeled and thinly sliced

1 jalapeño, Serrano, or other hot chili, seeded, ribs removed, and finely minced

3 cloves garlic, thinly sliced

16 chicken thighs (boneless and/or skin-less thighs also work)

Vegetable oil spray or neutral vegetable oil, such as canola, for greasing

Chopped fresh mint, basil, cilantro, or chives, for garnish

I know some people are adverse to dark meat chicken. If this is the case, use bone-in, skin-on breasts for this recipe, though the final result may be less juicy than when using thighs. If using breasts you may need to shorten the cooking time a bit.

1. To make the marinade, combine the coriander, cumin, and fennel seed in a small saucepan over medium heat. Toast, stirring constantly, until fragrant. Remove from the heat, transfer to a bowl, and set aside to cool temperature.

2. Grind the toasted spices in a spice or coffee grinder.

3. Combine the *ketjap manis*, mirin, brown sugar, fish sauce, ground spices, ginger, chili, and garlic in a covered container large enough to hold the chicken pieces. Stir until the sugar dissolves.

4. Add the chicken to the marinade. Toss, cover, and refrigerate for at least 6 hours and up to 2 days. If the chicken is not submerged, be sure to toss at least once a day during marinating.

5. Remove the chicken from the refrigerator and uncover.

6. Place 2 large sheet pans or large, shallow roasting pans in the oven and preheat to 525°F or as high as your oven will go.

7. Remove 1 of the pans from the oven. Quickly grease with the vegetable spray or oil. Use kitchen tongs to remove 1 thigh at a time from the marinade and place it, skin side down, on the hot pan. It will sizzle. Do this quickly so the pan stays hot. Repeat with 7 more thighs and then return the pan to the oven. Repeat by placing the 8 remaining thighs on the second pan. Roast for 10 minutes and then alternate the position of the pans in the oven. After 5 more minutes, reduce the oven temperature to 375°F and cook for 5 more minutes.

8. While the chicken is cooking, transfer the marinade to a medium saucepan and boil gently for 5 to 10 minutes, or until it has reduced by about half and thickened to a glaze. Add juices from the cooking chicken, if there are any, as you go along. Once reduced, remove from heat and set aside.

9. After 20 minutes total of cooking, turn the chicken pieces over using a metal spatula. Be careful, as they tend to stick. They may be already done at this point or need a few more minutes. If you can't tell if they are done, cut into one thigh to make sure it is no longer pink or check with an instant-read thermometer, which should register 160°F. (If the chicken is not done, bake for another 2 to 3 minutes and check again.) When done, remove from oven.

AFTER THE FIRST COURSE

10. Place the chicken on a serving platter, reheat the glaze, if necessary, over low heat, and pour the hot glaze over the chicken. Serve preferably hot or warm, or at room temperature. Sprinkle with the chopped herbs just before serving.

Asian Salsa Salad

Yield: 6–8 side-dish servings

1½ cups fresh pineapple, cut into small dice

1½ cups jicama, peeled and cut into small dice

2 large ripe mangos, peeled and diced

1 medium red onion, halved vertically and sliced into paper-thin half-rings

Freshly grated zest and freshly squeezed juice of 3 limes

1–2 small serrano chilies, seeded, ribs removed, and minced or cut into large pieces

½ cup chopped fresh cilantro

½ cup chopped fresh mint

2 teaspoons minced garlic

1 teaspoon fine sea salt, or to taste

½ teaspoon granulated sugar, or to taste

½ teaspoon ground cumin, or to taste

Freshly ground pepper, to taste

3 HOURS

1. Toss together all ingredients in a large bowl. Set aside for at least 1 hour to allow the flavors to marry. If using large pieces of the chilies, remove and discard.

SERVE

AFTER THE FIRST COURSE

2. Taste and adjust seasonings as needed. Toss and serve.

MICROPLANES AND ZESTING

I love microplanes. They are inexpensive and come in all shapes and sizes. I used to dread zesting and avoided recipes that called for it. A microplane changed all that, making the process almost fun and certainly speedy. However, when feeling really lazy or when I don't have the actual fruit on hand, I'll use a couple drops of Boyajian pure lemon, lime, or orange oil instead—and with the exact same results. The only thing these miracle oils don't duplicate is the zest's texture, but in almost all cases, I find smooth and silky preferable anyway.

Use this light, cool, fruity salsa to enliven all manner of fish, shellfish, and poultry.

Wild Rice Salad with Ginger Vinaigrette

Yield 6–8 side dish servings

8 cups cooked wild rice (or substitute cooked white or brown basmati rice)

¼ cup julienned fresh Thai or regular basil

¼ cup coarsely chopped fresh cilantro

¼ cup coarsely chopped fresh mint

4 whole scallions (both green and white parts), cut into paper-thin rings

½ cup toasted salted peanuts, coarsely chopped

1 recipe Ginger Vinaigrette (recipe follows), room temperature

Fine sea salt and freshly ground black pepper, to taste

3 HOURS

1. Toss the cooked rice, herbs, scallions, and peanuts with just enough of the Ginger Vinaigrette to moisten and flavor. Taste and adjust the seasoning as needed. Set aside for at least 1 hour before serving to allow the flavors to marry.

SERVE

2. Just before serving, taste and adjust the amount of vinaigrette and seasoning as needed. Serve.

Ginger Vinaigrette

Yield: About ¾ cup

½ cup neutral vegetable oil, such as canola

¼ cup unseasoned rice vinegar

1–3 teaspoons toasted sesame oil, or to taste

1 teaspoon freshly grated peeled fresh ginger, or to taste

2 cloves garlic, minced

Fine sea salt and freshly ground black pepper, to taste

Sriracha, Tabasco, or other hot sauce, to taste

1 DAY

1. Place all the ingredients in a lidded jar and shake vigorously until well combined. Set aside for at least 1 hour to allow flavors to marry. Taste and adjust the seasoning as needed.

2. Use immediately or refrigerate for up to 2 weeks. Bring to room temperature and reshake the jar before using.

Frozen Lemon Meringue Bombe

Yield: 8 generous servings

1½ cups heavy cream, very cold, whipped
1 recipe Lemon Curd (p. 304), cold*

1 Meringue Shell (p. 294), broken into
2-inch chunks*

If you prefer to or if you don't have a springform pan, you can freeze the bombe in a metal bowl and unmold as for the Baked Alaska (p. 87).

8 HOURS

1. In a large metal bowl, fold the whipped cream together with the Lemon Curd. Then fold in the meringue chunks.

2. Pour into a 9-inch or 10-inch springform pan, cover with aluminum foil, and freeze for at least 8 hours and up to 24 hours.

30 MINS

3. Remove the Bombe from the freezer, run a knife around its sides, and remove the springform. Transfer to a serving platter and return to the freezer.

SERVE

AFTER THE MAIN COURSE

4. Remove the Bombe from the freezer.

5. Slice with a large, sharp knife. If it's difficult to cut, dip the knife in hot water or let the Bombe thaw for 5 to 10 minutes before cutting. Serve right away.

If you don't care for frozen desserts or don't have the patience for them, make what I call a lemon Pavlova. The same three items in this bombe recipe can become a Pavlova in the time the it takes to whip the cream. Place the whole meringue shell on a large platter and fill it with the lemon curd. Pile the finished whipped cream on top, and you've got yourself an utterly delicious dessert.

* Make the Meringue Shell and Lemon Curd at least 1 day before assembling dessert.

ENTERTAINING BY
THE LIGHT OF DAY

ENTERTAINING BY THE LIGHT OF DAY

MENUS

Picnic Table
p. 108

Lunch with Friends
p. 116

Rustic Brunch
p. 124

Brunch, Italian Style
p. 134

La Dolce Vita Reprise
p. 140

Early Autumn Brunch
p. 146

Soup 'n' Sandwich
p. 154

Whether orchestrating a cozy get-together for the immediate family or including friends and neighbors as well, midday meals are tailor-made for laid-back entertaining. Of course you can turn a lunch/brunch event into a multicourse extravaganza, but why would you? For me, simple and easy define this casual territory.

Originating in 1890s England, "brunch" cleverly allowed people to skip breakfast, sleep in before church, and then—noonish and post-sermon—enjoy breakfast and lunch consolidated into a single meal.

These days, anything goes. Let your guest roster, your mood, the season, and whatever strikes your fancy at the market dictate the menu. *Chez moi*, occasions planned for late morning generally don't get going until afternoon anyway, at which point breakfast, lunch, and brunch edibles—often fairly interchangeable—are all welcome.

"Ease," however, is the one thing I do demand from these midday meals. I refuse to spend Sunday morning rushing around and stressed out. Thus, a primarily prepare-ahead repertoire of dishes works best.

Large, multi-ingredient salads, sandwiches, baked pastas, risottos, and hearty soups are my go-to main courses. And when I want something eggy, I lean toward frittatas, which can be whisked together a day in advance and even cooked several hours before guests arrive. An added bonus: they're equally good hot, warm, or room temperature, and when called upon, they provide portable picnic fare.

A soufflé and salad lunch is another eggy, host-friendly alternative. And guests will swoon. I realize the idea of an easy soufflé is counterintuitive, but once you get the basics down, they're actually a breeze.

When it comes to brunch, I'm biased toward knock-your-socks-off salads—both warm and cold, depending on the season. Do you have a selection of vinaigrettes stashed away in your fridge? If not, you easily can. Most other salad components can't be prepared weeks ahead like the dressings, but many can be prepped a day or two in advance, well wrapped, and refrigerated until needed.

A salad is an ideal repository for extraneous bits and pieces. If you're even marginally imaginative, any combination of leftover meat, poultry, fish, seafood, sausage, pasta, and vegetables—cannily tossed with a first-class vinaigrette—will result in a tasty creation. Or use the leftovers to brighten and resuscitate an otherwise pedestrian lettuce mix.

My former mother-in-law dreaded leftovers and was at a loss if anything at all remained uneaten. She insisted on second and third helpings and that we clean our plates. I'm exactly the opposite. Anticipating second-time-around meals—which I frequently prefer to the originals—I often double a recipe just to guarantee a surplus.

In general, I complement a brunch main event with artisanal bread, a simple salad, and a cheese or two. But do keep a few things in mind: With a salad-like main course, go light on side salads; with dairy-heavy meals, Asian menus, or cheese-based desserts, forgo cheese; and if serving sandwiches, there is no need for additional bread. Mix, match, remain flexible, make sure the food is as fresh as possible, and you won't go wrong.

If a midday cocktail is your idea of heaven, offer Bloody or Virgin Marys, mimosas, Bellinis, sangría, or flutes of iced bubbly as guests arrive. For years, my friends teased me relentlessly for my questionable habit of adding ice cubes to prosecco, Cava, and nonvintage Champagnes. I'm thrilled to report, however, that in Paris, Provence, and the Cote d'Azur, my long time favorite drink is now all the rage on hot summer days. The French shamelessly call it *une piscine*. So if, like me, you enjoy your bubbly with ice, don't let anyone talk you out of it, and add those cubes to your heart's content.

As for dessert, make-ahead or store-bought again works best. At casual midday gatherings, when not serving basic fruit and cheese, I offer bakery or gourmet shop items or something I've thrown together earlier in the week—usually an ice cream torte, poached fruit, or a fruit salad. Cupcakes, bars, and Basic Shortbread (p. 295) and Chocolate Chip Cookies (p. 300) are easy as well. And classic biscotti are irresistible on their own and even better dunked in Vin Santo.

My easiest frozen dessert is a basic *affogato,* and I serve it often. The Italian word translates as "drowned," and the dish traditionally features vanilla ice cream awash in rich espresso. For a divinely boozy dessert, replace the espresso with brandy, bourbon, dark rum, or Grand Marnier. Or play around with other flavors of ice cream—coffee, chocolate, and caramel are genius here.

Mix and match the Raspberry, Caramel, and Bitter Chocolate Sauces (p. 302) with various ice cream flavors in addition to traditional vanilla. And *amaretti*, pralines, biscotti, or Heath bars, crushed and sprinkled over any of the above—or over ice cream alone—results in a sweet treat dramatically better than the sum of the simple parts. But I digress . . .

If you're looking for meal and recipe ideas that are more specific, keep reading. This chapter includes seven relatively simple lunch/brunch menus with intriguing main courses ranging from Homemade Gravlax (p. 130) to Grilled Seafood Salad (p. 111) to Mixed Mushroom Risotto (p. 144) to a Caramelized Onion Crostata (p. 121). None of the recipes are complicated, and in the interest of relaxed entertaining, much of the work can, and should, be done in advance. These same basic menus—with minor additions, such as a starter or a extra side dish or two—easily become *sine qua non* Sunday suppers.

With only the rare exception, I prefer my midday feasts casual and relaxed. Brunch is a great time to try new recipes or to experiment in general. Don't hesitate to add, subtract, or combine. Tweaking a menu or recipe enough to make it your own is exceedingly satisfying.

SANDWICHES

Very few people can resist a really good sandwich, and there are many routes to making great ones. Here are some of my favorite tips:

- **Use leftovers.** An easy option is to park remnants of previous meals—including those in this book—between slices of bread. Best-quality loaves, English muffins, buns, or rolls—toasted or not—filled with last night's dinner can be even tastier than classic, tried and true combinations.

- **Load on the toppings.** Do include sweet onions, tomatoes, shredded greens (fresh herbs, interesting lettuces, arugula, cabbage, or spinach are good choices), and pickled anything. For me, the best sandwiches are overstuffed and messy. When in doubt, add something else.

- **Don't forget the condiments.** Last, no one wants a dry sandwich. Make sure to slather yours with a grainy mustard, flavored mayo, salsa, or vinaigrette of your choice, Thousand Island or Green Goddess Dressing (p. 158), or guacamole or Guacamole Salad (p. 36)—solo or in combination.

Recipes that Make Excellent Sandwiches

Pile **Grilled Whiskey-Marinated Salmon** (p. 195) and **Red Onion Confit** (p. 196) on mustard-slathered multigrain garlic toast for an irresistible combo, or try **Turkey Paillards** (p. 37) and salsa, with or without **Guacamole Salad**.

The **Butterflied Leg of Lamb** (p. 75) and **Rib-Eye Steaks** (p. 28) make scrumptious sandwiches garnished with just about anything. And hoagies or heroes composed of juicy slices of **Duck Magrets** (p. 172), **Pork Loin** (p. 206), or **Roast Turkey** (p. 240) are equally irresistible.

Open-face sandwiches provide a nice change of pace. Try serving your **Sizzling Cod Pan-Roast with Tomato–Caper Salsa** (p. 18) or **Roast Chicken with 40 Cloves of Garlic** (p. 64) leftovers warmed and spooned over toasted peasant bread, sourdough, or cornbread.

Concoct top-notch vegetable sandwiches by combining the **Fricassee of Mixed Mushrooms and Fresh Herbs** (p. 27) with arugula and melted fontina; the **Wilted Spinach Salad** (p. 171) with mozzarella; leftover **Frittata with Scallions** (p. 150) with green salad; or the **Caramelized Cauliflower** (p. 263) with watercress and thinly sliced sweet onion. (Prosciutto and crispy pancetta are delicious additions to both the frittata and the cauliflower sandwiches, if you're willing to veer from straight vegetarian) And employing yesterday's dressed greens as a sandwich condiment is one of the very few ways—other than as a frittata or omelet filling—I can think of to successfully recycle old salad.

Not the creative type, lacking leftovers, or just not in the mood to experiment? Use bacon, **Roast Turkey**, lettuce, tomato, and abundant **Green Goddess Dressing** or guacamole to create a sublime BLT.

Classic eggs Benedict—hollandaise-smothered poached eggs and Canadian bacon atop toasted English muffins—is hard to beat, but replacing the hollandaise with **Tomato–Caper Salsa**, a **Fricassee of Mixed Mushrooms**, or crisply sautéed onions, or replacing poached eggs with sunny-side up or scrambled, never disappoints. If you're willing to spend a few dollars more, substitute smoked salmon for the bacon and then top the eggs with dollops of sour cream or Greek yogurt and a sprinkling of minced chives or dill (or even caviar!). As with most things culinary, options are as far-reaching as your budget and imagination.

PICNIC TABLE

LUNCH FOR SIX

DISH	BEGIN PREP	PAGE
BUFFET		
Grilled Seafood and Chorizo Salad with Lemon–Shallot Vinaigrette	1 day ahead	111
Pan-Fried Mixed Pepper Polenta	1 day ahead	112
DESSERT		
Almond Marzipan Cake with Mixed Berries	1 day ahead	114

Guests appreciate the rustic Spanish and Italian overtones at play in this menu, and I serve it often. The lively main course (p. 111)—a palate-pleasing mélange of sweet and tender grilled seafood, spicy chorizo, and a tangy toss of dressed arugula and tomatoes—is brilliantly set off by red, pink, and black pepper–flecked Polenta (p. 112), a sumptuous side dish with the just the right amount of soothing "corniness" to balance the more complex salad.

The Almond Marzipan Cake (p. 114) is unusual: In the process of making the batter, I create my own marzipan—a trick I figured out some years back when playing around with a bushel of almonds gifted from a friend with a nut farm. In addition to saving money—as good marzipan is expensive—when prepared this way, the finished cake tastes particularly fresh, bright, and almondy. You can use this same method to make homemade marzipan for other uses. And once made, marzipan keeps almost indefinitely in the fridge. In the unlikely event you have leftover cake, try it for breakfast, toasted and slathered with Nutella or peach preserves.

Serve this flavorful menu all year long. The only adjustment I make in cooler weather is to replace the cake's fresh berry garnish with caramelized apples or pears or a drizzle of Bitter Chocolate Sauce (p. 302) and a sprinkling of crushed *amaretti*.

ORDER OF PREPARATION

START

1 DAY

1. Make the Lemon–Shallot Vinaigrette (p. 281) for the Seafood Salad (p. 111), cover, and refrigerate.

2. Complete Steps 1 through 5 for the Mixed Pepper Polenta (p. 112), cool, wrap, and refrigerate.

3. Complete Steps 1 through 9 for the Marzipan Cake (p. 114). Cool, cover, and store at room temperature.

2 HOURS

1. Remove the Lemon–Shallot Vinaigrette from the refrigerator.

2. Complete Step 6 for the Polenta.

3. Complete Step 10 for the Marzipan Cake and set aside.

45 MINS

1. If grilling the Seafood Salad, preheat the grill.

2. If baking the Polenta, preheat the oven to 450°F.

3. Complete Step 2 for the Seafood Salad and set aside.

30 MINS

1. If using a grill pan for the Seafood Salad, set it over medium–high heat.

2. Complete Steps 4 and 5 for the Seafood Salad.

20 MINS

1. If frying or grilling the Polenta, set a large, heavy pan or grill pan over medium–high heat.

2. Complete the Polenta (Step 9).

10 MINS

1. Complete Step 6 for the Seafood Salad.

SERVE

1. Complete the Seafood Salad (Step 7) and serve with the Polenta.

AFTER THE BUFFET

2. After clearing the table, complete the Marzipan Cake (Step 11) and serve with the mixed berries.

GET A HEAD START!

The **Lemon–Shallot Vinaigrette** for the **Seafood Salad** can be made in advance and refrigerated for up to 2 weeks.

The **Mixed Pepper Polenta** can be made ahead, unmolded, wrapped, and refrigerated for up to 4 days. Remove from the fridge and slice at least 2 hours before grilling.

The almond paste for the **Marzipan Cake** (Steps 1 and 2) can be made ahead, covered, and refrigerated for at least 4 weeks or frozen indefinitely. Bring to room temperature before using in the recipe. The finished cake itself can be frozen, well wrapped in foil, for at least 4 months.

Grilled Seafood and Chorizo Salad with Lemon–Shallot Vinaigrette

Yield: 8 generous first-course or 6 main-course servings

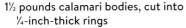

1½ pounds calamari bodies, cut into ¼-inch-thick rings

1½ pounds medium or large shrimp, peeled and butterflied

Fine sea salt and freshly ground black pepper, to taste

Extra virgin olive oil, as needed

4 large best-quality heirloom tomatoes or 2 baskets cherry tomatoes (whichever is in season and multiple colors if possible)

5 cups baby arugula

1 recipe Lemon–Shallot Vinaigrette (p. 281), room temperature

4 ounces imported Spanish chorizo, very thinly sliced and pan-fried until crisp

3 tablespoons chopped fresh Italian parsley, for garnish

The seafood may be pan-sautéed or broiled if no grill is available.

45 MINS

1. If grilling, preheat an indoor or outdoor grill.

2. Toss together the calamari rings and shrimp in a large bowl with the salt and pepper and just enough olive oil to coat generously. Set aside.

30 MINS

3. If using a grill pan, set it over medium–high heat.

4. Use tongs to transfer the seafood to the grill or grill pan. Do not crowd or the seafood will steam and not brown. If necessary, cook in 2 or 3 batches. Cook, turning frequently, for 5 to 10 minutes, or until done. Try not to overcook or the seafood may be tough. Remove from the heat and set aside.

5. While the seafood is cooking, slice the tomatoes and arrange on a serving platter.

10 MINS

6. Toss the arugula in a large bowl with enough of the Lemon–Shallot Vinaigrette to moisten and flavor.

SERVE

7. Scatter the dressed arugula, followed by the chorizo and grilled seafood, over the tomatoes. Garnish with the parsley and serve.

HOW TO PEEL, DEVEIN, AND BUTTERFLY SHRIMP

1. Pull off the shrimp's legs (and the head too, if it is attached).

2. Grip the shell at the head end and gently pull away from the body in one piece.

3. To butterfly, use a paring knife to slice down the center of the outer edge of the shrimp's back. Stop about ¼ inch before cutting all the way through. Press the shrimp open flat.

4. If not butterflying and wanting to devein, use a paring knife to slice about ¼-inch deep along the outer edge of the shrimp's back, down the center, and use the tip of the knife to remove the dark vein that runs along the center of the back and discard.

Pan-Fried Mixed Pepper Polenta

Yield: 6 side-dish servings

1 tablespoon extra virgin olive oil

1 small onion, chopped

1 clove garlic, minced

½ teaspoon crushed red pepper

¼ teaspoon dried thyme

1 small bay leaf, crumbled

1 quart liquid (water, milk, vegetable stock, chicken stock, or a mixture), plus more as needed

1 teaspoon fine sea salt, plus more to taste

8 ounces unseasoned instant polenta or finely ground cornmeal

2 tablespoons heavy cream or mascarpone cheese (optional)

2 teaspoons crushed pink peppercorns, or to taste

1 teaspoon cracked black peppercorns, or to taste

Unsalted butter or extra virgin olive oil, for browning

1. Heat the oil in a large saucepan over medium heat. Add the onion, garlic, crushed red pepper, thyme, and bay leaf and sauté, stirring frequently, for about 5 minutes, or until the onion begins to color.

2. Add the liquid and salt and bring to a boil over high heat. Remove from the heat. Slowly whisk in the polenta, a little at a time to avoid lumps.

3. Return to the heat and simmer, stirring constantly, for about 3 to 5 minutes, or until thick. If the polenta gets too thick, add more liquid.

4. Stir in the cream, if using, and simmer for 20 seconds. Remove from the heat. Add the pink and black peppercorns. Taste and adjust the seasoning as needed. The polenta will probably need more salt.

5. Pour the polenta into a greased loaf pan and set aside to cool. If not using within a few hours, unmold when cool, wrap well, and refrigerate. (The wrapped polenta will keep for up to 4 days in the refrigerator.)

TIP!

After slicing the polenta, let it come to room temperature before baking, frying, or grilling. This will take about 2 hours.

6. Place the polenta on a cutting board. Cut into ¾-inch slices and grease liberally on both sides with olive oil or butter. Set aside.

7. If baking, preheat the oven to 450°F.

8. If frying or grilling, set a large, heavy skillet or grill pan over medium–high heat.

9. If baking, transfer the polenta slices to a sheet pan and bake for about 5 to 7 minutes per side, or until light gold. If frying or grilling, place the polenta slices in the pan or on the grill and brown on both sides. Place the browned polenta in a 150°F oven for up to 20 minutes before serving to stay warm.

SERVE

10. Serve hot or warm.

Almond Marzipan Cake with Mixed Berries

Yield: 10–12 servings

You can toast the almonds in this recipe—and other nuts as well—up to 1 week in advance. Bake them on a sheet pan in a 350°F oven for about 10 minutes, or until very hot and lightly colored. Store cooled nuts in a covered container at room temperature or in the fridge.

Homemade marzipan (almond paste) tastes much fresher than store bought and is much less expensive. It's easy to make: Just follow Steps 1 and 2 of this recipe and store, covered, in the fridge for at least 4 weeks and in the freeze indefinitely.

1½ cups plus 1–2 tablespoons granulated sugar, divided

1 cup blanched almonds, toasted

¼ teaspoon best-quality pure vanilla extract

¼ teaspoon pure almond extract

2 tablespoons almond syrup (such as orgeat or orzata), room temperature

7 large egg whites, room temperature, divided

1¼ (2½ sticks) cups unsalted butter, room temperature

6 large egg yolks

1 cup all-purpose flour

½ teaspoon plus 2 generous pinches fine sea salt, divided

1½ teaspoons baking powder

½ teaspoon cream of tartar

5–7 cups fresh raspberries, blackberries, blueberries, sliced strawberries, or a mixture

Freshly grated zest and juice of ½ lemon

1–2 tablespoons confectioners' sugar, for garnish

1. To make the marzipan, combine the 1½ cups of granulated sugar and the almonds in the bowl of a food processor and process to form a smooth paste. Scrape down the sides as necessary with a rubber spatula.

2. Add the vanilla and almond extracts, almond syrup, and 1 egg white. Process until well blended, continuing to scrape down the sides of the bowl. Set aside.

3. Preheat the oven to 400°F. Butter and flour a 10-inch to 12-inch springform pan or 2 loaf pans, and place a piece of parchment paper on the bottom(s) of the pan(s). Butter the parchment paper and set aside.

4. To make the cake batter, using a stand mixer fitted with the paddle attachment or electric handheld mixer set on medium speed, beat the butter for 3 to 5 minutes, or until light and fluffy. Stir in the marzipan and continue to beat for 5 minutes, or until lightened. Add the yolks, 1 at a time, beating well after each addition.

5. Sift together the flour, the ½ teaspoon of salt, and the baking powder. Reduce the mixer's speed to low and add the dry mixture. Mix just until combined. Transfer the batter to a medium bowl and set aside.

6. Using a stand mixer fitted with the whisk attachment or an electric handheld set on low speed, beat the remaining 6 egg whites with 1 of the remaining pinches of salt for 1 minute, or until frothy. Add the cream of tartar and increase the speed to medium–low. Mix—continuing to slowly increase the mixer speed to medium and then medium–high—until the egg whites hold soft peaks but are not yet stiff.

7. Stir ⅓ of the egg white mixture into the batter and then very gently fold the batter into the remaining whites.

8. Transfer the batter to the prepared pan(s). Rap the pan(s) once on the counter to level the batter and eliminate air bubbles. Place in the oven and immediately turn the heat down to 350°F. If using the springform pan, bake for 40 to 50 minutes, or until done. If using the loaf pans, bake for 30 to 40 minutes, or until done. The cake is done when a toothpick inserted into the center comes out clean.

9. Remove from the oven and set aside to cool for 20 minutes. Remove the cake(s) from the pan(s). Cool completely, cover, and store at room temperature.

HOURS

10. Combine the berries, lemon zest and juice, and the remaining pinch of salt and 1 to 2 tablespoons of granulated sugar in a medium bowl and toss. Set aside.

SERVE

AFTER THE MAIN COURSE

11. Sift the confectioners' sugar over the cake and serve with the mixed berries.

LUNCH WITH FRIENDS

LUNCH FOR SIX

DISH	BEGIN PREP	PAGE
BUFFET		
Caramelized Onion and Goat Cheese Crostata	1 day ahead	121
Warm Green Bean and Bacon Salad with Sherry Vinegar Vinaigrette	2 hours ahead	123
Store-Bought Baguettes or Crusty Peasant Bread		
DESSERT		
Store-Bought Ice Cream with Crumbled Store-Bought *Amaretti* and Bitter Chocolate Sauce (p. 302)	1 day ahead	

Pie crust is one of my guilty pleasures, but I do feel slightly more virtuous when it includes whole-wheat flour and the tart is savory. First- and main-course tarts of all kinds—both large, communal ones and smaller, individual ones—are staples at my table. And I love making a Crostata (p. 121), just a fancy word for a freeform tart. Favorite fillings include mushrooms, roast vegetables, and in this case, a combination of caramelized onions and rich, salty goat cheese. If you prefer, replace the cheese with anchovies, sun-dried tomatoes, and/or sliced olives. Whichever option you choose, scatter a handful of chopped basil or another fresh herb over the crostata last minute for a fresh and colorful final touch.

The Warm Green Bean Salad (p. 123), decked out with bacon and pecans, is equally win-win. Though bacon is a delicious inclusion, vegetarians can omit it with impunity, as the meal has so much else going on. For a substantial starter or lunch main dish, add pieces of leftover pork, chicken, duck, or goose. And if you prefer, replace the pecans and pecan oil with hazelnuts, walnuts, or almonds and a matching nut oil.

Who doesn't "scream for ice cream" almost any time of day? I love the fun of making my own, but truthfully, there are so many fabulous brands out there—even at the corner deli—that there's no reason to become an ice cream manufacturer unless you really want to. And of course, you need an ice cream machine. However, I do strongly encourage you to make this Bitter Chocolate Sauce (p. 302), adapted from a recipe by Lutèce's André Soltner, and serve it over vanilla, chocolate, coffee, or caramel ice cream. In this menu, I've gilded the lily with crumbled *amaretti*, but crushed Heath bars, chopped toasted almonds, or Nut Praline (p. 302) are equally delicious. The deep chocolate elixir takes just minutes to prepare, keeps forever, and if you use ultra-fresh butter and best-quality cocoa powder, is better than any chocolate sauce you can buy. There's every reason to make it in huge batches— some for right now, some for the fridge, and some for the freezer.

ORDER OF PREPARATION

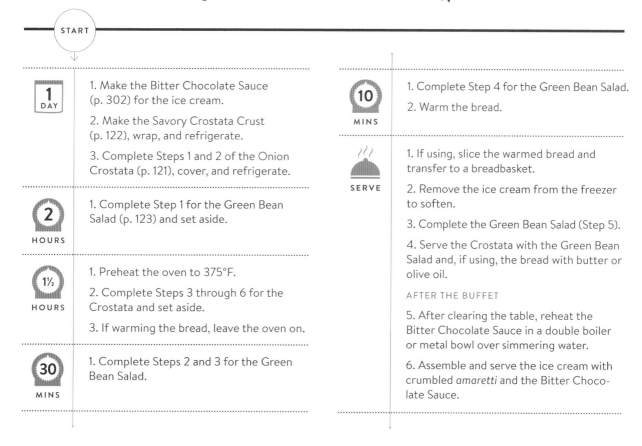

START

1 DAY

1. Make the Bitter Chocolate Sauce (p. 302) for the ice cream.

2. Make the Savory Crostata Crust (p. 122), wrap, and refrigerate.

3. Complete Steps 1 and 2 of the Onion Crostata (p. 121), cover, and refrigerate.

2 HOURS

1. Complete Step 1 for the Green Bean Salad (p. 123) and set aside.

1½ HOURS

1. Preheat the oven to 375°F.

2. Complete Steps 3 through 6 for the Crostata and set aside.

3. If warming the bread, leave the oven on.

30 MINS

1. Complete Steps 2 and 3 for the Green Bean Salad.

10 MINS

1. Complete Step 4 for the Green Bean Salad.

2. Warm the bread.

SERVE

1. If using, slice the warmed bread and transfer to a breadbasket.

2. Remove the ice cream from the freezer to soften.

3. Complete the Green Bean Salad (Step 5).

4. Serve the Crostata with the Green Bean Salad and, if using, the bread with butter or olive oil.

AFTER THE BUFFET

5. After clearing the table, reheat the Bitter Chocolate Sauce in a double boiler or metal bowl over simmering water.

6. Assemble and serve the ice cream with crumbled *amaretti* and the Bitter Chocolate Sauce.

GET A HEAD START!

The rolled out dough for the **Onion Crostata** can be wrapped in aluminum foil and frozen for up to 6 months. If frozen, allow to thaw in the fridge for 24 hours. The onions can be caramelized and refrigerated for up to 4 days or frozen for up to 6 months.

The entire **Crostata** can be baked up to 5 hours ahead and set aside. Reheat or not when ready to serve. Or assemble the Crostata up to 24 hours ahead, and refrigerate and bake off when needed.

The dressing for the **Green Bean Salad** can be made ahead, left in the pan, and set aside for up to 6 hours or refrigerated for up to 48 hours. The bacon, too, can be made ahead. Rewarm the dressing and recrisp the bacon before continuing.

Caramelized Onion and Goat Cheese Crostata

Yield: 6 generous main-course servings

4 tablespoons extra virgin olive oil

6 medium (about 2 pounds) Vidalia, red, or other sweet onions, very thinly sliced

2–3 sprigs fresh thyme or 1 teaspoon of dried thyme

½ teaspoon fine sea salt, plus more to taste

Freshly ground black pepper, to taste

½ recipe Savory Crostata Crust (recipe follows), cold but still pliable

½ cup crumbled goat cheese, feta, or ricotta salata

1 large egg, for egg wash (optional)

1 tablespoon heavy cream, for egg wash (optional)

1. Heat the oil in a large skillet set over medium heat. Add the onions, thyme, and salt. Cook, stirring frequently, for 30 minutes, or until the onions are lightly colored and the excess liquid has evaporated. Taste and adjust the salt and pepper as needed.

2. Transfer to a plate or bowl to cool completely. Warm onions will melt the dough. Cover and refrigerate if not using within a few hours.

3. Preheat the oven to 375°F. Place the Savory Crostata Crust (still on its parchment paper) on a cookie sheet and, leaving a 1½ inch border all around, evenly sprinkle it with the goat cheese. Top with the cooled onions.

4. If using, mix the egg with the cream to make an egg wash. Fold the dough's border up over the filling and press into place. The dough should be cool but not brittle. If it starts to break, let it warm up for a few more minutes. If it's too soft to work with, put the crostata in the fridge until the dough hardens up. If using, brush the crust edges with the egg wash. The wash is not necessary, but it does give the finished crust an attractive golden sheen.

5. Bake for 45 to 55 minutes, or until the filling is piping hot and the crust is golden brown.

6. Transfer the crostata to a wire rack to cool for at least 10 minutes. (The crostata will keep at room temperature for at least 5 hours.)

7. Serve warm or at room temperature.

Most fruit or vegetable crostatas, pies, and tarts can be assembled and stored in the refrigerator for up to 24 hours before baking.

If you've made the Onion Crostata earlier in the day but want to serve it warm, reheat it in a 375°F oven for 5 to 10 minutes.

Savory Crostata Crust

Yield: 2 crusts or 1 large crust

1½ cups all-purpose flour
½ cup whole-wheat flour*
¾ teaspoon fine sea salt

1 cup plus 2 tablespoons (2¼ sticks)
   unsalted butter, very cold and cut into
   small chunks
4–6 tablespoons ice water

Make the Crostata Crust with a food processor, electric mixer, or by hand. In each case, remember to work quickly and don't overprocess. Start with very cold butter and use as little liquid as possible.

Most people don't realize this, but when rolling out dough for any pie crust, it's perfectly fine to cut and piece the dough as you go along, perpetually adjusting to make sure the crust stays reasonably circular. If the dough becomes too sticky to do this easily, refrigerate until manageable. Once the crust is rolled into an acceptable circle, use a small sharp knife or pizza cutter to tidy up the edges.

1. Put both of the flours and the salt in the bowl of a food processor and pulse until combined.

2. Add the butter and toss with a fork. Pulse in 1 to 2 second bursts until most of the butter is the size of small peas.

3. With the motor off, pour 3 tablespoons of the ice water through the feed tube. Pulse until no dry patches remain and the dough begins to come together. Squeeze a handful of dough. If it does not cohere, add the remaining 1 tablespoon of water, pulse, and try again. The dough should remain fairly dry and under no circumstances should it form a ball when pulsed in the machine.

4. Turn the dough out onto a work surface. Form into 2 equal balls and place 1 in the center of a large piece of parchment paper and flatten into a disk. Place another piece of parchment paper on top of the disk and hit it a few times with a rolling pin to flatten somewhat more. Then roll the dough into a circle approximately 13 inches in diameter.

5. Repeat with the other disk.

6. Fold the parchment sheets around each of the rolled crusts and. refrigerate for at least 1 hour or overnight before using. For longer storage, also wrap in foil.

* This dough can be made entirely with all-purpose flour instead of including whole wheat.

Warm Green Bean and Bacon Salad with Sherry Vinegar Vinaigrette

Yield: 8 side-dish servings

½ pound lean smoky bacon

1 small clove garlic, finely minced

Large pinch baking soda (optional)

3 pounds fresh green string beans, trimmed

½ cup toasted pecans, roughly chopped

8 whole scallions (green and white parts), cut into very thin rounds

¼ cup chopped fresh Italian parsley

¼ cup minced fresh tarragon

¼ cup minced fresh chives

4 tablespoons sherry vinegar

2 teaspoons Dijon mustard

½ cup extra virgin olive oil or a mixture of olive oil and pecan oil, or less oil as needed

Fine sea salt and freshly ground black pepper, to taste

For a more substantial salad, add 2 cups of cooked, diced potatoes. Or for a great vegetarian starter or lunch main course, replace the bacon with shaved Gruyère or crumbled feta, blue cheese, or goat cheese.

2 HOURS

1. Fry the bacon in a large skillet over medium–high heat, until golden brown on both sides but not overly crisp. Remove from the heat, transfer the bacon to paper towels, and blot well. Reserve the fat in the skillet. Chop the bacon coarsely and mix it with the garlic. Set aside.

30 MINS

2. Bring a large pot of salted water to a boil over high heat. Add the baking powder, if using, followed by the string beans and boil for 5 minutes, or until tender. Drain immediately and spread on clean kitchen towels to dry and cool a bit.

3. While still warm, transfer the beans to a large salad bowl. Add the bacon–garlic mixture followed by the pecans, scallions, parsley, tarragon, and chives.

10 MINS

4. Warm the reserved bacon fat over low heat, and then whisk in the vinegar and mustard. Add ½ of the mixed oils and taste. Add more oil until the dressing tastes right to you. You should have about ¾ cup of vinaigrette. Whisk thoroughly, taste, and season generously with the salt and pepper as needed.

To insure that green vegetables retain their intense color once cooked, add a large pinch of baking soda to the boiling water just before adding the vegetables. But don't add too much or your vegetables may become mushy or lose nutrients. This works for most green vegetables, including sugar snap peas, green peas, broccoli, and asparagus as well as for the green beans in this recipe.

SERVE

5. Pour the warm dressing over the salad, toss, taste, and adjust the seasoning as necessary. Serve while still warm.

RUSTIC BRUNCH

BRUNCH FOR SIX

DISH	BEGIN PREP	PAGE
BUFFET		
Roasted Cauliflower and Watercress Salad with Walnuts and Gruyère	4 hours ahead	129
Homemade Gravlax with Sweet Mustard–Dill Sauce	3 days ahead	130
Irish Brown Bread	1 day ahead	132
DESSERT		
Golden Coconut–Chocolate Chunk Brownies	1 day ahead	133

T**he recipes in this small but perfect menu** are gems on their own and exquisite in combination. The Roasted Cauliflower (p. 129) starter is almost too rich and sumptuous to be called a salad, although crisp, red Treviso and spicy watercress do balance out the lushness of the other ingredients: caramelized cauliflower, toasted walnuts, and thick shavings of Gruyère. And a few spoonfuls of Walnut Vinaigrette (p. 280) pulls everything together. For a more substantial dish, toss in 1½ pounds of steamed, boiled, or roasted potatoes, cooled and cut into slices or a large dice.

If, in warm weather, the hearty salad seems a bit much, replace it with any of the lighter ones in this book: the My Favorite Caesar (p. 84); Grilled Asparagus Mimosa (p. 194); or Arugula with Green Apples (p. 143). Or just toss some watercress, fennel, and endive together with your favorite vinaigrette.

Luxurious yet inexpensive, Gravlax (p. 130)—salt-, sugar-, and dill-cured salmon—offers abundant bang for the buck. And it's genius. Buy a whole fillet, which per pound is usually the most economical option, and serve a crowd. Most of my guests prefer gravlax to even the most expensive smoked Scotch and Irish varieties. I do, too.

Though the idea of curing your own fish may sound intimidating, there's not much to it. You can certainly serve store-bought smoked salmon instead, but why not give gravlax a try? It takes literally five minutes to doctor up the raw salmon with sugar, salt, pepper, and fresh dill. After that, just refrigerate and turn daily for two or three days. I prefer my gravlax less salty and cure for only two, but play around and see what works for you. If you inadvertently overcure it, a 30-minute soak in cold water should fix the problem.

The tangy Sweet Mustard–Dill Sauce (p. 131) is quick, easy, and good enough to consume by the spoonful. When not serving it with Gravlax, slather it on a salmon and red onion sandwich, dollop it alongside a perfectly grilled salmon fillet, or spread it between the pastry and the fish when making a salmon and caramelized onion *coulibiac*. And surprisingly, it's also particularly tasty alongside a juicy pork or veal chop.

My Irish Brown Bread (p. 132) is another must-have recipe. Anyone who's been to Ireland will tell you: Nothing beats the local brown bread. Since its lift derives from baking soda, not yeast, the dough demands no kneading or rising and is oven-ready in under 10 minutes. Bake for 50 minutes, and voilà: two fragrant, crusty loaves. Ideally make extra, as the bread easily keeps in the fridge for two weeks and in the freezer for months.

I got this brown bread recipe from my friend David's Dubliner mother, who warned me it could not be replicated off the Emerald Isle—an Irish tall tale for sure since I make it with perfect results here in Manhattan. Chock-full of oatmeal, whole wheat, wheat germ, and bran, it's amazingly good for you, but I'd eat this brown bread compulsively even if it weren't. Rough, moist, and grainy, whether fresh or toasted, it's a match made in heaven with almost everything. Use it for sandwiches or serve alongside soups, salads, and roast or grilled meats, poultry, and fish. In addition to Gravlax, top it with any other smoked fish, lump crabmeat, or a couple of briny oysters. And don't forget breakfast—thick slices, toasted and plastered with butter and marmalade or honey, are an auspicious way to start the day.

Like many other baby boomers, when I bite into a brownie, blondie, lemon square, or congo bar, I'm awash in Proustian nostalgia and find myself reflecting back on the lunchbox treats, afterschool snacks, and slumber-party baking sprees of childhood.

I inherited my mother's recipe box filled with fairly foolproof prescriptions for basic bars: spread the batter in a pan, bake, cool, and cut into squares. When my kids were young, my daughters and I made these confections that I remembered from my youth. The kids and their friends loved them, but even beloved basics are often ripe for creative updates.

A slightly more complex variation on the theme, this menu's divine Golden Coconut–Chocolate Chunk Brownie (p. 133) recipe—adapted from Lisa Slater's book, *Brownie Points*—is one of my most successful recent discoveries. Brownies may sound a bit old hat, but don't underestimate these bars, which are rich and chocolaty, topped with a chewy, macaroon-like coconut crust, and nothing short of spectacular.

ORDER OF PREPARATION

START

3 DAYS

1. Complete Steps 1 through 3 of the Gravlax (p. 130) and refrigerate, turning at least once a day.

2. Make the Mustard–Dill Sauce (p. 131), cover, and refrigerate.

1 DAY

1. Complete Steps 1 through 7 for the Brownies (p. 133). Cool, cover, and store at room temperature.

2. Complete Steps 1 through 6 for the Irish Brown Bread (p. 132). Cool, cover, and store at room temperature.

3. Make the Walnut Vinaigrette (p. 280) for the Cauliflower Salad (p. 129) and refrigerate.

4 HOURS

1. Preheat the oven to 400°F.

2. Complete Steps 2 and 3 for the Cauliflower Salad and set aside.

2 HOURS

1. Remove the Walnut Vinaigrette from the refrigerator.

2. Remove the Mustard–Dill Sauce from the refrigerator.

20 MINS

1. Complete Steps 4 and 5 for the Gravlax and set aside.

10 MINS

1. Complete Step 4 for the Cauliflower Salad.

SERVE

1. Complete the Cauliflower Salad (Step 5) and the Irish Brown Bread (Step 7).

2. Serve the Gravlax with the Mustard–Dill Sauce, Cauliflower Salad, Irish Brown Bread, and butter or olive oil, if using.

AFTER THE BUFFET

3. After clearing the table, complete the Brownies (Step 8) and serve.

GET A HEAD START!

Both the **Walnut Vinaigrette** for the **Roasted Cauliflower Salad** and the **Sweet Mustard–Dill Sauce** can be made ahead and refrigerated for up to 2 weeks.

Gravlax will keep in the refrigerator for 1 to 2 weeks after the salt, sugar, and dill have been removed.

Irish Brown Bread can be made, cooled, wrapped in aluminum foil, and refrigerated for up to 2 weeks or frozen for at least 6 months.

The **Brownies** can be made, cooled, covered, and stored at room temperature for 2 days, refrigerated for 1 week, or frozen for at least 3 months.

Roasted Cauliflower and Watercress Salad with Walnuts and Gruyère

Yield: 6–8 first-course servings

1 large head cauliflower, broken into medium-size florets

4–6 tablespoons extra virgin olive oil, as needed

Fine sea salt and freshly ground black pepper, to taste

3 bunches watercress, trimmed and coarsely chopped

⅔ cup coarsely grated Gruyère cheese

⅓ cup walnuts, toasted and coarsely chopped

1 large Treviso, sliced crosswise into ¼-inch-thick pieces

1 recipe Walnut Vinaigrette (p. 280), room temperature

Almost any cheese, including Gruyère, can be grated up to 1 week in advance and refrigerated in a covered container. However, grated Parmesan will keep at least 4 weeks.

4 HOURS

1. Preheat the oven to 400°F.

2. Toss the cauliflower, oil, salt, and pepper in a medium bowl until well coated. Transfer to a sheet pan and roast for 35 to 50 minutes, or until very tender, dark golden, and crispy in spots.

3. Remove from the oven and set aside. When cool enough to handle, cut into smaller florets. Set aside.

10 MINS

4. In a large salad bowl, combine the roasted cauliflower with the watercress, Gruyère, walnuts, and Treviso. Toss with just enough of the Walnut Vinaigrette to moisten and flavor.

The Roasted Cauliflower Salad also works well as a first course. And the roasted cauliflower component, on its own, is a tasty side dish served hot, warm, or at room temperature.

SERVE

5. Taste and adjust the salt and pepper as needed. Serve right away.

Homemade Gravlax with Sweet Mustard–Dill Sauce

Yield: 8 generous main-course servings

1 (3-pound) fresh center-cut salmon fillet, skin on

½ cup kosher salt

½ cup granulated sugar

2 tablespoons white and/or black peppercorns, crushed

1 tablespoon fennel seed, toasted and cooled

1 large bunch fresh dill

3–4 sprigs fresh dill, chopped, for garnish

1 recipe Sweet Mustard–Dill Sauce (recipe follows), room temperature

You can sauté gravlax to serve as a main course. Rather than slicing it thinly, cut the finished gravlax into 6-ounce sections and sauté with a bit of olive oil until heated through. Serve hot or warm and pass the mustard sauce and optional lemon wedges separately.

1. Cut the salmon fillet in half crosswise and place 1 piece, skin side down, in a deep dish.

2. Combine the salt, sugar, peppercorns, and fennel seed. Sprinkle ½ of the curing mixture evenly over the piece of salmon. Place the 1 bunch of dill on top of the curing mixture. Then place the second piece of salmon, skin side up, on top of that, making sure both pieces of fish line up exactly.

3. Cover the dish with aluminum foil. Refrigerate the salmon for 48 to 72 hours, turning it at least once a day and basting it with the liquid that collects in the pan.

4. Remove the salmon from the refrigerator and uncover. Discard the dill and marinade. Run cold water over the salmon to rinse off any remaining curing mixture. Pat dry with paper towels.

5. Place the 2 pieces of salmon—cut end to cut end—on an attractive cutting board. Slice the salmon crosswise in thin slices as for smoked salmon. Arrange on the cutting board or on a long serving platter and sprinkle with the chopped dill. Set aside.

6. Serve with the Sweet Mustard–Dill Sauce. Refrigerate extra salmon, covered, for 1 to 2 weeks.

Sweet Mustard–Dill Sauce

Yield: About 1½ cup

6 tablespoons honey mustard
3 tablespoons white wine vinegar
½ cup extra virgin olive oil

½ cup chopped fresh dill
¾ teaspoon fine sea salt, plus more to taste
Freshly ground black pepper, to taste

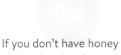

If you don't have honey mustard on hand, you can replace it with 4 tablespoons Dijon or German mustard and 2 tablespoons honey.

3 DAYS

1. Combine the mustard and vinegar in a medium bowl. Gradually whisk in the oil. Stir in the dill, salt, and pepper. Alternatively, pulse everything together in a food processor. Taste and adjust the seasoning as needed.

2. Cover and refrigerate for at least 1 hour to allow flavors to marry. Use right away or refrigerate for up to 2 weeks.

Irish Brown Bread

Yield: 2 medium sized loaves

16 ounces (3½ cups) whole-wheat flour

8 ounces (1¾ cups) self-rising flour

8 ounces (1¼ cups) steel-cut (pinhead) oats

4 ounces (1½ cups) natural bran

2 ounces (⅔ cup) wheat germ

4 teaspoons baking soda

4 teaspoons dark brown sugar

1½ teaspoons fine sea salt

4½ cups buttermilk, room temperature

It's easy to make your own self-rising flour. Sift 4 cups of all-purpose flour together with 2 teaspoons salt and 2 tablespoons baking powder 6 times. You will have approximately 1 pound (4 cups) of self-rising flour. You can scale up or down depending on the recipe. I like to make extra and keep it in a canister for next time.

1. Preheat the oven to 400°F. Grease 2 (9-inch or 10-inch × 5-inch) loaf pans and set aside.

2. In a very large bowl and using a large spoon, mix together the dry ingredients until well combined.

3. Add the buttermilk and stir until everything is evenly moist.

4. Divide the dough equally between the 2 prepared pans.

5. Bake on the center rack of the oven for 50 minutes.

6. Unmold and cool completely on wire racks. Cover and store at room temperature.

SERVE

7. Slice and serve.

Try slices of avocado and red onion sprinkled with salt and pepper and sandwiched between slices of this brown bread, which have been toasted with Garlic Oil (p. 273). When high season and at their best, tomatoes are a great substitute for the avocados. It's even better if you add fresh basil and sliced mozzarella.

Golden Coconut–Chocolate Chunk Brownies

Yield: 16 (2-inch) brownies

For the Brownie Batter

¾ cup all-purpose flour

¼ teaspoon fine sea salt

¼ teaspoon baking powder

½ cup (1 stick) unsalted butter

1¾ ounces unsweetened chocolate, cut into small chunks

1¾ ounces semisweet chocolate, cut into small chunks

3 large eggs, room temperature

½ cup granulated sugar

½ cup dark brown sugar

1½ teaspoons best-quality pure vanilla extract

1 cup semisweet chocolate chips or coarsely chopped semisweet chocolate

For the Macaroon Topping

2 large egg whites

½ cup sugar

2 cups sweetened, shredded coconut

½ teaspoon best-quality pure vanilla extract

¼ teaspoon fine sea salt

1. With a rack adjusted to the highest position, preheat the oven to 350°F. Line an 8-inch square baking pan with aluminum foil, leaving enough foil overhang on 2 opposite sides to use as handles.

2. *Start the Brownie Batter:* Mix the flour, salt, and baking powder together and set aside. Melt the butter and unsweetened and semisweet chocolate chunks in a medium saucepan set over very low heat, stirring frequently, until about ¾ melted. Remove from the heat and stir until smooth and completely melted. Set aside.

3. Using a stand mixer fitted with the paddle attachment or an electric handheld mixer set on medium–high speed, beat the eggs, granulated and brown sugars, and vanilla for 5 minutes, or until tripled in volume. With the motor running, slowly pour in the chocolate mixture, continuing to mix until well combined. Turn off the mixer.

4. Add the dry ingredients and mix on low speed until just combined, scraping down the sides of bowl once or twice. Add in the chocolate chips and continue to mix for 30 to 60 seconds, or until combined. Pour into the prepared pan and set aside.

5. *Start the Macaroon Topping:* Place the egg whites and sugar in a medium saucepan set over medium–low heat and whisk constantly until the sugar has dissolved and a candy thermometer registers 140°F. Remove from the heat and stir in the coconut. Return the pan to low heat and cook, stirring constantly, for exactly 5 minutes. Remove from the heat and stir in the vanilla and salt.

6. Carefully spread the macaroon topping over the brownie batter. Bake for 30 minutes, or until the topping is golden. Remove from the oven, and place on a wire rack to cool completely.

7. Store, covered, at room temperature.

AFTER THE MAIN COURSE

8. Cut into 16 (2-inch) squares, transfer to a serving platter, and serve.

BRUNCH, ITALIAN STYLE

BRUNCH FOR SIX

DISH	BEGIN PREP	PAGE
BUFFET		
Heirloom Tomato Salad with Fresh Herbs and Marjoram–Balsamic Vinaigrette	1 day ahead	138
Baked Pasta with Asparagus, Green Peas, and Lemon	4 hours ahead	139
Store-Bought French or Italian Bread		
DESSERT		
Chocolate–Ginger Biscotti	1 day ahead	298

The baked pasta of my childhood was synonymous with macaroni and cheese. Though my mother's crunchy-on-top and velvety-within specialty was loved by all, as a young adult with my own kitchen, I was more than ready to branch out.

The best baked pastas are rich and rustic—the dreamiest of comfort foods. I look to them for cozy sustenance when temperatures fall. However, this particular recipe (p. 139), adapted from Al Forno in Providence, Rhode Island, is replete with spring vegetables, is relatively light, and works well even in warmer weather. Green peas and asparagus nestling in crusty, golden pasta provide visual appeal while caramelized onions, tangy lemon, and four savory cheeses contribute serious depth of flavor.

Even in August and September, the dish provides a deeply satisfying lunch when served lukewarm rather than hot. Precede it with a platter of peak-season heirloom tomatoes. My Tomato Salad (p. 138) displays a rainbow of reds, greens, yellows, and purples and is glorious, especially when strewn with a confetti of fresh green herbs. If you're a gardener—or can befriend one—a scattering of spicy nasturtium blossoms, tasting as good as it looks, is the perfect addition.

When tomatoes are less than optimal, replace them with My Favorite Caesar Salad (p. 84) or an Arugula Salad with Green Apples (p. 143) instead. Or forget the salad entirely, take advantage of always ripe, always delicious canned San Marzanos, and begin the meal with Tomato–Cumin Soup (p. 74).

Biscotti, unlike tomatoes, taste great any time of year. I've loved these crunchy, twice-baked Italian cookies ever since my father took me to Rome in my early teens. Sitting on the Via Veneto and biting into this unfamiliar treat, after giving it a dunk in a glass of smooth, syrupy Vin Santo, made me feel like the ultimate sophisticate. The experience was short-lived, however, as I didn't taste the cookie again until the 1980s, when waves of fancy Italians invaded Manhattan bringing with them their impeccable, less-is-more style and great food. The Chocolate–Ginger version (p. 298) is one I created for Dean & DeLuca in the early 1990s. They're divine but nontraditional. If you want to dip your biscotti in Vin Santo, try making a more classic variety. Or feel free to buy biscotti if you aren't up for making them—no one has to know.

ORDER OF PREPARATION

START

1 DAY

1. If not using store-bought biscotti, make the Chocolate–Ginger Biscotti (p. 298), cover, and store at room temperature.

2. Make the Marjoram–Balsamic Vinaigrette for the Tomato Salad (p. 138) and refrigerate.

4 HOURS

1. Complete Steps 1 through 6 for the Baked Pasta (p. 139) and set aside.

2 HOURS

1. Remove the Vinaigrette from the refrigerator.

45 MINS

1. With a rack adjusted to the upper-third position, preheat the oven to 500°F.

2. Make the Tomato Salad.

3. Complete the Baked Pasta (Step 8).

5 MINS

1. If using, place the French or Italian Bread in the hot oven.

SERVE

1. Serve the Tomato Salad with the Baked Pasta and, if using, the warmed bread and butter or olive oil.

AFTER THE BUFFET

2. After clearing the table, pass the plate of Biscotti.

GET A HEAD START!

Like most vinaigrettes, the one for the **Heirloom Tomato Salad** can be made ahead and refrigerated for up to 2 weeks.

Like most **baked pastas**—including lasagnas—this one can be assembled and refrigerated for up to 48 hours before baking. Bring to room temperature before baking or to bake pasta straight from the fridge, increase the baking time by at least 10 minutes.

The **Biscotti** can be made up to 4 weeks ahead and stored in a covered container. They can also be frozen for at least 6 months.

Heirloom Tomato Salad with Fresh Herbs and Marjoram–Balsamic Vinaigrette

Yield: 6 side-dish servings

Use only the best, most flavorful tomatoes when making a tomato salad. In a pinch, lackluster tomatoes can be somewhat improved by a scant sprinkling of sugar and finely minced garlic. Or take advantage of cherry tomatoes, which off-season tend to be more flavorful than the larger ones. And remember, like potatoes, tomatoes require lots of salt.

6–8 large heirloom tomatoes, mixed in color

1 small red onion or a very large shallot

1 recipe Marjoram–Balsamic Vinaigrette (recipe follows), room temperature

6 tablespoons coarsely chopped fresh basil, Italian parsley, chives, or a mixture

45 MINS

1. Cut the tomatoes into ½-inch slices and arrange on a serving platter. Halve the onion and slice into paper-thin half-rings.

2. Drizzle the tomatoes with enough of the Marjoram–Balsamic Vinaigrette to flavor. Scatter the onion over the top and sprinkle with the fresh herbs. Set aside.

SERVE

3. Serve at room temperature.

Marjoram–Balsamic Vinaigrette

Yield: About ½ cup

¼ cup extra virgin olive oil

1 tablespoon sherry, red wine, or balsamic vinegar

2 teaspoons finely minced fresh marjoram

Pinch granulated sugar

1 clove garlic, finely minced

Fine sea salt, freshly ground black pepper, and Tabasco sauce, to taste

1 DAY

1. Place all vinaigrette ingredients in a lidded jar and shake vigorously until well combined. Set aside for at least 1 hour to allow the flavors to marry. Taste and adjust the seasoning as needed.

2. Use immediately or refrigerate for up to 2 weeks. Bring to room temperature and reshake the jar before using.

Baked Pasta with Asparagus, Green Peas, and Lemon

Yield: 6 main-course servings or 8 generous first-course servings

2½ cups heavy cream

1½ cups frozen green peas, thawed

½ cup grated fontina cheese

½ cup grated Pecorino Romano cheese

½ cup grated Italian Parmesan cheese, plus more for sprinkling

¼ cup finely minced onion

2 tablespoons fresh ricotta

2 teaspoons freshly grated lemon zest

1¼ teaspoons kosher salt, plus more to taste

1 teaspoon freshly ground black pepper, plus more to taste

Dash Tabasco sauce

1 pound fresh asparagus, trimmed and cut on a diagonal into ⅛-inch-thick slices

1 medium red onion, sliced into paper-thin rings

2 tablespoons melted unsalted butter

1 pound imported pasta shells, penne, or fusilli

Tip!

When a recipe calls for only part of an onion, you don't have to discard the remainder. Just wrap it really well in foil and refrigerate for up to 2 weeks.

4 HOURS

1. Bring a very large pot of salted water to a boil over high heat.

2. While the water is heating, combine the cream, peas, fontina, Pecorino, Parmesan, minced onion, ricotta, and zest in a large bowl. Add the salt, pepper, and Tabasco. Set aside.

3. Toss together the asparagus, red onion, and melted butter in a separate bowl. Season with the salt and pepper.

4. Add the pasta to the boiling water. Stir and then boil for 4 minutes. Drain the pasta well and add it to the cream mixture.

5. Transfer the pasta mixture to a large gratin dish. The pasta should be no more than 1½-inches deep. If necessary, use a second dish.

6. Evenly divide the asparagus–onion mixture over the top of the pasta and sprinkle generously with Parmesan. Set aside until ready to bake.

45 MINS

7. With a rack adjusted to the upper-third position, preheat the oven to 500°F.

8. Bake for 15 to 18 minutes, or until the pasta is very hot and bubbly and the asparagus begin to brown. Let rest a few minutes before serving.

SERVE

9. Serve hot.

LA DOLCE VITA REPRISE

BRUNCH FOR EIGHT

DISH	BEGIN PREP	PAGE
BUFFET		
Arugula Salad with Green Apples and Marcona Almonds	5 mins ahead	143
Mixed Mushroom Risotto	75 minutes ahead	144
DESSERT		
Venetian Polenta Cake with Dried Fruit and Cognac	1 day ahead	145

This northern Italian menu is a classic—straightforward and perfectly balanced. The Arugula Salad (p. 143) is my loose take on a Tuscan friend's favorite recipe. Depending on my mood and on the season, I often replace the apples with pears, peaches, plums, or nectarines.

A mushroom lover's dream, this Mixed Mushroom Risotto (p. 144) is as full-flavored as they come. An abundance of dried mushrooms, combined with Parmesan, garlic, onion, and parsley, results in a complexity that makes the dish hard to forget. You can add sautéed fresh mushrooms at the end for texture, but—other than to extend the dish a bit—they're unnecessary, as two ounces of dried porcini, chanterelles, and/or morels goes a long way and will provide all the taste you need—and more. If you have leftovers (which you probably won't), add a beaten egg the next day and fry up a batch risotto cakes.

In 2006, when I was writing *Lost Desserts*, Barbara Kafka gave me this unusual Polenta Cake recipe (p. 145), saying she'd gotten it directly from James Beard. Beard, in turn had told Kafka that because it produced a "perfect cake . . . fruity and luscious but not too rich," he'd gone to great lengths to wheedle the prized recipe away from a bakeshop in Venice.

For me, the subtle crunch of cornmeal elevates this special confection sky high and makes it equally appealing—toasted or not—at breakfast, teatime, or after dinner. Orange slices or a glass of Vin Santo are both excellent accompaniments.

ORDER OF PREPARATION

 START

 1 DAY

1. Make the Lemon–Shallot Vinaigrette (p. 281) for the Arugula Salad (p. 143), cover, and refrigerate.

2. Complete Steps 1 through 8 for the Polenta Cake (p. 145). Cool, wrap, and store at room temperature.

 75 MINS

1. Remove the Vinaigrette from the refrigerator.

2. Complete Steps 1 through 3 for the Mushroom Risotto (p. 144) and set aside.

 45 MINS

1. Complete Steps 4 through 7 for the Mushroom Risotto.

 5 MINS

1. Make the Arugula Salad.

 SERVE

1. Complete the Mushroom Risotto (Step 8) and serve with the Arugula Salad. Pass extra Parmesan.

AFTER THE BUFFET

2. After clearing the table, finish the Polenta Cake (Step 9) and serve.

GET A HEAD START!

The vinaigrette for the **Arugula Salad** can be made ahead and refrigerated for up to 2 weeks.

Cook the **Risotto** halfway through earlier in the day and spread the mixture out on sheet pans to cool quickly. Set aside and then, about 15 minutes before serving, place 1 cup of the remaining broth—or water—in the original casserole and bring to a simmer. Add the cooled Risotto, finish the recipe, and serve.

The dried mushrooms for the **Risotto** can be soaked and chopped in advance, covered, and refrigerated up to 3 days.

The **Polenta Cake** can be made, cooled, wrapped in foil, and stored at room temperature for up to 24 hours, in the refrigerator for up to 1 week, or in the freezer for at least 4 months.

Arugula Salad with Green Apples and Marcona Almonds

Yield: 8 first-course servings

12 large handfuls baby arugula

2 large fennel bulbs, trimmed and thinly sliced

2 Granny Smith apples, peeled (or not) and very thinly sliced

1 large frisée, cut or torn into bite-size pieces

¾ cup toasted Marcona almonds (toasted blanched almonds can be substituted), very coarsely chopped

2 cups thinly sliced celery

1 cup golden or regular raisins

1 cup coarsely grated or shaved Italian Parmesan cheese

1 recipe Lemon–Shallot Vinaigrette (p. 281), room temperature

1. Place all salad ingredients in a large bowl and toss. Add enough of the Lemon–Shallot Vinaigrette to moisten and flavor. Taste and adjust seasoning as needed.

2. Serve right away.

Marcona almonds, hailing from Spain, are shorter, rounder, sweeter, and more delicately textured than regular almonds. They are traditionally lightly fried in oil before serving, although you can just toast them in the oven, as I do, before tossing with a bit of olive oil and some salt. They're an ideal nibble with cocktails or added to a green salad.

Nuts for most uses taste fresher and more flavorful after being toasted in a 350°F oven for about 10 minutes. Cool before using.

Mixed Mushroom Risotto

Yield: 8 main-course servings

2 ounces dried porcini or mixed dried wild mushrooms

2 cups water, warm

4–6 cups chicken stock, plus more as needed

2 tablespoons unsalted butter

1 tablespoon extra virgin olive oil

Large pinch crushed red pepper

⅓ cup finely minced onion or shallot

1 large clove garlic, finely minced

1½ cups risotto rice such as Arborio, Carnaroli, or Vialone Nano

½ cup dry white wine

1 tablespoon Truffle Butter (p. 274), unsalted butter, or I tablespoon truffle oil

½ cup freshly grated Italian Parmesan cheese, plus more for passing

3 tablespoons finely minced fresh Italian parsley

Fine sea salt and freshly ground pepper, to taste

75 MINS

1. Rinse the dried mushrooms in cold water. Remove and discard any pebbles. Strain. Place the mushrooms in a bowl with the warm water. Set aside for at least 30 minutes.

2. To make the broth, strain the mushroom soaking liquid through a fine sieve into a medium saucepan and add the stock. Set aside.

3. Coarsely chop the strained mushrooms. Set aside.

45 MINS

4. Bring the broth to a low steady simmer over medium–low heat.

5. In a large casserole, heat the unsalted butter and oil over low heat. Add the crushed red pepper. Add the onion and garlic and sweat for about 5 minutes, or until soft. Do not brown.

6. Add the rice to the casserole and stir for 2 minutes with a wooden spoon. Raise the heat to medium and add the wine, stirring until it is completely absorbed. Add the chopped mushrooms and ½ cup of the simmering broth. Stir until the broth is almost completely absorbed. Continue to add the broth, ½ cup at a time, stirring and waiting for the broth to be absorbed before adding more. If the broth runs out, continue with ½ cups of simmering water.

7. When the rice is al dente, stir in a final ¼ cup of simmering broth or water and remove from the heat. Stir in the truffle butter, Parmesan, and parsley. Season with plenty of salt and pepper. Cover if not serving right away.

SERVE

8. Serve hot with passed Parmesan.

Dried mushrooms are one of God's major gifts to the home cook. After a quick rinse in cool water, just rehydrate them with a 30-minute soak in warm water. And don't waste their soaking liquid. It's packed with flavor. If you don't need it for a risotto or soup right off, freeze for future use.

Venetian Polenta Cake with Dried Fruit and Cognac

Yield: 8 generous servings

1½ cups plus 3 tablespoons all-purpose flour, divided

1 cup yellow cornmeal

1 tablespoon baking powder

½ teaspoon fine sea salt

½ cup chopped candied citrus fruit, such as citron, lemon, grapefruit, or orange

½ cup raisins; currants; chopped dried figs, apricots, or peaches; or a mixture

1 cup (2 sticks) unsalted butter, room temperature

1 cup granulated sugar

3 large eggs, room temperature

2 tablespoons cognac

1. Preheat the oven to 350°F. Butter a 9-inch springform pan. Line with parchment paper, butter and flour the paper, and set aside.

2. Sift together the 1½ cups of flour, the cornmeal, the baking powder, and the salt. Set aside.

3. In a small bowl, toss the candied fruit and the dried fruit together with the remaining 3 tablespoons of flour until coated. Put in a strainer, shake off the excess flour, and set aside.

4. Using an stand mixer fitted with the paddle attachment or an electric handheld mixer set on medium–high speed, cream together the butter and sugar for 5 minutes, or until very light and fluffy. Add the eggs, 1 at a time, beating well after each addition. Scrape down the sides of the bowl. Reduce the mixer speed to low and add the flour–cornmeal mixture and the cognac, and beat until just combined. Add the candied and dried fruits and beat 15 seconds more.

5. Scrape the batter into the prepared pan. Knock the pan on the counter a couple of times to settle the batter.

6. Bake for 45 minutes, or until the cake is lightly golden, pulling away from the edges, and a toothpick inserted into its center comes out clean. Don't overbake.

7. Remove from the oven. Cool for 10 minutes.

8. Run a small knife around the sides of the cake to loosen. Remove the pan sides. Transfer to a wire rack to cool completely. Wrap and store at room temperature.

AFTER THE MAIN COURSE

9. Slice and serve.

SERVE

EARLY AUTUMN BRUNCH

BRUNCH FOR EIGHT

DISH	BEGIN PREP	PAGE
BUFFET		
Fresh Melon and Fig Platter with Prosciutto and Fresh Lime	2 hours ahead	
Roast Potato and Feta Frittata with Scallions and Dill	45 mins ahead	150
Creamy Green Polenta	1 day ahead	151
DESSERT		
Miniature Cream Scones with Crème Fraîche and Jam	1 day ahead	153

often make a full meal of Miniature Cream Scones (p. 153), and after tasting them, you'll understand why. However, this time around, they are just one component of a particularly appealing brunch buffet.

I developed several varieties of these scones in the early 1990s specifically for the tearoom at Felissimo on Manhattan's Upper East Side, and I made them religiously until the tearoom closed almost 10 years later. A cross between the real thing and a big cookie, they were a huge hit and even commended a *New York Times* article. Comprising nothing but basic dry ingredients, cream, sugar, and whatever add-ins strike your fancy, they couldn't be easier to make.

Scones freeze perfectly and are great to always have within reach. They're ideal breakfast and snack foods, and when halved horizontally and decked out with fruit or berries, ice cream, and whipped cream, they're divine for dessert as well.

But this meal is not just about scones. Although you can serve the melon, fig, and prosciutto combination all year long, it's a classic autumnal treat. Drape slices of cantaloupe, honeydew, or Crenshaw melon with prosciutto, and then scatter figs over and around. Be sure to halve or quarter the figs to expose their deep pink interiors. When figs are out of season, just fill in with extra melon. Lime wedges, their tart juice the perfect foil to the sweet fruit and salty ham, are the ideal garnish. Small bunches of red or green grapes are an amusing addition, particularly in late summer and early fall when tiny Champagne grapes make a brief appearance.

A frittata is the most practical egg dish I can think of and a seamless pairing with the fruit and prosciutto. As opposed to scrambled, fried, poached, baked, or soft boiled eggs, frittatas are equally appealing whether served hot, warm, or at room temperature. For most frittatas, whisk the ingredients together up to a day in advance and cook up to several hours before guests arrive. Sturdy and portable, this versatile egg dish also represents quintessential picnic food. Like those of its quiche and omelet cousins, fillings are infinite and ideal repositories for leftovers. Cooked vegetables, pastas, meats, fish, and poultry—solo or combined with cheese and fresh herbs—are all good bets. This Roast Potato and Feta Frittata (p. 150) is a winner as is, but for variation, try adding cooked asparagus and a half pound of smoked salmon. Artichokes; caramelized onions; ham, chives, and Gruyère; or simply cooked penne with coarsely ground black pepper are favorite fillings as well.

The Creamy Green Polenta (p. 151) is my simplification of a more complicated April Bloomfield recipe and adds color and pizzazz to any plate. Stirring Bloomfield's Kale Purée (p. 152)—or a pesto, green vegetable purée, or salsa verde—into polenta provides a pleasing change of palette from standard yellow and imparts extra flavor to this popular side dish. If you're running late and can't prepare the real thing, substitute instant polenta, a last minute time-saver. The greens provide added taste, distraction, and visual appeal, so the absence of the more complex "slow" polenta won't be missed. When lacking the time and energy and even instant yellow polenta sounds overwhelming, just serve a good loaf of bread instead. In any case, keep the gorgeous green polenta in mind to accompany more relaxed future meals, especially when they include roast or grilled chicken, steak, fish, or chops.

ORDER OF PREPARATION

START

1 DAY

1. Complete Steps 1 through 4 of the Cream Scones (p. 153), wrap, and refrigerate.

2. Make the Kale Purée (p. 152) for the Polenta (p. 151), cool, cover, and refrigerate.

2 HOURS

1. Slice the fresh melon and figs and arrange it on a platter with the lime wedges. Set aside.

1½ HOURS

1. Preheat the oven to 375°F.

2. Complete Steps 6 and 7 for the Cream Scones, cover, and set aside.

75 MINS

1. Make the Polenta.

45 MINS

1. With a rack adjusted to the highest position, preheat the oven to 475°F.

2. While the oven preheats, complete Steps 2 through 7 for the Frittata (p. 150).

20 MINS

1. Drape slices of prosciutto over the melon and figs.

SERVE

1. If reheating the Scones, complete Step 8.

2. Complete the Frittata (Step 8) and the Scones (Step 9).

3. Serve the melon and fig platter, Frittata, Polenta, and Cream Scones as a buffet. Pass the crème fraîche, jam, and/or butter, if using.

GET A HEAD START!

Placed in a bowl of cold water, the sliced potatoes for the **Frittata** can be set aside for up to 4 hours or refrigerated for up to 12.

Refrigerate the **Kale Purée** in a covered container for up to 4 days.

The **Miniature Scones** can keep in a covered container for 24 hours at room temperature, 3 days in the fridge, and at least 3 months in the freezer.

Roast Potato and Feta Frittata with Scallions and Dill

Yield: 8 main-course servings

Many professional bakers leave their eggs out on the counter overnight to come to room temperature. You can too!

5 tablespoons unsalted butter

1 tablespoon neutral oil, such as canola

3 large baking potatoes, peeled and cut into ½-inch dice

⅔ cup minced shallots or red onion

10 large eggs, room temperature

⅓ cup heavy cream

6 tablespoons thinly sliced scallions (white and green parts)

4 tablespoons chopped fresh dill

3 tablespoons chopped fresh Italian parsley

Fine sea salt and freshly ground black pepper, to taste

5 ounces feta cheese, crumbled or cut into ¼-inch dice

45 MINS

1. With the rack adjusted to the highest position, preheat the oven to 475°F.

2. While the oven preheats, heat the butter and oil together in a 10-inch or 11-inch ovenproof nonstick (or well-seasoned) heavy metal skillet set over medium–high heat. Add the potatoes and cook, stirring frequently, for 10 minutes. Add the shallots and continue to cook, stirring frequently, for 5 minutes, or until the potatoes are tender and golden.

3. While the potatoes are cooking, whisk together the eggs, cream, scallions, and herbs in a large bowl. Season with the salt and pepper. Set aside.

4. When the potatoes are ready, remove the pan from the heat and scatter the feta evenly over the potatoes. Slowly pour the egg mixture on top of the feta.

5. Cover the pan and return to medium heat. Let the frittata cook without stirring for about 2 minutes, or until a crust begins to form underneath. Use a spatula to lift up an edge of the frittata and check.

6. Uncover the skillet and place in the oven for about 5 minutes, or until the eggs are just set while the center remains a bit creamy. If you prefer a firmer frittata, bake for 1 to 2 minutes longer.

7. Remove the skillet from the oven and slide the frittata onto a serving platter. If the frittata does not want to slide, loosen it with a spatula.

SERVE

8. Cut the frittata into 8 wedges and serve hot, warm, or at room temperature.

Creamy Green Polenta

Yield: 8 side-dish servings

7 cups water

4 teaspoons kosher salt

2 cups coarse stone-ground polenta, such as Anson Mills

¼ cup extra virgin olive oil

½ recipe Kale Purée (recipe follows), or more to taste

2 ounces Italian Parmesan cheese, finely grated, divided

5 tablespoons mascarpone cheese, divided

Fine sea salt and freshly ground black pepper, to taste

In a hurry? Use instant polenta instead of the stone ground. Start boiling the water for the polenta about 20 minutes before eating rather than 75. Follow the instructions on the package—or in the Mixed Pepper Polenta recipe (p. 112)—and then, pick up with Step 3.

75 MINS

1. In a large pot, bring the water and kosher salt to a boil over high heat.

2. Remove from the heat and gradually add the polenta, whisking as you pour. Return to the heat and cook, whisking continuously, for 2 minutes, or until the polenta starts to thicken and looks like it's one with the water. Reduce the heat to low. The polenta should steam and tremble but only rarely erupt with bubbles. Cook, stirring occasionally, for 45 minutes, or until the polenta is tender but still slightly coarse in texture.

3. Stir in the olive oil, the Kale Purée, and most of the Parmesan. Keep cooking, stirring occasionally, for 2 to 3 minutes. Remove from the heat and fold in 2 tablespoons of the mascarpone. (It's nice to run into little pockets of mascarpone, so don't stir too much.) Transfer to a serving bowl and top with the remaining 3 tablespoons of mascarpone and the remaining Parmesan. Taste and season with the sea salt and black pepper as needed.

SERVE

4. Serve right away.

Kale Purée

Yield: 1½–2 cups

This recipe makes up to twice as much Kale Purée as you need for the Creamy Green Polenta recipe. Use the rest as a sauce for pasta or freeze for future use. You can substitute ½–¾ cup of pesto or salsa verde for the Kale Purée.

5 cloves garlic, divided
Kosher salt, for boiling
1 pound Tuscan kale, thick stems removed

¾ teaspoon fine sea salt
½ cup extra virgin olive oil

1. Fill a large saucepan with water and add 4 cloves of the garlic. Cover and bring to a boil over high heat. Add enough of the kosher salt so that the water tastes slightly salty and then add the kale, prodding to submerge. Cook, uncovered, for 2 to 3 minutes, or until the kale is tender and tears easily.

2. Remove the boiled garlic and set aside. Drain the kale in a colander. When it's cool enough to handle, squeeze out as much water as you can. Roughly chop the kale.

3. Combine the chopped kale, cooked and raw garlic and the sea salt in the bowl of a food processor. Process for about 45 seconds, stopping occasionally to scrape down the sides of the bowl. With the motor running, add the oil through the feed tube in a steady stream.

4. Use right away or transfer to a covered container and refrigerate for up to 4 days.

Miniature Cream Scones with Crème Fraîche and Jam

Yield: 10–20 scones, depending on size

2 cups all-purpose flour
⅓ cup plus 2–3 tablespoons granulated sugar, divided
1 tablespoon baking powder
½ teaspoon fine sea salt

1⅓ cups toasted pecans, walnuts, or skinned hazelnuts, chopped
1 cup heavy cream, cold
2–3 tablespoons melted unsalted butter
Butter, crème fraîche, and/or jam, for serving

1. Line a cookie sheet with parchment paper and set aside. Use a second cookie sheet if needed.

2. Sift the flour, ⅓ cup of the sugar, the baking powder, and the salt together into a large bowl or into the bowl of a stand mixer fitted with the paddle attachment. Stir in the nuts.

3. Add the cream to the bowl. With the stand mixer or an electric handheld mixer set on low speed, mix the ingredients until just combined.

4. Squeeze the dough together on lightly floured work surface. Flatten and then pat into a 1¼-inch-thick square. Use a rolling pin if necessary. Using a sharp knife, cut into 20 equal squares. Alternatively, pat or roll the dough into a 1¼-inch-thick circle and cut into 8 to 10 equal wedges. Place the squares or wedges on the prepared cookie sheet(s), wrap, and refrigerate.

5. Preheat the oven to 375°F

6. Paint the scone tops with the melted butter and sprinkle with the remaining 2 to 3 tablespoons of sugar. Bake for 15 to 25 minutes (timing will depend on the size of the scones), or until they're cooked through and the tops are golden.

7. Transfer the scones to a wire rack to cool completely. Place in a covered container and set aside.

8. If desired, reheat the scones in a 350°F oven for 5 to 10 minutes, or until hot.

9. Place on a serving platter and serve warm or at room temperature with butter, crème fraîche, and/or jam.

Tip! To vary the flavor, replace the nuts with 1⅓ cups of chocolate chips, raisins, or chopped mixed dried fruits. To make candied-ginger scones, replace the nuts with 1⅓ cups of chopped candied ginger and add 1 teaspoon of powdered ginger to the dry ingredients.

Tip! You can make this recipe straight through, if necessary, but the scones will be more tender if refrigerated for at least 1 hour and up to 3 days before baking. If you want to make the scones the day you serve them, allow about 45 minutes to complete the entire recipe.

SOUP 'N' SANDWICH

LUNCH FOR SIX

DISH	BEGIN PREP	PAGE
FIRST COURSE		
Cold Yogurt Soup with Fresh Herbs, Cucumber, Cumin, Feta, and Pink Peppercorns	1 day ahead	46
ENTRÉE		
Pan-Fried Soft-Shell Crab Sandwiches with Bacon and Green Goddess Dressing	3 hours ahead	157
ON THE SIDE		
Gingered Cabbage and Tomato Slaw	1 day ahead	159
DESSERT		
Store-Bought or Homemade Cookies and/or Biscotti		

f you're a soft-shell crab fan, this is probably the best sandwich on the planet. And if you're not, substituting chicken or Turkey Paillards (p. 37) produces great results as well. For those not acquainted with Green Goddess Dressing (p. 158), you'd do well to familiarize yourself with it. The 1950s combination of avocados, garlic, anchovies, and lemon juice is a real find and a no-brainer to make. Originally served on iceberg lettuce, it remains utterly contemporary to this day when dolloped on chicken, fish, shellfish, salads, and of course—as in this menu—on sandwiches.

Riffing off a basic BLT, this Soft-Shell Crab Sandwich (p. 157) incorporates bacon, tomato, and sweet onion in addition to the crusty crab. For brunch, I highly recommend including the optional fried egg. The unwieldy result—you may end up using a knife and fork rather than your hands to eat it—is well worth every bit of the scrumptious mess. Be sure to have extra napkins on hand.

I've paired this sandwich with the Cold Yogurt Soup (p. 46) from the Summer Refresher menu, which is perfect for summer. For spring, try

GET A HEAD START!

Make the soups 2 or 3 days ahead and refrigerate.

Fry the bacon for the **Sandwiches** up to 3 days ahead, refrigerate, and re-crisp before using.

Make the **Green Goddess Dressing** up to 8 hours ahead and store as directed.

Make the **Slaw** up to 2 days ahead and refrigerate.

Green Pea Soup (p. 224), and for winter, I recommend Tomato–Cumin Soup (p. 74).

The Cabbage and Tomato Slaw (p. 159), featuring a tasty mayonnaise-based dressing and adapted from a dish Jeremiah Tower served me with hamburgers last 4th of July, creamily completes the plate. I can never get enough summer tomatoes, and in this menu, they play major roles in both the sandwich and the slaw. However, for taste and color, add julienned red or yellow bell peppers and shaved carrots to the slaw instead. Or adhere to my "too much is not enough" way of thinking and include everything.

A mix of cookies and biscotti—or one or the other—suffices for dessert. When in season, however, a big bowl of ripe cherries on ice is an irresistible addition. Or scatter cherries over a bowl of fresh peaches or nectarines. Better still, serve cookies, biscotti, *and* a bowl of gorgeous fruit.

ORDER OF PREPARATION

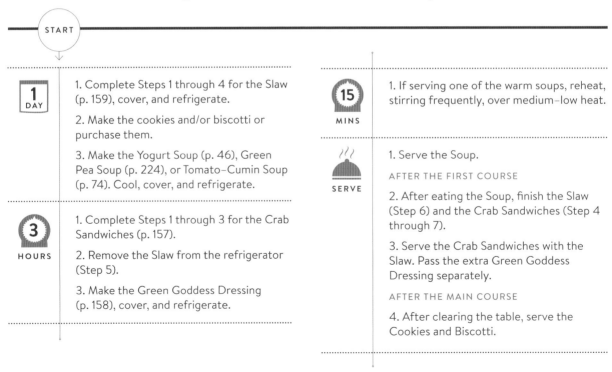

START

1 DAY

1. Complete Steps 1 through 4 for the Slaw (p. 159), cover, and refrigerate.

2. Make the cookies and/or biscotti or purchase them.

3. Make the Yogurt Soup (p. 46), Green Pea Soup (p. 224), or Tomato–Cumin Soup (p. 74). Cool, cover, and refrigerate.

3 HOURS

1. Complete Steps 1 through 3 for the Crab Sandwiches (p. 157).

2. Remove the Slaw from the refrigerator (Step 5).

3. Make the Green Goddess Dressing (p. 158), cover, and refrigerate.

15 MINS

1. If serving one of the warm soups, reheat, stirring frequently, over medium–low heat.

SERVE

1. Serve the Soup.

AFTER THE FIRST COURSE

2. After eating the Soup, finish the Slaw (Step 6) and the Crab Sandwiches (Step 4 through 7).

3. Serve the Crab Sandwiches with the Slaw. Pass the extra Green Goddess Dressing separately.

AFTER THE MAIN COURSE

4. After clearing the table, serve the Cookies and Biscotti.

Pan-Fried Soft-Shell Crab Sandwiches with Bacon and Green Goddess Dressing

Yield: 6 main-course servings

18 slices best-quality smoky bacon

1½ cups self-rising cake or all-purpose flour

1½ cups yellow cornmeal

⅜ teaspoon ground cayenne pepper

Fine sea salt and freshly ground black pepper, to taste

2¼ cups buttermilk or whole milk

5 large eggs, lightly beaten

6 large very fresh, soft-shell crabs, cleaned

Canola oil, for pan-frying

6 brioche buns, English muffins, onion rolls, or Ciabatta rolls, halved

6 fried eggs (optional)*

1 large Bermuda or Vidalia onion, very thinly sliced

2 large ripe tomatoes, very thinly sliced

1 bunch watercress, trimmed, washed, and well dried

1 recipe Green Goddess Dressing (recipe follows)

Soft-shell crabs are highly perishable. Buy them the day you plan to use them and store them on ice in the refrigerator until ready to use. Ideally they should still be alive when cleaned. Cleaning is not hard, but I suggest you let the fishmonger do it for you. I certainly do.

3 HOURS

1. Place the bacon in a large skillet set over medium heat, and cook for 3 to 5 minutes per side, or until crisp. Remove from the heat and transfer the bacon to a plate lined with paper towels. Discard all but a thin film of the bacon fat and set the skillet aside.

2. Stir together the flour, cornmeal, cayenne, salt, and pepper in a large, shallow bowl. In a medium bowl, whisk together the buttermilk and lightly beaten eggs. Set both bowls aside.

3. Dip 1 crab into the flour mixture, shaking off the excess. Dip the floured crab into the egg mixture and then dip it once more into the flour mixture. Place the battered crab on a sheet pan and repeat the process until all 6 crabs are battered. Refrigerate the crabs until needed.

SERVE

AFTER THE FIRST COURSE

4. Heat 1 inch of the oil in a very large saucepan or casserole over medium–high heat until a deep-fry thermometer registers 370°F. Adjust the heat while frying to keep the temperature as close to 370°F as possible.

CONTINUED

* If using fried eggs, cook them in the bacon fat before you toast the buns in Step 6.

Pan-Fried Soft-Shell Crab Sandwiches with Bacon and Green Goddess Dressing

CONTINUED

5. Fry the crabs for 3 to 5 minutes per side, or until golden brown. Transfer to a plate lined with paper towels and season with the salt and pepper as needed. You will probably need to fry the crabs in several batches.

6. Set the skillet of reserved bacon fat over medium–high heat. Once the fat is hot, place the buns, cut-side down, in the pan and toast for about 3 minutes, or until golden. You will probably have to do this in batches as well.

7. Transfer the buns to 6 plates. Top the bottom half of each bun with 1 of the fried eggs (if using), 3 slices of bacon, a scattering of onions, tomato slices, and 1 crab. Place a handful of watercress and a large spoonful of Green Goddess Dressing atop the crabs. Close the sandwiches and serve.

Green Goddess Dressing

Yield: 1½–2 cups

8 oil-packed anchovy fillets

2 large ripe Haas avocados

Freshly squeezed juice and freshly grated zest of 2 lemons

2 tablespoons extra virgin olive oil

4 teaspoons white wine vinegar

2 large cloves garlic

Fine sea salt and freshly ground black pepper, to taste

Few drops Tabasco sauce

3 HOURS

1. Place all the ingredients in a blender or the bowl of a food processor and purée until smooth. Taste and adjust the seasoning as needed.

2. Use right away or transfer to a covered container and refrigerate.

Tip!

When storing the Green Goddess Dressing, bury the avocado pits in the dressing—as with guacamole—to prevent discoloration. Then press a sheet of plastic wrap flat on the surface of the dressing to keep all air out. Refrigerate for up to 8 hours.

Gingered Cabbage and Tomato Slaw

Yield: 8 side-dish servings

¾–1 cup Hellman's or Basic Mayonnaise (p. 275)

¼ cup whole milk or buttermilk, plus more if needed

2 tablespoons rice vinegar or freshly squeezed lime juice

2–3 teaspoons powdered ginger, or to taste

3 large cloves garlic, minced

1 large head green cabbage, cored and cut into 2-inch dice

Fine sea salt and freshly ground black pepper, to taste

5 small ripe tomatoes halved and cut into ¼-inch wedges or 2 baskets cherry tomatoes, halved

1. To make the dressing, whisk together the mayonnaise, milk, vinegar, ginger, and garlic in a small bowl until well combined. Set aside.

2. Place the cabbage in a large bowl, add the dressing, and toss to combine. Taste and adjust the salt and pepper as needed.

3. Gently stir in the tomatoes.

4. Cover and refrigerate for at least 8 hours to allow the flavors to marry.

5. Remove from the refrigerator.

6. Taste and adjust the seasoning as needed before serving. Serve cool or at room temperature (not cold).

DINNER
FOR 8

DINNER FOR 8

MENUS

Candlelight Soirée
p. 166

Shanghai Nights: East Meets West
p. 178

Genteel Grilling
p. 190

Autumn Flavors
p. 200

Whether as guest or host, I take real pleasure in an elegant, seated dinner. For me, settling in for the duration with table companions is infinitely more gratifying than flitting from one (often trivial) conversation to the next at cocktail events where the people with whom I'm speaking are usually looking over my shoulder for greener pastures. Sit-down dinners are win-win. At home, there's the satisfaction of introducing friends to one another and the cozy security of familiar faces, while a meal hosted by another is a great opportunity to meet new people. A close friend aptly reflected: "A dinner party allows me to flirt with impunity, knowing I'll leave with my husband at the end of the evening."

A couple of mandatory hours at the table can jolly even the dullest dinner partner into an interesting interchange, something hardly possible when alternating between standing, flitting, and grabbing at passed hors d'oeuvres. And what an unexpected thrill when that initially unpromising tablemate tells you that she's Princess Anastasia come back from the dead or lets on that he's just won a Pulitzer.

My fascination with formal dinners—at least sufficiently formal that no one arrives in jeans or barefoot—once more goes back to early childhood. In the late '50s, we'd just moved from a Santa Monica starter apartment to a house in Beverly Hills, and my mother felt free to entertain in earnest. Our new residence, a labor of love owing at least as much to my mother's dogged creativity as to the architect himself, was state-of-the art modern with each room flowing seamlessly into the next. The dining room was differentiated from the living room only by a delicate, Japanese-inspired floor-to-ceiling bamboo curtain that was pulled shut only to hide the settings and clearings of the table.

The walls of the house were primarily glass doors opening onto multiple courtyards brimming with semitropical plantings. Before dinner guests wandered, drinks in hand, in and out of my fairyland: birds of paradise; banana, ginkgo, and coral trees; papyrus; a small citrus grove; roses; lantana; and tiny-leaved dichondra pillowing between paving stones.

Stirred cocktails, shaken martinis, and Camels arranged in small ebony cigarette canisters were *de rigueur* when my parents entertained and intriguingly unfamiliar "forbidden fruit" to a small child. Equally foreign were uniformed waiters offering silver trays of cocktails and hors d'oeuvres to formally clad guests.

These guests, like everyone else back then, were still carnivorous, and, though I hate to admit it, menu planning was much simpler. Mom's excellent beef—well-marbled steaks or a succulent prime rib accompanied by Béarnaise sauce—was a guiltless pleasure served at virtually every soirée. The only exceptions I remember were an occasional leg of lamb, the Thanksgiving turkey, and a very 1950s shrimp–Velveeta chafing dish concoction gleaned from *Sunset* magazine.

I also have Technicolor memories of Mom's killer desserts, especially her lemon chiffon pie, baked Alaska, and rum-heavy, intricately layered trifle pudding, ceremoniously presented in a magnificent cut-crystal bowl. However, other than a good-enough Caesar salad, corn succotash, and Idaho potatoes baked in foil and doused with sour cream and chives, there were almost no side dishes.

I, on the other hand, out of necessity, now double (or even triple) up on side dishes. I used to inquire ahead about guests' food preferences

Cocktail nibbles such as Truffled Almonds (p. 291), Curry Coins (p. 290), Gourmet Trail Mix (p. 289), Parmesan–Rosemary Coins (p. 289), and Marinated Olives (p. 292) are always appreciated with drinks—alcoholic or otherwise—and are especially convenient if already stockpiled in the pantry, fridge, or freezer.

and was met with requests for dairy-free, gluten-free, nut-free, low-carb, low-fat, vegan, and vegetarian menus. It became too complicated. I decided to stop asking, and I now offer a larger selection from which guests can pick and choose. And I keep my fingers crossed that things will work out. So far, they always have.

While I do have sympathy for the allergies and medical conditions out there, as well as for the vagaries of the individual palate, I sometimes miss the "olden days" when hosts just served what they felt like serving, and guests "politely" kept their mouths shut and simply pushed the food around on the plate if they chose not to eat it. You could opt for a snack or even a second meal after the event. Or like Scarlett O'Hara, you could eat dinner before you ever left home.

Speaking of snacking, I only serve small savory tidbits before dinner. Even a tiny nibble can cut hunger and counteract the effects of a cocktail without spoiling the appetite for the meal to come. Why self-sabotage with a platter of cheeses and salamis—a dinner in itself—before serving a meal you've spent hours, or even days, creating? I do love passed hot hors d'oeuvres, but they're labor intensive, and I prefer to relegate my kitchen hours to the main event.

When hosting a meal composed of a series of courses, I cannot repeat myself often enough: *plan ahead.* Get organized and do as much as you possibly can before guests arrive. I've said it before and I'll say it again: Getting a handle on culinary timing is absolutely key if you're planning to enjoy your own party.

Also, if you can swing it, hire help. A person or two in the wings serving, pouring drinks, and tidying up allows you to focus on your guests, who in turn are more relaxed when they don't feel on call to assist. If you can't get a professional waiter, is there a housekeeper, babysitter, or responsible teenager—your own or one from the neighborhood—for hire? There are no hard and fast rules, but when hosting a seated dinner for more than eight people, I suggest enlisting help. And if you don't, discouraging general guest assistance is still a priority. I like to designate a single helper (a close friend, partner, or spouse is useful here).

Assemble green salads in advance, but don't dress until time to serve.

Otherwise, everyone is hopping up to help, the kitchen is overrun, and the table left with the odd person or two at loose ends and feeling unnecessarily guilty for not having hopped up as well. Possibly the most convincing reason for hiring help is to put your guests at ease.

CANDLELIGHT SOIRÉE

DINNER FOR EIGHT

DISH	BEGIN PREP	PAGE
FIRST COURSE		
Wilted Spinach Salad with Dates and Crispy Bacon	1 day ahead	171
ENTRÉE		
Pan-Seared Duck Magrets with Raspberry–Port Sauce	3 days ahead	172
ON THE SIDE		
Mixed Cheese, Garlic, and Fresh Herb Soufflé	3 days ahead	174
Mushy Peas	3 hours ahead	176
DESSERT		
Fané	3 days ahead	177

In southwest France, oversized duck breasts, or *magrets de canard*, are a common main course. Sadly, they are still underutilized and underappreciated in the United States. However, if you like steak, you'll love these "duck steaks," which are similar in taste and texture. Almost all of their fat is right under the skin, and as it melts away during cooking, the magrets have the added bonus of scrumptious, enticingly crisp, golden skin. And if that doesn't rope you in, the meat—with its compelling flavor that is deeper and more complex than that of beef, pork, or lamb—will. Like venison or buffalo, these Pan-Seared Duck Magrets (p. 172) are much better for you than grocery-store beef. But be careful: The magrets are juicy and beautifully pink when properly cooked, but past medium rare, they lose all appeal. So please don't overcook.

The succulent duck breasts do not need enhancing, but if you choose to gild the lily, virtually any savory fruit sauce complements the rich meat. This one, a raspberry elixir heightened with port, Armagnac, and aromatics, is ideal with all manner of duck, chicken, goose, pork, and game. Replace the raspberries with cherries or another stone fruit for a change of pace, and off-season, use frozen berries or try figs, pears, or

apples. During the holidays, quince or brandy-soaked dried fruit works perfectly as well.

The duck is accompanied by two equally commendable sides. The Mixed Cheese Soufflé (p. 174), though scrumptiously cheesy, incorporates enough airily whipped egg whites to make it a light and ethereal accompaniment to the richly sauced duck. When baked and served in individual ramekins, the little soufflés have been my most popular dinner-party starter for years. And, with nothing but bread and a green salad alongside, they make a great main course for a ladies' lunch. For this menu though, I bake the single soufflé in a large, shallow oval baking dish instead of a classic soufflé mold, as it cooks more quickly and rises higher.

Britain's beloved Mushy Peas (p. 176), a scrumptiously versatile, spring-green veggie preparation, completes the main course. When I first tasted it at London's J. Sheekey in the 1990s, I couldn't imagine how the sum could be so much better than the simple parts—frozen peas, cream, onion, fresh mint, and butter—but it was. Instantly addicted, I've made the dish regularly ever since. Even better, my then-small children were hooked. In contrast to the myriad vegetables they wouldn't touch, on the increasingly frequent nights I served mushy peas, they'd clean their plates and ask for seconds.

My Wilted Spinach Salad (p. 171) is a warm starter for cool weather. With the addition of bacon, feta, and dates, the old comfort food classic is once again new—and extra tasty to boot. To customize the menu for hot weather, consider replacing the wilted spinach with the Arugula Salad with Green Apples (p. 143) or Cold Yogurt Soup (p. 46).

I first tasted *Fané* (p. 177), this menu's delectable frozen finale, over the Christmas holidays in 2001 while staying with French friends, the Comte and Comtesse de Vogue, at their legendary chateau, Vaux-le-Vicomte. The kitchen produced one luxe dish after another, an opulent succession of caviar followed by smoked salmon, followed by white truffles, followed by foie gras, followed again by caviar . . . and the wine pairings were perfectly chosen for each dish. But my most distinct memories are of the remarkable desserts, and the most remarkable of these was *Fané*, a riotous combination of ice cream, whipped cream, meringue chunks, and white nougat topped with two sweet sauces and chocolate shavings.

Virtually the whole dish can be prepared in advance—much of it weeks in advance. All that's required last minute is to warm a sauce or two, unmold the dessert, plaster it with meringue chunks, slice, and serve.

I've now been making *Fané* for almost 15 years; many of my friends and students claim it's their favorite dessert ever. And it just may be mine as well. With a *Fané* finale, even the humblest repast becomes legendary. Distinctly festive, it's tailor-made for birthdays, anniversaries, and major dinner parties as well as for Christmas and New Year's Eve.

ORDER OF PREPARATION

3 DAYS

1. Complete Steps 1 through 3 for the Cheese Soufflé (p. 174). Cool, cover, and refrigerate.

2. Complete Step 1 for the Magrets (p. 172). Cool, cover, and refrigerate.

3. Complete Steps 1 and 2 for the *Fané* (p. 177), cover, and freeze.

4. Make the Meringue Shell (p. 294) for the *Fané*. Cool, wrap, and store at room temperature.

1 DAY

1. Complete Steps 1 through 3 for the Spinach Salad (p. 171). Cool, cover, and refrigerate in the skillet.

2. Complete Step 2 for the Magrets and refrigerate.

3. If using, make the Bitter Chocolate Sauce (p. 302) and/or Caramel Sauce (p. 303) for the *Fané* and store at room temperature.

3 HOURS

1. Complete Steps 1 through 3 for the Mushy Peas (p. 176). Cool, cover, and set aside.

2 HOURS

1. Remove the dressing for the Spinach Salad from the refrigerator (Step 4).

2. Remove the magrets and raspberry–port reduction from the refrigerator (Step 3).

3. Complete Steps 3 and 4 for the *Fané* and freeze.

45 MINS

1. Preheat the oven to 400°F.

2. Complete Steps 4 through 8 for the Soufflé.

15 MINS

1. Complete Steps 4 through 8 for the Magrets and set aside.

2. Complete Step 5 for the Spinach Salad and set aside.

SERVE

1. Before serving the Spinach Salad, complete Step 9 for the Soufflé.

2. Complete the Spinach Salad (Steps 6 and 7) and serve.

AFTER THE FIRST COURSE

3. After eating the Spinach Salad, complete the Mushy Peas (Step 4) and Magrets (Steps 9 and 10).

4. The Soufflé should be nearly done, but if not, remember that soufflés are well worth waiting for and they do not wait for you.

5. When the Soufflé is done, serve it—immediately so it doesn't fall—along with the Magrets and Mushy Peas.

AFTER THE MAIN COURSE

6. Complete the *Fané* (Steps 5 through 9) and serve.

GET A HEAD START!

Duck Magrets can be browned or even cooked ¾ through a few hours ahead of serving and finished off last minute.

The **Cheese Soufflé** base can be made ahead, covered with plastic wrap touching its surface, and refrigerated for up to 3 days. Warm to tepid over very low heat before continuing with the recipe.

The Meringue Shell for the *Fané* can be made, cooled, wrapped in foil, and stored at room temperature for at least 4 months. The **Sauces** can be made up to 4 months ahead and refrigerated.

Wilted Spinach Salad with Dates and Crispy Bacon

Yield: 8 to 10 side-dish servings

12 pieces thick-sliced bacon

3 tablespoons balsamic vinegar, plus more to taste

1½ tablespoons grainy mustard

2 tablespoons honey

Dash Tabasco sauce

Fine sea salt and freshly ground black pepper, to taste

1 pound fresh baby spinach, washed, dried, and room temperature

18 best-quality dates, pitted and quartered

2 large red onions, sliced into paper-thin rings

1 bulb fennel, sliced paper thin

½ cup crumbled Bulgarian feta, ricotta salata, or crumbly goat cheese

2 tablespoons extra virgin olive oil, plus more as needed

1. Fry the bacon on both sides in a large skillet over medium–high heat, until very crisp, periodically pouring off and reserving the grease.

2. Remove from the heat and transfer the bacon to a plate lined with paper towels and blot. Return 9 tablespoons of the bacon grease to the skillet and discard the rest. Crumble the cooled bacon, cover, and refrigerate.

3. Warm the reserved bacon grease over medium heat. Add the vinegar, mustard, honey, Tabasco, salt, and pepper. Heat to a simmer, scraping up the accumulated bits. Remove from the heat, cool, cover the skillet, and refrigerate.

4. Remove the dressing skillet from the refrigerator.

5. Recrisp the crumbled bacon in a small pan set over low heat. Place the crumbled bacon, spinach, dates, onions, fennel, and feta in a large salad bowl. Set aside.

6. Place the skillet of dressing over medium–low heat, whisking frequently, until hot. Whisk in the olive oil. Taste and adjust the salt, pepper, vinegar, and olive oil as needed.

7. Add enough of the hot dressing to the salad to moisten, wilt, and flavor. Adjust seasoning as needed. Serve right away.

Pan-Seared Duck Magrets with Raspberry–Port Sauce

Yield: 8 main-course servings

Are you confused when a recipe called for a "whole chicken breast"? A whole duck magret (or duck breast) causes the same confusion. The breast is actually the underside of a chicken or duck when the animal is walking around. Each bird has two breasts. When a recipe calls for a chicken or duck breast, it generally means half the breast. When a recipe calls for a whole breast, it means both halves.

1 (10-ounce) bag frozen raspberries
½ cup ruby port
3 tablespoons cognac, brandy, or Armagnac
1 tablespoon balsamic vinegar, plus more to taste
1 large carrot, peeled and coarsely chopped
1 large stalk celery, trimmed and coarsely chopped
1 small onion, coarsely chopped

½ teaspoon dried thyme
1 large clove garlic, chopped
Fine sea salt and freshly ground black pepper, to taste
Tabasco sauce, to taste
2 (2-pound) whole duck magrets, halved (about 4 pounds total)
½–1 cup very strong duck or chicken stock
2 cups fresh raspberries
¼ cup chopped fresh Italian parsley or minced fresh chives, for garnish

1. To make the raspberry–port sauce, combine the first 11 ingredients in a medium saucepan over low heat and simmer for 10 to 25 minutes, or until the mixture is reduced by ½. Remove from the heat, cool to lukewarm, strain into a container, pressing the solids with a spoon to extract all possible flavor, cover, and refrigerate.

You can make the reduction (Step 1) ahead and freeze for at least 6 months. Thaw before using. This same sauce can be used with pan-sautéed pork chops. If using pork, use pork or chicken stock instead of duck stock.

2. Rinse the magrets in cool water and pat dry. With a sharp knife, score the skin in a diagonal 3/16-inch grid. Cut through most of the fat, but don't cut into the meat. Cover and refrigerate.

3. Remove the magrets and reserved raspberry–port sauce from the refrigerator.

4. Place a large, heavy skillet over high heat until very hot

5. Place the magrets in the skillet, skin side down, and cook for 6 to 10 minutes, or until the skin is dark brown and crispy. If necessary, reduce the heat so the skin doesn't burn. Lots of duck fat will melt into the pan. Periodically pour it off into a heatproof container and discard when cool.

6. Reduce the heat to medium–low and cook the magrets on the other side for about 3 to 5 minutes, or until done. When cut, the meat should look like rare steak.

7. Transfer the magrets to a serving platter, cover loosely with aluminum foil, and let rest for at least 8 minutes before slicing.

8. While the magrets rest, set the skillet back over medium heat and deglaze with the stock. Add the reduction and reduce, stirring occasionally, until the sauce has the consistency of heavy cream. Taste and adjust the salt, pepper, and Tabasco as needed. Remove from the heat and set aside.

SERVE

AFTER THE FIRST COURSE

9. Reheat the raspberry–port sauce over low heat. When hot, remove from the heat and stir in ¾ of the fresh raspberries. Taste and adjust the seasoning as needed.

10. While sauce is reheating, slice the duck and arrange on a warm (if possible) platter. Pour the heated sauce over the sliced duck and sprinkle with the remaining raspberries. Garnish with the parsley or chives and serve.

Mixed Cheese, Garlic, and Fresh Herb Soufflé

Yield: 8 side-dish servings

This recipe can also make 8 individual soufflés. If making individual soufflés, follow the same recipe but divide the batter among 8 (12-ounce) buttered and Parmesan-dusted molds or ramekins, and bake for only about 20 minutes.

6 tablespoons unsalted butter

3 cloves garlic, minced

6 tablespoons all-purpose flour

2 cups whole milk, simmering

1⅛ teaspoons fine sea salt, or more to taste, divided

¼ teaspoon freshly ground black pepper, plus more to taste

⅛ teaspoon ground cayenne pepper, plus more to taste

⅛ teaspoon freshly grated nutmeg, plus more to taste

6 large egg yolks

Softened butter and grated Italian Parmesan cheese, to prepare the mold

10 large egg whites, room temperature

1 teaspoon cream of tartar

¼ cup finely minced fresh chives

¼ cup minced fresh Italian parsley

6 tablespoons coarsely grated Gruyère and/or Italian Parmesan cheese

3 DAYS

1. To make the soufflé base, melt the butter with the garlic in a large saucepan set over medium heat. Cook, stirring constantly, for 1 minute. Whisk in the flour and cook over medium heat, stirring with a wooden spoon, until the butter and flour foam together for 2 minutes without browning.

2. Remove from the heat and pour in the simmering milk, beating vigorously with a wire whisk, until well blended. Add the 1 teaspoon of salt, the pepper, the cayenne, and the nutmeg and return to medium heat. Boil gently, stirring constantly, for 1 minute. The sauce should be very thick.

Separate your eggs cold! Even if you need room temperature whites or yolks, separate them cold. When warmer, the yolks are much more likely to break and ruin the whites.

3. Whisk in the yolks, 1 at a time. Run a rubber spatula around the corners of the pan and then whisk again to make sure everything is homogenous. Taste and adjust the seasoning as needed. The seasoning should be strong, as flavors will be diluted when the whites are added in Step 6. Cover with plastic wrap, touching the surface of the hot soufflé base to prevent a skin from forming, cool, then refrigerate.

45 MINS

4. Preheat the oven to 400°F. Generously butter an approximately 9-inch × 13-inches oval ceramic baking dish and dust with the grated Parmesan. Place on a large sheet pan and set aside.

5. Warm the soufflé base to tepid over very low heat, stirring constantly. Transfer the warmed base to a very large bowl.

6. Using a stand mixer fitted with the whisk attachment or an electric handheld set on low speed, beat the room-temperature egg whites with the remaining ⅛ teaspoon of salt for 1 minute, or until frothy. Add the cream of tartar and increase the speed to medium–low. Mix—continuing to slowly increase the mixer speed to medium and then medium–high—until the egg whites hold soft peaks but are not yet stiff.

7. Stir ⅓ of the whipped whites into the warmed soufflé base along with the fresh herbs. Then, using a large rubber spatula, slowly and very gently fold the lightened base and all but 3 tablespoons of the grated cheese into the remaining whites until no streaks of white are showing. Do not overfold.

8. Gently scrape the mixture into the prepared dish, smoothing the top just a bit with the spatula. Sprinkle the remaining 3 table-spoons of cheese over all.

SERVE

9. Place the soufflé and sheet pan in the oven. Immediately lower the heat to 375°F and bake for 30 to 45 minutes, or until just set.

AFTER THE FIRST COURSE

10. When the soufflé is ready, serve immediately. Remember, your main course will wait for the soufflé, not the other way around!

Tip!

Contrary to traditional thinking, the soufflé base can be folded together with the beaten whites, poured into the mold(s), covered with a large inverted bowl or pot, and set aside for up to 1 hour before baking.

Tip!

When folding whipped eggs whites into something else—a soufflé base, a cake batter, a mousse—take your time and be very gentle. Fold, do not stir or mix. The point is to be so gentle that you do not deflate the air bubbles you've spent so much time incorporating into the egg whites by whipping. Those air bubbles are exactly the thing that will make your soufflé rise.

Mushy Peas

Yield: 8 side-dish servings

4 tablespoons extra virgin olive oil

1½ cups finely chopped onion

2 (14–16 ounce) bags frozen green peas, thawed

½ cup heavy cream, plus more for thinning if needed

4 tablespoons unsalted butter

2–3 tablespoons chopped fresh mint

½ teaspoon sea salt, or to taste

¼ teaspoon freshly ground black pepper, or to taste

3 HOURS

1. Warm the oil in a large saucepan set over medium–high heat. Add the onions and cook, stirring occasionally, for about 5 minutes, or until softened and beginning to color. Add the thawed peas and cream and cook for 5 more minutes, or until piping hot. Remove from the heat.

2. Place ½ of the pea mixture, the butter, and the mint in a food processor or blender and pulse a few times.

3. Add the processed pea mixture back to the saucepan, season with the salt and pepper, and stir. If you like your mushy peas a bit runny, add a bit more heavy cream. Remove from the heat, cool, cover, and set aside.

SERVE

AFTER THE FIRST COURSE

4. Uncover the mushy peas and warm, stirring frequently, over low heat. If the pea mixture is still too thick, once hot, add a bit more cream, taste, and adjust the salt and pepper and cream as needed. Serve right away.

Fané

Yield: 10–12 servings

3 pints best-quality vanilla ice cream, somewhat softened

6 cups of heavy cream, very cold

6 tablespoons of granulated sugar

½ teaspoon best-quality pure vanilla extract

16 ounces best-quality white nougat, cut into ¼-inch chunks or 1¼ cup coarsely chopped Nut Praline (p. 302)

1 Meringue Shell (p. 294) broken into irregular, 1-inch chunks

2–3 ounces semisweet chocolate, coarsely chopped

Bitter Chocolate (p. 302) and/or Caramel Sauce (p. 303), for serving (both optional)

If you don't have the time or energy to make meringue, substitute store-bought meringue cookies or meringue shells purchased from a local bakery and broken into pieces.

3 DAYS

1. Place a 4-quart metal bowl in the freezer for at least 20 minutes to chill.

2. Using a large rubber spatula, evenly line the sides of the bowl with the softened ice cream, cover the bowl with foil, and freeze for at least 4 hours.

2 HOURS

3. Using a stand mixer fitted with the whisk attachment or an electric handheld mixer set on medium–high speed, beat the cream. When the cream begins to thicken, add the sugar and vanilla and continue to beat until soft peaks form. Reserve 3 cups of the whipped cream, cover, and refrigerate. Fold the remaining whipped cream together with the nougat.

4. Remove the ice cream-lined bowl from the freezer and fill it with the nougat–whipped cream mixture. Cover the bowl and return to the freezer.

This recipe works well with almost any flavor of ice cream. Raspberry, strawberry, caramel, chocolate, and coffee are my faves when not using vanilla.

SERVE

AFTER THE MAIN COURSE

5. If using, warm the Bitter Chocolate and/or Caramel Sauce(s) in a microwave or in a saucepan set over very low heat.

6. Remove the bowl from the freezer and set it in a basin or larger bowl of very hot water. After 15 seconds, invert the bowl and unmold the ice cream onto a large round platter.

7. Spread the reserved whipped cream over the ice cream and push the meringue chunks into the whipped cream.

8. Sprinkle the chopped semisweet chocolate over all.

9. Present at the table and cut into wedges with a large, heavy knife. Serve with the Bitter Chocolate and/or Caramel Sauce(s), if using.

If too hard to cut easily, wait 5 and 10 minutes and try again and/or dip the knife in hot water before cutting each slice. *Fané* tastes best somewhat softened so your patience will be rewarded.

SHANGHAI NIGHTS: EAST MEETS WEST

DINNER FOR EIGHT

DISH	BEGIN PREP	PAGE
FIRST COURSE		
Shrimp and Lemongrass Bisque with a Confetti of Stir-Fried Vegetables	1 day ahead	182
ENTRÉE		
Shanghai Beef Short Ribs	2 days ahead	184
ON THE SIDE		
Wasabi Rémoulade with Cucumber and Radish (optional)	1 day ahead	185
Sweet 'n' Spicy Cabbage Salad	2 days ahead	187
Steamed or Boiled White or Brown Rice	1 hour ahead	
DESSERT		
Ginger-Caramelized Pears with Vanilla Crème Fraîche	5 hours ahead	188

This East meets West fantasy is an updated version a menu I've been teaching for years. My attempts to retire it and move on continue to be met with someone begging me to teach it "just one more time." The best I've been able to do is tweak it a bit.

I have, however, held onto the original starter, a Shrimp and Lemongrass Bisque (p. 182) that is a fusion-lover's dream come true and too perfect to mess with. Pale coral in color and strewn with a rainbow of stir-fried vegetables, the soup—a simplified take on a recipe picked up years ago when my daughter Kate and I took a full-day cooking class at Raymond Blanc's Belmond Le Manoir aux Quat'Saisons in Oxfordshire—tastes as exquisite as it looks. The lemongrass, ginger, garlic, and coconut milk exemplify the Michelin-starred chef's creative vision of gastronomy while evoking gutsy Asian street food. The classic shellfish bisque preparation showcases Blanc's flawless French cooking techniques. This recipe holds a prime position in my recipe Hall of Fame. I think you'll love it.

The bisque is a hard act to follow, but the Short Ribs (p. 184) do the trick nicely. For a change of pace and because they're even more succulent, I've recently been substituting beef short ribs for the original menu's pork baby back ribs. The meat stands up exceedingly well on its own, but to enhance it still further, consider serving a pungent Wasabi Rémoulade (p. 185) adapted from Chef Daniel Boulud.

And speaking of great chefs, if you aren't familiar with Yotam Ottolenghi, you're missing out. An Israeli-born food writer, master chef, and restaurant owner now based in London, he's penned the *Guardian*'s weekly food column for almost two decades and more recently has written five groundbreaking, award-winning cookbooks. Thus I've replaced a humdrum sesame noodle preparation with an Ottolenghi-inspired Sweet 'n' Spicy Cabbage Salad (p. 187). Its colorful cacophony of mixed cabbages, mango, cashews, mint, chilies, cilantro, sesame, and soy sauce results in a seductive combination of flavors that will wow any crowd.

And for dessert, a platter of Ginger-Caramelized Pears (p. 188) lives up to the meal that precedes it. The recipe comes from my close friend and favorite photographer, Eric Boman, who is almost as good at creating recipes as he is at taking pictures. To complement this Asian menu, the addition of fresh ginger is mine, but Eric's original version, using a vanilla bean instead, pairs perfectly with more traditional Western menus. The recipe is super easy; you don't even peel the pears! Just halve them, scoop out the seeds, and let the fruit simmer along, making its own caramel while you prepare the rest of the meal. You can even finish the entire dish up to a day ahead and leave it out to reheat—or not—when ready to serve.

ORDER OF PREPARATION

START

2 DAYS

1. Make the Sweet 'n' Spicy Dressing for the Cabbage Salad (p. 187), cover, and refrigerate.

2. Complete Step 1 for the Short Ribs (p. 184), cover, and refrigerate.

1 DAY

1. Complete Steps 2 through 4 for the Short Ribs. Cool, cover, and refrigerate.

2. Complete Steps 1 through 3 for the Shrimp Bisque (p. 182). Cool, cover, and refrigerate.

3. If using, make the Wasabi Rémoulade (p. 185), cover, and refrigerate.

5 HOURS

1. Complete Steps 1 through 8 for the Ginger-Caramelized Pears (p. 188) and set aside.

2. Prepare the vanilla crème fraîche for the Ginger-Caramelized Pears, cover, and refrigerate.

3 HOURS

1. Remove the Sweet 'n' Spicy Dressing from the refrigerator.

2. Remove the Short Ribs and glaze (Step 5), Shrimp Bisque (Step 4), and Wasabi Rémoulade from the refrigerator.

1 HOUR

1. Complete Step 1 for the Cabbage Salad, cover, and set aside.

2. Cook rice according to package instructions and set aside.

15 MINS

1. Preheat the broiler and complete Step 7 for the Short Ribs.

2. Make the Stir-Fried Vegetables (p. 183) for the Bisque.

3. Complete Step 5 for the Shrimp Bisque.

SERVE

1. Complete the Shrimp Bisque (Step 6) and serve topped with the Stir-Fried Vegetables.

AFTER THE FIRST COURSE

2. After finishing the Shrimp Bisque, complete the Short Ribs (Steps 8 and 9), and complete the Cabbage Salad (Step 2).

3. Serve the Short Ribs dolloped with the Wasabi Rémoulade, if using, and the Cabbage Salad and rice.

AFTER THE MAIN COURSE

4. After clearing the table, complete the Ginger-Caramelized Pears (Step 9) and serve with the vanilla crème fraîche.

GET A HEAD START!

Slice, wrap, and refrigerate the vegetables for the **Shrimp Bisque** stir-fry up to 24 hours in advance. The bisque itself can be made ahead and refrigerated for up to 48 hours or frozen for at least 6 months.

The glaze for the **Beef Short Ribs** can be made ahead and refrigerated for up to 2 months or frozen for up to 1 year. The ribs themselves can be cooked through Step 4 up to 4 days in advance. Cool, cover, and refrigerate. Remove the fat that has risen to the top and hardened before continuing with the recipe.

The dressing for the **Cabbage Salad** can be made and refrigerated for several months.

Caramelize the pan for the **Ginger-Caramelized Pears** up to 2 days ahead.

Shrimp and Lemongrass Bisque with a Confetti of Stir-Fried Vegetables

Yield: 8 first-course servings

2 pounds medium shrimp, shells removed and reserved*
2 tablespoons unsalted butter
2 tablespoons neutral oil, such as canola
½ cup Asian dried shrimp
½ cup chopped lemongrass
½ cup thinly sliced or roughly chopped unpeeled ginger
½ cup roughly chopped garlic

4 tablespoons tomato paste
3 tomatoes, chopped
3 cups water
3 cups coconut milk
Fine sea salt and freshly ground black pepper, to taste
Stir-Fried Vegetables (recipe follows), for serving

Tip!

Fresh lemongrass can be hard to cut. Pounding it first with a kitchen mallet helps, and I then find it easier to cut with a scissors than with a knife.

COOKING WITH ASIAN DRIED SHRIMP

Asian dried shrimp are highly flavorful. For a shrimp stock facsimile, simmer a couple of tablespoons of the tiny shrimp in a pot of fish stock or light chicken stock and then strain out. Asian dried shrimp are a genius way to infuse something with shrimpiness. Simmer them in seafood soups, stews, and sauces for extra flavor. Just keep in mind, the shrimp are salty so adjust the amount of added salt in your recipe accordingly.

1 DAY

1. Use scissors to cut the shrimp shells in halves or thirds. In a large saucepan, stockpot, or casserole, cook the shells over medium heat with the butter, oil, and dried shrimp for 10 to 15 minutes, or until golden. Add the lemongrass, ginger, and garlic and cook for another 2 minutes.

2. Add the tomato paste and tomatoes. Cook for 1 minute then add the water and the coconut milk. Simmer, partially covered and stirring occasionally, for 25 minutes. Remove from the heat.

3. Blend the mixture directly in the saucepan with an immersion blender for 1 to 2 minutes. Pass the mixture through a sieve into another large saucepan. Press to extract as much liquid as possible. Cool, cover, and refrigerate.

3 HOURS

4. Remove the bisque from the refrigerator.

15 MINS

5. Bring the bisque to a simmer over medium heat. Cut the raw shrimp in half and add to the bisque. Remove from the heat, cover, and set aside for 2 to 5 minutes, or until the shrimp are cooked through. Taste and adjust the salt and pepper as needed.

SERVE

6. Serve in warmed (if possible) soup bowls, topped with the Stir-Fried Vegetables.

Have your fishmonger shell the shrimp (or do it yourself) and save the shells. If the fishmonger has extra shells, ask him for them and use them too. Shrimp shells can be frozen for up to 3 months if you want to collect them for future use.

Stir-Fried Vegetables

Yield: 8 generous garnish servings or 4 generous side dish servings

2 tablespoons neutral vegetable oil, such as canola

1 tablespoon toasted sesame oil, or more to taste

2 large cloves garlic, finely chopped

1 tablespoon finely chopped peeled fresh ginger

1 mild fresh red chili, seeded, deveined, and finely minced

1 small red bell pepper, very thinly sliced

1 carrot, peeled and thinly sliced

½ cup sugar snap peas or snow peas, strings removed and cut in half lengthwise

1 small zucchini, very thinly sliced

1 head bok choy, thinly sliced

6 large shiitake mushrooms, stems removed, very thinly sliced

½ cup bean sprouts

2 tablespoons best-quality soy sauce, or more to taste

2 whole scallions (white and green parts), very thinly sliced

1 bunch fresh cilantro, roughly chopped

Freshly squeezed lime juice, to taste (optional)

Speed is important in stir-frying these vegetables, so be sure to cut them very thin and cook over very high heat.

15 MINS

1. Warm the vegetable and sesame oils in a wok or a large, heavy skillet over very high heat.

2. When very hot—just before smoking—add the garlic, ginger, and chili. Stir and then add all the vegetables, mushrooms, and bean sprouts.

3. Stir-fry for 1 minute. Then add the soy sauce. Cover and cook 2 minutes more. Stir in the scallions and cilantro. Taste and adjust the seasoning (with the lime juice, soy sauce, and/or toasted sesame oil) as needed.

Shanghai Beef Short Ribs

Yield: 8 main-course servings

For the Glaze

1 cup hoisin sauce

½ cup soy sauce

½ cup honey

4 tablespoons Champagne vinegar

2 dried Thai chilies

2 cloves garlic, minced

1 teaspoon freshly grated orange zest

¼ teaspoon five-spice powder

For the Ribs

6 tablespoons safflower oil

10 bone-in meaty beef short ribs, halved crosswise by butcher

10 ounces (about 5 inches) fresh peeled ginger, thinly sliced

6 cloves garlic, sliced

½ cup finely chopped lemongrass

2 dried Thai chilies or ¼ teaspoon Sriracha

10 cups water

1⅓ cups soy sauce

2 teaspoons kosher salt

1 teaspoon granulated sugar

For Garnish

3 tablespoons chopped fresh cilantro, Thai or regular basil, and/or chives

1 recipe Wasabi Rémoulade with Cucumber and Radish (recipe follows), room temperature (optional)

1. *Make the Glaze:* Combine all the glaze ingredients in a medium saucepan set over medium–high heat. Simmer for 10 minutes, or until the mixture coats the back of a spoon. Remove from the heat and set aside to cool. Cover and refrigerate.

2. *Start the Ribs:* Heat the oil in a large casserole or Dutch oven set over medium–high heat. Add the ribs and sauté, working in batches if necessary, for 3 to 4 minutes per side, or until deeply browned all over. Transfer the ribs to a plate, leaving the drippings in the casserole.

3. Reduce the heat to medium and add the ginger, garlic, lemongrass, and chilies to the drippings. Cook, stirring frequently, for 5 minutes, or until golden and fragrant.

4. Add the water, soy sauce, salt, sugar, and ribs. Cover, and gently simmer for 60 to 75 minutes, or until ribs are very tender. Remove from the heat and cool. Cover and refrigerate.

5. Remove the ribs and glaze from the refrigerator. Remove any fat that has hardened on top of the ribs.

6. Preheat the broiler.

7. While the broiler preheats, transfer the ribs to a sheet pan. Generously brush the glaze on both sides of the ribs. Reserve any extra glaze in a small pitcher.

AFTER THE FIRST COURSE

8. Broil for 3 minutes per side, or until the glaze starts to bubble. Transfer to a serving platter and drizzle with some of the reserved glaze.

9. Garnish with the herbs. If using, dollop with the Wasabi Rémoulade. Spoon any extra rémoulade into a small serving bowl and pass separately. Serve the ribs hot and pass the remaining glaze.

Wasabi Rémoulade with Cucumber and Radish

Yield: 2–3 cups

¼ cup Hellman's or Basic Mayonnaise (p. 275)

2 tablespoons Dijon mustard

4 teaspoons wasabi paste

Fine sea salt and freshly ground black pepper, to taste

2 pounds cucumbers, peeled, seeded, and cut into 1½-inch sticks

1 pound red radishes, thinly sliced

½ cup finely minced fresh chives

1. In a large bowl, combine the mayonnaise, mustard, wasabi paste, salt, and pepper. Fold in the cucumbers, radishes, and chives. Cover and refrigerate. (This will keep in the refrigerator for up to 1 day.)

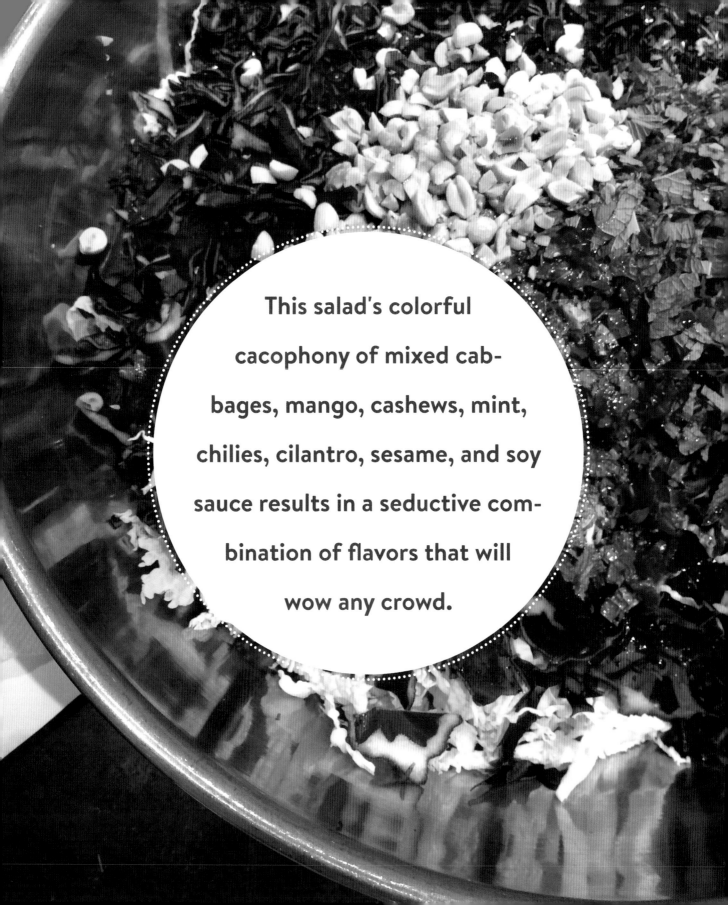

This salad's colorful cacophony of mixed cabbages, mango, cashews, mint, chilies, cilantro, sesame, and soy sauce results in a seductive combination of flavors that will wow any crowd.

Sweet 'n' Spicy Cabbage Salad

Yield: 8 first-course servings

½ Savoy cabbage, finely shredded

½ red cabbage, finely shredded

2 mangoes, peeled and cut into thin strips

1 small fresh red chili, seeded, ribs removed, and finely minced, or more to taste

¼ cup finely shredded fresh mint leaves

1 cup chopped fresh cilantro

½ cup roasted salted cashews or peanuts, coarsely chopped, divided

1 recipe Sweet 'n' Spicy Dressing (recipe follows), room temperature

1 HOUR

1. Place both of the shredded cabbages in a large salad bowl. Add the mangoes, chili, mint, cilantro, and ¼ cup of the nuts. Toss with enough of the Sweet 'n' Spicy Dressing to moisten and flavor. Taste and adjust the salt and pepper as needed. Set aside.

SERVE

AFTER THE FIRST COURSE

2. Toss, taste, and adjust salt and pepper as needed. Top with the remaining ¼ cup of nuts and serve.

Sweet 'n' Spicy Dressing

Yield: About ½–¾ cup

¾ cup unseasoned rice wine vinegar

1 stalk lemongrass, finely chopped

2 cloves garlic, minced

6 tablespoons pure maple syrup

1 tablespoon soy sauce, or more to taste

½ teaspoon crushed red pepper

2 tablespoons neutral oil, such as canola

Fine sea salt and freshly ground black pepper, to taste

2–4 tablespoons toasted sesame oil, or to taste

Freshly squeezed juice of 1½ limes, or more to taste

Tip!

This dressing is delicious and comes in handy. I make extra as it keeps in the fridge for several months.

2 DAYS

1. Put all the dressing ingredients, except the sesame oil and lime juice, in a medium saucepan set over high heat and reduce for 10 to 25 minutes, or until thick and syrupy.

2. Remove from the heat and set aside to cool. Add the sesame oil and lime juice. Taste and adjust the salt, pepper, soy sauce, and lime as needed. Set aside for up to 4 hours or refrigerate for up to 3 weeks.

Ginger-Caramelized Pears with Vanilla Crème Fraîche

Yield: 8 servings

1¾ cups granulated sugar

Pinch fine sea salt

8 hard-ripe Bosc or Bartlett pears, halved lengthwise

1 (3-inch) piece fresh peeled ginger, cut into ¼-inch-thick rounds

2 tablespoons water or Poire Williams, for deglazing

1¾ cups crème fraîche mixed with 1 teaspoon best-quality pure vanilla extract, for serving

These gingered pears are perfect following an Asian meal. However, the pears are equally delicious infused with vanilla. Just replace the ginger with a vanilla bean sliced in half lengthwise.

5 HOURS

1. Set a lidded skillet, large enough to hold all the pears in a single layer, over high heat and cover the bottom with ⅛ inch of water.

2. Sprinkle the sugar evenly over the water. Add the salt. Stir.

3. Heat the sugar mixture for about 5 minutes, or until it boils and becomes clear. At this point, stop stirring, and reduce the heat to medium. When browning begins, turn the heat down to low and tilt the skillet to mix, until the sugar is deep caramel. Remove from the heat.

4. Use a melon baller or a sharp knife to remove the seeds from the pear halves. Leave stems intact and do not peel.

5. Place the ginger rounds in the caramel. Then, starting from the edge of the skillet, place the pear halves, cut side down and pointing inward, in a concentric circle on top of and in between the ginger. Then, fill in the middle as best you can.

6. Place the skillet over very low heat and cover.

7. Cook the pears for 40 to 70 minutes, or until very tender. (They may take longer to cook. Check frequently.)

8. Transfer the pears to a large serving platter, cut side up. Remove and discard the ginger and set the skillet aside.

If you overcook the pears, don't worry. Overcooked, they shrivel up a bit but are no less delicious. Better overcooked than undercooked, in this case.

SERVE

AFTER THE MAIN COURSE

9. Warm the skillet over medium heat and deglaze with the water or Poire Williams. Pour the caramel over the pears.

10. Serve warm or at room temperature with the vanilla crème fraîche or sour cream on the side.

GENTEEL GRILLING

DINNER FOR EIGHT

DISH	BEGIN PREP	PAGE
FIRST COURSE		
Grilled Asparagus Mimosa	4½ hours ahead	194
ENTRÉE		
Grilled Whiskey-Marinated Salmon with Ginger–Garlic Mayonnaise	4 days ahead	195
ON THE SIDE		
Red Onion Confit	3 days ahead	196
Doubly Corn Pudding	1½ ahead	197
DESSERT		
Mixed Berry Pavlova	4 days ahead ahead	198

Salmon is one obvious answer to the how-to of easy entertaining. It's insanely popular, cooks in no time, and is equally good hot, warm, or at room temperature. This particular take on America's favorite fish is melt-in-your-mouth delicious and has been one of my most frequent dinner party offerings ever since my brother prepared it for me decades ago over a Malibu bonfire.

Johnny was always an avid fisherman. When barely 20, he ratcheted his hobby up a notch when he began summering on a remote Alaskan island and catching an abundance of salmon. What he and his fellow fishermen didn't consume raw or give away was flash-frozen to take home. Though fresh salmon tartare remains Johnny's favorite fast food to this day, I prefer the grilled version—marinated in Canadian Club, soy sauce, toasted sesame oil, brown sugar, and garlic—that he fed us that evening in Malibu. The piquant fillets were flavorful, juicy, and cooked to perfection.

Over the years, I've served the Whiskey-Marinated Salmon (p. 195) in salads, as kebabs, and sandwiched. But currently I prefer my whiskey salmon straight up, accompanied by Ginger–Garlic Mayonnaise (p. 275), creamy Corn Pudding (p. 197), and Red Onion Confit (p. 196).

The Asparagus Mimosa (p. 194) that kicks off the meal is seasonal and sensational. Though this simple spring preparation veers from the classic version of the dish, it remains a delicious example of the age old pairing of asparagus and egg. The green spears are grilled—rather than steamed or boiled—and capers and fresh tarragon stand in for bread-crumbs and parsley. The simple ingredients command center stage so get your asparagus, eggs, and tarragon from a farmers' market if you possibly can.

This brilliant medley of colors and distinct flavors—purple onions and yellow corn pudding along with the pink salmon and green aspar-agus—pleases the eye as well as the palate. Dessert extends the edible rainbow. Red and blue berries against snow-white meringue are gor-geous and mouthwatering.

Getting the hang of the meringue—an airy and versatile confection that can be made even months in advance—is well worth the minimal time and effort required. This particular berry-topped Pavlova (p. 198) is first rate, but you can fill a meringue shell with almost anything. Even crunchy crumbled scraps of meringue, served under or over fruit and ice cream or folded into whipped cream along with sliced stone fruits or fresh berries, will leave guests begging for more—and for the recipe.

GET A HEAD START!

The eggs for the **Asparagus Mimosa** can be hard boiled and refrigerated up to 2 weeks ahead. They can be grat-ed, covered, and refrigerated up to 24 hours before needed.

The **Salmon** marinade can be made ahead and refrigerated for 3 weeks or frozen for at least 6 months.

The **Red Onion Confit** can be made, cooled, and refrigerated for at least 4 days or frozen for up to 6 months. Reheat in a microwave or in a skillet set over low heat. You may need to add a tablespoon or 2 of water when reheating.

Doubly Corn Pudding can be held for up to 1 hour in a still-warm, turned off oven or be baked up to 5 hours ahead, set aside, and reheated—covered with foil—at 350°F for about 20 minutes or until hot.

Meringue shells—well wrapped in foil—keep for at least 4 months at room temperature.

ORDER OF PREPARATION

START

4 DAYS

1. Make the Meringue Shell (p. 294) for the Pavlova (p. 198), wrap, and store at room temperature.

2. Complete Step 1 for the Grilled Salmon (p. 195), cover, and refrigerate.

3 DAYS

1. Complete Steps 1 through 3 for the Onion Confit (p. 196). Cool, cover, and refrigerate.

1 DAY

1. Make the Ginger–Garlic Mayonnaise (p. 275) for the Salmon, cover, and refrigerate.

8 HOURS

1. Complete Step 2 for the Salmon and refrigerate.

4½ HOURS

1. If using a grill for the Asparagus Mimosa (p. 194), preheat it.

4 HOURS

1. If using a grill pan for the Asparagus Mimosa, set it over high heat.

2. Complete Steps 3 and 5 for the Asparagus Mimosa and set aside.

2 HOURS

1. Complete Step 1 for the Pavlova and set aside.

2. Remove the Onion Confit from the refrigerator (Step 4).

1½ HOURS

1. Preheat the oven to 400°F.

2. While the oven preheats, complete Steps 2 through 6 for the Corn Pudding (p. 197).

30 MINS

1. Remove the Ginger–Garlic Mayonnaise and the Salmon from the refrigerator (Step 3).

2. If using, prepare a grill for the Salmon.

3. Complete the Asparagus Mimosa (Step 6).

10 MINS

1. If using, set a grill pan over high heat for the Salmon.

2. Complete Steps 6 for the Salmon

SERVE

1. Complete Step 7 for the Corn Pudding and set aside.

2. Serve the Asparagus Mimosa.

3. If reheating, complete Step 5 for the Onion Confit.

AFTER THE FIRST COURSE

4. Complete Steps 2 and 3 for the Pavlova.

5. After eating the Asparagus Mimosa, complete the Salmon (Step 7) and serve with the Ginger–Garlic Mayonnaise, Onion Confit, and Corn Pudding.

AFTER THE MAIN COURSE

6. After clearing the table, complete the Pavlova (Steps 4 and 5) and serve.

Grilled Asparagus Mimosa

Yield: 8 first-course servings

2½ pounds asparagus

4 tablespoons extra virgin olive oil, plus more as needed, divided

2 teaspoons fine sea salt, or more to taste

Freshly ground black pepper, to taste

4 large hard-boiled eggs, peeled and coarsely grated

4 tablespoons roughly chopped fresh tarragon

4 teaspoons small capers, rinsed, drained, and patted dry

When I don't have access to a grill, I roast the asparagus in a hot oven. Within 5 hours of the time you plan to serve them, lay the asparagus in a single layer on 1 or 2 sheet pans, brush with extra virgin olive oil or Garlic Oil (p. 273), season with salt and pepper, and roast at 450°F for 15 to 20 minutes, or until just tender. Set aside at room temperature until ready to dress and serve.

4½ HOURS

1. If using a grill, preheat it.

4 HOURS

2. If using a grill pan, set it over high heat.

3. Toss or paint the asparagus with 2 tablespoons of the olive oil (or more as needed). Season with the salt and pepper.

4. Grill, turning once or twice, for about 15 minutes, or until tender.

5. Arrange the grilled asparagus attractively on a serving platter. Adjust the salt and pepper as needed. Set aside. (This will keep at room temperature for up to 5 hours).

30 MINS

6. Top with the grated egg, staying close to the center of the stalks so that the tips remain visible. Sprinkle with the tarragon and capers. Set aside. (This will keep at room temperature for up to 1 hour.)

SERVE

7. Serve at room temperature.

Grilled Whiskey-Marinated Salmon with Ginger–Garlic Mayonnaise

Yield: 8 main-course servings

¾ cup Canadian Club whiskey or bourbon

7 tablespoons light soy sauce or tamari sauce

½ cup olive extra virgin oil

3 tablespoons dark brown sugar

2 teaspoons dark toasted sesame oil

4 cloves garlic, finely minced

Few drops Tabasco or other hot chili sauce

3 pounds center-cut salmon fillet, skin on and left whole or cut into 2 or 3 pieces

Fine sea salt and freshly ground black pepper, to taste

1 recipe Ginger–Garlic Mayonnaise (p. 275), for serving

1. To make the marinade, put the whiskey, soy sauce, olive oil, brown sugar, sesame oil, garlic, and Tabasco in a lidded jar and shake vigorously to combine. Set aside for at least 6 hours to allow flavors to marry and then refrigerate.

2. Put the salmon and the marinade in a large zip-lock bag or covered container. Refrigerate for 6 to 24 hours, turning the salmon once or twice.

3. Remove salmon from the refrigerator.

4. If using, preheat a grill.

5. If using, set a grill pan over high heat.

6. Season the salmon with the salt and pepper and grill for 3 to 4 minutes per side or broil for 6 to 8 minutes with or without turning.

AFTER THE FIRST COURSE

7. Dollop with the Ginger–Garlic Mayonnaise or pass it separately. Serve the salmon hot, warm, or at room temperature.

If you aren't up for grilling, bake the fish in an oven preheated to 500°F. Place a sheet pan on the top rack for 5 minutes. Lay the salmon, skin side down, on the hot pan and bake for about 8 to 12 minutes or until done. Cooking time will vary depending on desired doneness and thickness of the fish.

If you don't have a grill pan, use a preheated large, heavy skillet. You won't get the grill marks, but the fish will still taste delicious.

Red Onion Confit

Yield: 8 side-dish servings

8 large red onions, very thinly sliced

½ cup extra virgin olive oil

4 cloves garlic, roughly chopped, or more to taste

3 tablespoons balsamic vinegar

3 tablespoons water

½ teaspoon dried thyme

¼ teaspoon granulated sugar

Fine sea salt, freshly ground black pepper, and Tabasco sauce, to taste

1. Preheat the oven to 400°F.

2. Toss all the ingredients together in a large bowl. Divide the onions between 2 large sheet pans and spread evenly. Place the pans on 2 separate racks in the oven. Bake 20 minutes, then toss with a metal spatula and switch the positions of the sheet pans on the racks.

3. Bake, tossing occasionally, for another 20 to 30 minutes, or until the onions begin to darken and caramelize with even darker spots here and there. Remove the pans from the oven, taste, and adjust the seasoning as needed. Set aside to cool. Cover and refrigerate.

4. Remove the confit from the refrigerator.

5. If serving warm or hot, place the pan in a 400°F oven for about 5 minutes. Alternatively, reheat in a microwave or in a large skillet set over low heat. You may need to add 1 to 2 tablespoons of water when reheating.

AFTER THE FIRST COURSE

6. Serve hot, warm, or at room temperature.

Doubly Corn Pudding

Yield: 8 side-dish servings

1 medium onion, chopped

4 tablespoons unsalted butter, plus more for preparing the baking dish

1 clove garlic, minced

2 cups water

1 teaspoon kosher salt, or more to taste

¼ teaspoon freshly ground black pepper

¾ cups stone-ground yellow cornmeal

4 large eggs, room temperature well beaten

¾ cups buttermilk, room temperature

¼ cup heavy cream, room temperature

1½ cups fresh or thawed frozen corn kernels (do not use canned)

1½ HOURS

1. Preheat the oven to 400°F.

2. While the oven preheats, butter a 10-inch × 12-inch ceramic baking dish (or an equivalent round or oval baking dish) and set aside.

3. Sauté the onion with the butter in a large, heavy saucepan set over medium heat for 3 minutes. Add the garlic and continue to cook, stirring frequently, until the onions begin to color. Add the water, salt, and pepper and simmer for 2 minutes.

4. Remove from the heat and whisk in the cornmeal, making sure that no lumps form. Return to low heat and cook, stirring, for about 3 minutes, or until very thick.

5. Remove from the heat and whisk in the eggs, buttermilk, and cream followed by the corn kernels. Scrape into the prepared baking dish.

6. Place the baking dish on a sheet pan. Bake for 45 minute to 1 hour, or until the pudding is just set and the top has browned.

This recipe can be made last minute; prepared up to 4 hours ahead, set aside, and reheated to serve; or finished about 1 hour ahead and kept warm in the turned off oven.

SERVE

7. When done, remove from the oven and set aside to rest for at least 10 minutes. For a longer wait, leave in the turned off oven with the door ajar to stay warm.

AFTER THE FIRST COURSE

8. Serve hot or warm from the baking dish.

Mixed Berry Pavlova

Yield: 8 servings

6 cups mixed strawberries, raspberries, blueberries, or blackberries, or a mixture, cut as for fruit salad

Pinch fine sea salt, to taste

¼ teaspoon granulated sugar, or more to taste

1 Meringue Shell (p. 294)

2 pints best-quality vanilla ice cream

1½ cups heavy cream, very cold

¼ teaspoon best-quality pure vanilla extract

2 HOURS

1. Mix the berries with the salt and sugar. Set aside.

SERVE

AFTER THE FIRST COURSE

2. Place the Meringue Shell on a 13- to 14-inch round platter.

3. Remove the ice cream from the freezer to soften.

AFTER THE MAIN COURSE

4. Using a stand mixer fitted with the whisk attachment or an electric handheld mixer set on medium–high speed, whip the cream with the vanilla until soft peaks form.

5. Spread the ice cream in the Meringue Shell and top with the whipped cream and then with the berries. Bring to the table and then slice into wedges.

Berries not in season?

Make this Pavlova with

Lemon Curd (p. 304) or

Chocolate Mousse (p. 40) and

whipped cream instead.

AUTUMN
FLAVORS

DINNER FOR EIGHT

DISH	BEGIN PREP	PAGE
FIRST COURSE		
Arugula Salad with Green Apples and Marcona Almonds	1 day ahead	143
ENTRÉE		
Pan-Roasted Pork Loin with Honeyed Figs and Caramelized Fennel	1 day ahead	206
ON THE SIDE		
Delmonico Potatoes Gratin	1 day ahead	208
DESSERT		
Caramelized Plum and Rosemary Polenta Pound Cake	3 days ahead	210

The dishes comprising this fruit-centric fall menu are individually appealing and even more so in concert. The apple, fig, and plum recipes play off each other surprisingly well. In late spring and early fall, when weather cool enough to comfortably consume fat-marbled pork coincides with the fig harvest, I serve this dinner as often as possible.

I have no patience for "the other white meat" kind of pork, which I find tough, dry, and unappealing. If you buy pork that is deep pink or darker in color and has a hefty fat content, your Pan-Roasted Pork Loin (p. 206) will be juicy, flavorful, and truly spectacular. Just don't overcook it! Other than a few cases a year triggered by bear meat, undercooked game, and home-reared pigs, instances of trichinosis have been almost nonexistent in the United States for decades, so there is no need to ruin good meat by roasting it into oblivion.

This recipe produces a distinctively succulent loin, even when served with nothing but defatted pan juices. However, in conjunction with caramelized, melt-in-your-mouth vegetables and honeyed figs, it's a gourmet feast.

If you're counting calories, swap out the pork for chicken or a meaty white fish—such as Roast Cod (p. 18), halibut, swordfish, or haddock—all of which pair equally well with the fig and fennel garnish. The substitution results in a menu light enough even for high summer, especially if you replace the Potatoes Gratin (p. 208) with a simple potato and red onion pan-roast; a rice, grain, or pasta salad; or nothing but thick slices of garlic toast for sopping up the flavorful sauce.

One last comment regarding substitutions: off-season dried figs—halved and soaked in warm water, tea, wine, or stock for at least 30 minutes before using—or fresh pears can stand in seamlessly for fresh figs. Just add the drained, reconstituted figs or sliced pears to the vegetables for the last 25 minutes of cooking.

I often serve this menu's classic Potatoes Gratin—named for Delmonico's, the legendary New York City eatery where Chef Charles Ranhofer invented it in the 1860s—with a green salad and some good bread and call it dinner. But whether presented as a side dish or as the main event, layers of tender, nutmeg-spiked spuds interspersed with Gruyère and garlic-thickened cream, all under a crispy, golden gratin, are irresistible. And what host can ignore the practicality of something you can assemble days in advance and bake off when needed? One final plus for the unconverted: By definition, gratins are served from the dish in which they are baked. Thus, one less item to wash, dry, and put away.

And save room for my favorite plum dessert. Plums are my stone fruit of choice both to eat out of hand and to caramelize for use in sauces, pancakes, pie fillings, ice cream bases, and—as in this recipe—in cake batters. Black Ruby, El Dorado, Elephant Heart, Seneca, Friar, Hollywood, Queen Rosa—if plums had nothing going for them but their spectacular names, I would still be a fan. However, given their superb flavor—tending to be deeper and more complex than that of their what-you-see-is-what-you-get peach and nectarine cousins—I'm utterly hooked.

Once apricots and peaches are long gone, enjoy figs and plums through early fall.

When it comes to cooked plums, roasting, stewing, or grilling all suffice, but nothing beats the depth of flavor achieved by caramelizing in a skillet. This may sound complicated, but actually requires nothing more than sautéing the sliced fruit with butter and sugar—and sometimes also with aromatics, spices, or alcohol—until their juices partially evaporate, and then thicken and darken in color.

For this plummy Polenta Pound Cake (p. 210), just alternate layers of the cooked fruit and batter in a loaf pan and bake until golden. A few tablespoons of cognac add extra tenderness to the crumb, and the unusual inclusion of fresh rosemary pairs brilliantly with the rustic fruit. Cornmeal adds gusto and provides a bit of adventure.

Served warm with whipped cream and extra plums—fresh or sautéed—on the side, this cake tops my list of sweet treats for early fall. The prepared plums are good served separately—on toast, muffins, waffles, and pancakes as well as on ice cream and custards—so make extra, especially as they keep in the fridge for weeks (in the unlikely event someone doesn't finish them off first).

PLUMS

Plums come into season in early summer and abound for at least a month once peaches and nectarines have gone by the wayside. Like most fruit, flavor is dramatically enhanced by caramelizing. Plums are ideal in baked goods: tarts, pies, cobblers, crisps, gratins, soufflés—not to mention ice creams and sauces. The simplest of my yummy plum recipes caramelizes the fruit with citrus zests and juices, and then finishes off the mixture with a splash of Grand Marnier. Spoon over vanilla ice cream, frozen yogurt, custard, or panna cotta. You can add crunch and a soupçon of elegance by placing individual Meringue Shells (p. 294) on dessert plates (or place one large shell on a platter) before topping with ice cream and this ambrosial sauce.

ORDER OF PREPARATION

 START

 3 DAYS
1. Make the Prepared Plums for the Polenta Pound Cake (p. 211). Cool, cover, and refrigerate.

 1 DAY
1. Make the Lemon–Shallot Vinaigrette (p. 281) for the Arugula Salad (p. 143). Cover and refrigerate.

2. Complete Steps 1 through 7 for the Potatoes Gratin (p. 208). Cool, cover, and refrigerate.

3. Complete Step 1 and 2 for the Pork Loin (p. 206), cover, and refrigerate.

4. Complete Steps 1 through 6 for the Pound Cake. Cool, cover, and store at room temperature.

 5 HOURS
1. Remove the Potatoes from the refrigerator (Step 8).

 4 HOURS
1. Remove the Pork from the refrigerator (Step 3).

 2½ HOURS
1. With racks adjusted to the lower-third and center positions, preheat the oven to 400°F.

 2 HOURS
1. Complete Step 5 for the Pork.

2. Remove the Vinaigrette from the refrigerator.

 1½ HOURS
1. Confirm that racks are adjusted to the lower-third and center positions and the oven is at 400°F.

 1 HOUR
1. Complete Step 6 for the Pork and set aside.

2. Complete Step 10 for the Potatoes.

 5 MINS
1. Make the Arugula Salad.

 SERVE
1. Serve the Arugula Salad.

2. Remove the Pork from the oven and raise the oven temperature to 425°F (Step 7). Then, complete Step 8.

3. Complete Step 11 for the Potatoes.

AFTER THE FIRST COURSE

4. After finishing the Salad, complete the Pork (Step 9) and serve with the Potatoes.

5. If using, remove the ice cream from the freezer to soften.

AFTER THE MAIN COURSE

6. After clearing the table, whip the cream, if using. Complete the Pound Cake (Step 7) and serve with the ice cream and/or whipped cream, if using.

GET A HEAD START!

Marinate the **Pork Loin** up to 3 days ahead. This timing works for most meat and poultry. If there is acid (citrus or vinegar) in the marinade, 1 day or even just a few hours is better.

Make the prepared plums for the **Polenta Pound Cake** up to 2 weeks ahead and store in the fridge. The cake itself can also be baked ahead. Cool, wrap well, and refrigerate for up to 3 days or freeze for at least 3 months.

Pan-Roasted Pork Loin with Honeyed Figs and Caramelized Fennel

Yield: 8 main-course servings

5 cloves garlic, minced

7–9 tablespoons extra virgin olive oil, divided

1 tablespoon kosher salt

1 tablespoon fresh thyme leaves or 2 teaspoons dried thyme

1 bone-in pork loin (8 chops), fat on*

15 cloves garlic, peeled or unpeeled

3 organic lemons, thinly sliced crosswise and seeds removed

3 red onions, each cut into 8 wedges

2 bulbs fresh fennel, trimmed and each cut vertically into 8–10 pieces

2 teaspoons ground fennel

Fine sea salt and freshly ground black pepper, to taste

3 tablespoons honey

12 fresh figs, trimmed and cut in half vertically

½ cup chopped fresh cilantro or Italian parsley, for garnish

1. Place the minced garlic, 3 tablespoons of the oil, the kosher salt, and the thyme in a food processor and process until well combined.

2. Place the pork, fat side up, in a roasting pan just large enough to hold it. Rub the marinade mixture all over it. Cover and refrigerate. (The pork can marinate for up to 3 hours at room temperature before roasting or refrigerating. It will keep in the refrigerator for up to 3 days.)

3. Remove the pork from the refrigerator.

4. With racks adjusted to the lower-third and center positions, preheat the oven to 400°F.

5. On a sheet pan, toss the whole garlic, lemon slices, onions, fresh and ground fennel, sea salt, and pepper with 4 to 6 tablespoons of the oil or enough to coat them well. The vegetables should be in a single layer. If too crowded, use a second sheet pan. Place the vegetables on the lower rack of the oven or on both racks if using a second pan. Roast, tossing occasionally, for 40 to 60 minutes, or until the vegetables are tender and a bit caramelized. If using 2 pans, reverse their positions in the oven about half way through cooking. Remove from the oven and set aside.

Have the butcher crack the bones so you can cut the chops apart easily after cooking.

1
HOUR

6. Roast the pork on the center rack for 50 to 75 minutes, or until an instant-read thermometer inserted into the thickest part of the loin registers 138°F.

SERVE

7. When done, transfer the pork to a cutting board and let it rest for at least 20 minutes. Raise the oven temperature to 425°F.

8. While the meat is resting, toss the honey with the cooked vegetables. Add the figs and return to the oven for 10 to 15 minutes, or until the figs and vegetables are piping hot. Remove from the oven and toss in any pork juices that have accumulated on the cutting board. Taste and adjust the sea salt and pepper as needed.

AFTER THE FIRST COURSE

9. Slice the rested pork between the bones into chops and place them on a platter. Spoon the vegetable–fig mixture over the top of the chops and drizzle with any newly accumulated pork juices. Garnish with the cilantro or parsley and serve.

Delmonico Potatoes Gratin

Yield: 8–10 side-dish servings

¾ cup freshly grated Italian Parmesan cheese

¾ cup coarsely grated Gruyère cheese

3 cups chopped onions

1¾ cups whole milk

2 cups heavy cream

4 cloves garlic, very finely minced or put through a press

1 teaspoon fine sea salt, plus more to taste

½ teaspoon freshly ground pepper, plus more to taste

½ teaspoon dried thyme or 2 teaspoons chopped fresh thyme leaves

¼ teaspoon freshly grated nutmeg

10 tablespoons (1¼ sticks) unsalted butter, room temperature, divided

8 large Yukon gold potatoes, peeled and cut crosswise into ⅛-inch slices, divided

1. Mix the Parmesan and Gruyère together and set aside.

2. Combine the onions, milk, cream, garlic, salt, pepper, thyme, nutmeg, and 8 tablespoons of the butter in a medium saucepan set over medium heat. Bring to a simmer.

3. Remove the pan from the heat and give it a stir. Set aside.

4. Use the remaining 2 tablespoons of butter to grease an approximately 10-inch × 12-inch oval ceramic gratin dish.

5. Evenly cover the bottom of the buttered dish with ½ of the potatoes.

6. Pour ½ of the warm milk mixture over the potatoes and then sprinkle with ¾ of the cheese mixture.

7. Repeat with the remaining potatoes, and then the remaining milk and cheese. Cool, cover, and refrigerate if not baking right away.

8. Remove the assembled potatoes from the refrigerator.

9. With an over rack adjusted to the lower-third position, preheat the oven to 400°F.

If you don't have time to bring the Potatoes Gratin to room temperature, bake straight from the refrigerator but add at least 15 minutes to the baking time.

HOUR

10. Place the gratin dish on a sheet pan and bake on the lower rack of the oven (beneath the Pork Loin) for 45 to 60 minutes, or until the liquid is absorbed and the potatoes are piping hot, bubbly around the edges, golden, and very tender when the tip of a sharp knife is inserted into the center. If the potatoes are not browning enough, rearrange the racks and move them above the Pork Loin for the last 15 to 20 minutes of baking, or broil them at the last minute. If broiling, keep a close watch so they don't burn.

Tip!

If you have a second oven at your disposal, bake the potatoes gratin on the center rather than the bottom rack.

SERVE

11. Remove from oven and set aside to rest for 10 to 20 minutes before serving.

AFTER THE FIRST COURSE

12. Serve hot or very warm.

Caramelized Plum and Rosemary Polenta Pound Cake

Yield: 8–10 servings

When plums are out of season, you can make this cake with most other fruits, but save the rosemary for the stone fruits of summer and early fall. Pears, apples, and quince are better complemented by cinnamon, nutmeg, allspice, or ginger.

1½ cups all-purpose flour
1 cup yellow cornmeal
1 tablespoon baking powder
½ teaspoon fine sea salt
1 cup (2 sticks) unsalted butter, room temperature, plus more for greasing
1 cup granulated sugar
2 tablespoons finely minced fresh rosemary leaves

3 large eggs, room temperature
Freshly grated zest of 1 lemon
2 tablespoons cognac or brandy
Prepared Plums (recipe follows), room temperature
Sliced fresh plums, for serving (optional)
Whipped cream or vanilla ice cream, for serving (optional)

1 DAY

1. Preheat the oven to 350°F. Butter a 5½-inch × 10-inch loaf pan and line the bottom with parchment paper. Butter the paper and set aside.

2. Sift the flour, cornmeal, baking powder, and salt together. Set aside.

3. Using a stand mixer fitted with the paddle attachment or an electric handheld mixer set on medium–high speed, cream the butter with the sugar and rosemary for 3 to 5 minutes, or until very light and fluffy.

4. Add the eggs, 1 at a time, beating well after each addition. Add the lemon zest.

5. Scrape down the bowl. With the mixer on low speed, add the dry ingredients, alternating with the cognac. Mix until just combined. Scrape down the sides of the bowl and mix a few more seconds. Spoon ½ of the batter into the prepared pan. Evenly distribute ½ of the Prepared Plums over the batter. Top with the rest of the batter and smooth with a rubber spatula. Spoon the remaining fruit over the top and, using a spoon or fork, push the pieces down into the batter here and there.

6. Place on a sheet pan and bake for 45 minutes, or until golden and a toothpick or skewer inserted into the center of the cake comes out clean. Don't overbake. Cool in the pan for 10 minutes, then invert the cake onto a wire rack and quickly reinvert. When completely cool, store, covered, at room temperature for up to 24 hours. For longer storage, refrigerate.

SERVE

AFTER THE MAIN COURSE

7. Serve with the sliced fresh plums and whipped cream or vanilla ice cream, if using.

Prepared Plums

Yield: 2 cups

6–8 large plums, pitted and each cut into 6–8 wedges
⅓ cup granulated sugar
Pinch fine sea salt

Freshly grated zest of 1 lemon
1 teaspoon finely minced fresh rosemary
2 tablespoons cognac, rum, or amaretto, or more to taste

Instead of serving the Polenta Cake with fresh plums, make extra Prepared Plums to serve on the side.

1. Place the plums, sugar, salt, lemon zest, and rosemary in a medium saucepan and cook, stirring occasionally, over medium heat for 10 to 15 minutes, or until the fruit is very soft. Remove from the heat and add the liquor.

2. Cool, cover, and refrigerate. (The plums will keep in the refrigerator for up to 2 weeks.)

CHAPTER 5

HOLIDAYS

HOLIDAYS

MENUS

Easter or Passover
p. 218

Thanksgiving
p. 234

Christmas
p. 252

For most of us in 21st-century America, the holidays are no longer "holy" days, but they are still special. This is particularly true in November and December, a unique period each year that—along with much else—involves a lot of eating, drinking, and partying. The "good news" is that your children are out of school; you're inundated with houseguests—family and friends you normally don't see—and you host and attend as many parties at this time as in the other 10 months of the year combined. If you're not careful, all of this is also the "bad news," with too much fun and togetherness often tipping over into chaos, anxiety, and ill temper.

Planning ahead, as usual, can save the day as well as the season. Make your calendar your new best friend. View the holidays in the big picture. Don't schedule events for more nights per week than you and your family can comfortably manage. It's pointless to attend so many potentially enjoyable parties that each becomes drudgery. I realize I sound like a stick-in-the-mud, but moderation is even more important in November and December than in general. And this is particularly true when the lion's share of the entertaining is scheduled to fall on you.

The last six weeks of the year often entail quite a bit of time spent entertaining the family. And many of us are called on to host work-related festivities as well. I glide through the holidays with relative ease when I manage to entertain no more than once a week. To this end, I combine events when even marginally appropriate. You never know: The most unlikely bedfellows might hit it off, and one less evening of hosting might be the deciding factor in retaining your sanity. When in charge of the family Thanksgiving, I do my best to make sure that Christmas, Hanukkah, New Year's Eve, and New Year's Day are delegated to others. I am not always able to make this happen, but I try.

When throwing the party does land on me, planning is the first priority. Apologies for being a broken record, but *order of preparation* is the name of the game if you're going to enjoy your own party and the days leading up to it. And isn't that the least you deserve? Focus on chronology—the steps involved in making dinner—and prepare as much as humanly possible as far ahead as humanly possible.

Stash finished dishes or their components in the freezer, check them off the list, and forget about them—often for weeks or months—until needed. Some items can also be relegated to the fridge up to a week or more in advance. All this "stashing" will make day-of a breeze . . . or at least verging on one.

All of that being said, I do want to add that potluck thinking, on top of careful planning and organization, can be a lifesaver. Dessert—with side dishes as a close second—is the easiest part of a holiday feast to pawn off on others or to purchase. So when you're on overload (despite my magical order of preparation suggestions), remember that most cities have at least a couple of good bakeries, gourmet stores, and supermarket counters where you can pick up perfectly acceptable tarts, pies, and cakes. In a pinch, there's always the Internet. And on another note, if you can persuade someone who is not bringing food to provide wine and champagne, so much the better.

In any case, whether you're cooking the whole shebang yourself or have enlisted help, an order of preparation chart allows you to negotiate holiday madness in a timely fashion while remaining calm and sane. In this chapter, I detail the Easter or Passover, Thanksgiving, and Christmas menus for 12 that have performed best for me over the years. I've

At Thanksgiving, pecans are traditional, but the Candied Nut Tart is equally good made with walnut, hazelnuts, or almonds.

worked out the kinks, and season after season, returning guests greet these meals with enthusiasm.

Nonetheless, variety is the spice of life, and I do occasionally tweak, substitute, add, and omit. Follow these menus to the letter or regard them as general templates. And remember that the recipes can be scaled up or down, as it's unlikely you'll have exactly 12 people anyway. Nothing here is written in stone.

Flexibility is almost as important as planning, and these menus can easily be adjusted to work for other festive occasions and for other numbers of guests. And though I've suggested serving prime rib at Christmas, Easter's leg of lamb would be delicious then as well.

It's important to do what feels right for you. If your family insists on a bird and all the trimmings at both Christmas and Thanksgiving, go for it. In that case, however, consider replacing the very Thanksgiving-specific Crème Caramel with the *Fané* (p. 177), Frozen Lemon Bombe (p. 101), and/or a Devil's Food (p. 264) or Coconut Layer Cake (p. 231). The Candied Pecan Tart (p. 251), on the other hand, is evergreen—an all-time favorite and ideal choice if you want to treat your guests to a second or third dessert.

The trick is to balance planning and flexibility. Expect the unexpected. Because everyone—not just you—is on overload, the holidays are a particularly unpredictable time of year. Know there will be factors you can't control: guests are delayed or cancel last minute, someone has the flu, your cousin arrives with unannounced houseguests. Don't panic. You've planned ahead, but now it's time to go with the flow. There is clearly much you can't control, but your holidays will go more smoothly if you focus primarily on what you can. This chapter will show you what those things are and will lay out instructions for making it all come to pass stress free.

EASTER OR PASSOVER

DINNER FOR TWELVE

DISH	BEGIN PREP	PAGE
FIRST COURSE		
Green Pea, Lettuce, and Celery Soup	2 days ahead	224
ENTRÉE		
Mustard-Coated Leg of Lamb	2 days ahead	225
ON THE SIDE		
Asparagus with Lemon–Shallot Vinaigrette	2 days ahead	226
Scalloped Potatoes with Onions, Tomatoes, Anchovies, and Fresh Herbs	1 day ahead	227
DESSERT		
For Passover: Individual Chocolate–Espresso Soufflés	1 day ahead	229
For Easter: Coconut Layer Cake	1 day ahead	231

Easter and Passover come along in early spring just as we are gratefully shedding the drabness of winter and appreciating the arrival of daffodils, tulips, flowering fruit trees, and the sun. Along with leg of lamb—traditional fare for both Easter and Passover repasts—the rest of this this March-April menu works for both holiday feasts and includes its fair share of spring green vegetables. It opens with a velvety smooth, and lovely-to-look-at delicate Pea, Lettuce, and Celery Soup (p. 224), which is complemented and greatly enhanced by a number of contrasting garnishes. Choices—use one or more—include chopped chorizo, pancetta, hazelnuts, and tiny croutons.

Classically Julia Child, the crustily golden Leg of Lamb (p. 225), takes me back to the early days in my very first kitchen. Julia got it right. With a mustard marinade that renders the meat at once succulent, meltingly tender, and incredibly tasty, this is still the lamb roast against which I measure all others. And FYI, the mustard coating also works wonders when broiling a butterflied lamb leg or grilling pork chops or chicken pieces.

The Scalloped Potatoes (p. 227), also adapted from Child, continue the robust Mediterranean thrust of the meal. Since the dish can be served hot, warm, or at room temperature, it's a great recipe all year long for the make-ahead cook. As all the required cooking liquid is provided by the tomatoes, the robust flavors of garlic, onions, and anchovies coalesce with the reducing tomato juices and results in a dish that just screams South of France. These hearty potatoes are an equally fitting accompaniment for beef, pork, steak, and chops as well as for grilled swordfish, tuna, salmon, and mackerel.

The heavier lamb and potato dishes cry out for a less substantial balancing act. The Asparagus with Lemon–Shallot Vinaigrette (p. 226) adds a palate-enlivening element to the menu while echoing the spring green of the starter. If you prefer, instead of the asparagus, get the same effect with a mixed green salad.

The Coconut Layer Cake (p. 231) and the Individual Chocolate–Espresso Soufflés (p. 229) are both genius ways to finish off this meal. Even when not baked in a bunny-shaped cake pan, the fluffy coconut dessert reminds me of the Easter bunny; so at Easter, I do generally opt for the beautiful cake with its brilliantly white icing and blizzard of shredded coconut topping. The confection tastes as good as it looks (or even better). Though not visible, a heavenly vanilla pudding–whipped cream concoction is generously slathered between its three layers. This is no cake for sissies.

And it's convenient. If you prefer to get a head start, make and freeze the cake layers months in advance. Then assemble and ice the cake up to two days ahead of time and refrigerate until needed. It goes without saying that with the addition of a few candles, it's also perfect for a special birthday.

With a base that keeps for up to three days in the fridge, the soufflés can also be partially prepared ahead. And they're a dream for Passover,

If Chocolate–Espresso Soufflés or a Coconut Cake are not up your alley, a Frozen Lemon Bombe (p. 101), *Fané* (p. 177), and Baked Alaska (p. 87) are all excellent substitutes and flourless for Passover as well.

as they taste fantastic but contain no flour whatsoever. The already glorious flavor of deep, dark chocolate is accentuated further by the addition of espresso. The result is decadent but, miraculously, still relatively low in calories. Of course, this disclaimer does not apply when you add an ice cream or whipped cream garnish.

SOUFFLÉS

Most people don't realize that you can make soufflé bases up to three days in advance and store them in the fridge until needed. To finish and serve, preheat the oven, whisk up the egg whites, fold them into the warmed premade base, fill the molds, and bake. Timing is of the essence, as the mini masterpieces will collapse if not served straight from the oven. However, if misfortune strikes, my close friend Chef Jeremiah Tower suggests moving right along and telling guests that the fallen soufflés are your favorite grandmother's favorite puddings. Deflated, they are a bit homely but no less delicious.

Ideally, though, they won't collapse until after presentation. In cooking school, we were taught that "people wait for soufflés; soufflés do not wait for people." So be sure to seat guests at least five minutes before you expect your little triumphs to emerge from the oven. I prefer individual soufflés to a single large one, as the small ones cook more quickly and are easier to time. And—humans being humans and therefore proprietary—who wouldn't choose their own personal soufflé over a sloppy portion scooped from a communal dish?

ORDER OF PREPARATION

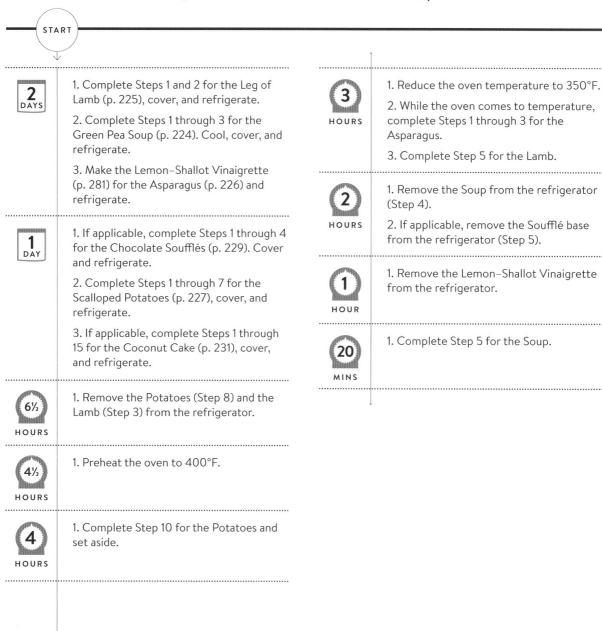

START

2 DAYS

1. Complete Steps 1 and 2 for the Leg of Lamb (p. 225), cover, and refrigerate.

2. Complete Steps 1 through 3 for the Green Pea Soup (p. 224). Cool, cover, and refrigerate.

3. Make the Lemon–Shallot Vinaigrette (p. 281) for the Asparagus (p. 226) and refrigerate.

1 DAY

1. If applicable, complete Steps 1 through 4 for the Chocolate Soufflés (p. 229). Cover and refrigerate.

2. Complete Steps 1 through 7 for the Scalloped Potatoes (p. 227), cover, and refrigerate.

3. If applicable, complete Steps 1 through 15 for the Coconut Cake (p. 231), cover, and refrigerate.

6½ HOURS

1. Remove the Potatoes (Step 8) and the Lamb (Step 3) from the refrigerator.

4½ HOURS

1. Preheat the oven to 400°F.

4 HOURS

1. Complete Step 10 for the Potatoes and set aside.

3 HOURS

1. Reduce the oven temperature to 350°F.

2. While the oven comes to temperature, complete Steps 1 through 3 for the Asparagus.

3. Complete Step 5 for the Lamb.

2 HOURS

1. Remove the Soup from the refrigerator (Step 4).

2. If applicable, remove the Soufflé base from the refrigerator (Step 5).

1 HOUR

1. Remove the Lemon–Shallot Vinaigrette from the refrigerator.

20 MINS

1. Complete Step 5 for the Soup.

SERVE

1. Remove the Lamb from the oven (Step 6), and if reheating the Potatoes, complete Step 11.

2. If applicable, remove the Coconut Cake from the refrigerator (Step 16).

3. Complete the Soup (Step 6) and serve.

AFTER THE FIRST COURSE

4. After eating the Soup, remove the Potatoes from the oven (Step 12) and, if making the Soufflé, raise the temperature to 400°F.

5. Complete the Lamb (Step 7) and the Asparagus (Step 4).

6. Serve the Lamb with the Asparagus and the Potatoes.

AFTER THE MAIN COURSE

7. Before clearing the table, if making the Soufflés, complete Steps 7 through 12.

8. If applicable, when the Soufflés are done, serve them immediately—so they don't fall—along with the whipped cream or ice cream

9. If applicable, complete Step 17 for the Coconut Cake and serve.

GET A HEAD START!

The **Green Pea Soup** can be made and refrigerated up to 2 days ahead.

The marinade for the **Leg of Lamb** can be made up to 4 days ahead and refrigerated.

The **Chocolate–Espresso Soufflé** base can be made up to 3 days ahead and refrigerated. Heat to lukewarm before completing the recipe.

The layers for the **Coconut Cake** can be made ahead and frozen for up to 4 months. Thaw before completing the recipe. The filling can be made up to 24 hours before assembling the cake, and the entire cake can be assembled, iced, and refrigerated a day in advance.

Green Pea, Lettuce, and Celery Soup

Yield: 12 first-course servings

3 tablespoons neutral oil, such as canola

3 tablespoons unsalted butter

3 stalks celery, finely sliced

2 medium onions, finely sliced

1 large leek, finely sliced and washed well

6 cups vegetable stock, plus more for thinning as needed

2 teaspoons fine sea salt, or more to taste

¾ teaspoon freshly ground white or black pepper, or more to taste

2⅓ (14- to 16-ounce) bags frozen green peas, thawed

2 heads Bibb or 1 large head Boston lettuce, leaves separated

½ cup coarsely chopped fresh Italian parsley

⅓ cup fresh mint leaves

¾ teaspoon granulated sugar, or to taste

⅓ cup heavy cream or half and half

Fried diced chorizo or pancetta, tiny croutons, and/or chopped toasted hazelnuts, for garnish (optional)

Tip!

I sometimes add 1 to 2 tablespoons of West Indian (a mild, sweet) curry powder in Step 1. In that case, I use a scattering of scallions and/or the tiny croutons on top of each portion rather than one of the other suggested garnishes.

2 DAYS

1. Heat the oil and butter in a heavy saucepan set over medium–low heat. Add the celery, onions, and leek and cook for 10 minutes, or until soft. Add the 6 cups of stock and bring to a boil over high heat. Reduce the heat to low, and simmer for 8 minutes. Season with the salt and pepper, and then add the thawed peas and simmer 2 minutes more. Remove from the heat.

2. Add the lettuce, parsley, mint, and sugar, and use an immersion blender to purée until very smooth. Alternatively, once cool, purée in a blender. Taste and adjust the salt, pepper and sugar as needed.

3. Set aside to cool. Transfer to a covered container and refrigerate.

2 HOURS

4. Remove the soup from the refrigerator.

20 MINS

5. Return soup to the saucepan and reheat over medium–low heat. Do not boil. Stir in the cream and heat through. If too thick, add a bit more stock. Taste and adjust the salt, pepper, and sugar as needed.

SERVE

6. Ladle into warmed (if possible) soup bowls. If using, garnish each portion with a scattering of the chorizo, pancetta, tiny croutons, or chopped toasted hazelnuts. Serve right away.

Mustard-Coated Leg of Lamb

Yield: 12 main-course servings

1 cup Dijon mustard

4 tablespoons soy sauce

2–3 large cloves garlic, finely chopped or put through a garlic press

2 tablespoons dried rosemary leaves or thyme

½ teaspoon powdered ginger

4 tablespoons extra virgin olive oil

1 (10-pound) bone-in leg of lamb*

2 DAYS

1. Combine the mustard, soy sauce, garlic, rosemary, and ginger together in a small bowl. Add the oil, a few drops at a time, while whisking to make a mayonnaise-like cream. Alternatively, use a food processor: process everything but the oil. Then, with the motor running, add the oil slowly through the feed tube.

2. Using a rubber spatula, slather the lamb all over with the mustard mixture. Use it all. If there is extra, spoon it on top. Set on a rack in a low roasting pan, cover, and refrigerate.

6½ HOURS

3. Remove the lamb from the refrigerator.

3 HOURS

4. Preheat the oven to 350°F.

5. Place the lamb in the center of the oven. Roast for 2 to 2½ hours for rare (120°F), 2½ to 3 hours for medium rare (130°F), and 3 to 3¼ hours for well done (140°F). Use an instant-read thermometer to check the temperature and remember that the lamb will continue to cook a bit as it rests.

SERVE

6. Remove lamb from oven and let it rest for 20 to 30 minutes.

AFTER THE FIRST COURSE

7. Carve, arrange on a serving platter, and serve.

* It's easier to carve the lamb if you ask the butcher to remove the hip bone.

Asparagus with Lemon–Shallot Vinaigrette

Yield: 12 side-dish servings

50–60 medium or large asparagus
Kosher salt, for salting the water
Large pinch baking soda

½ cup Lemon–Shallot Vinaigrette (p. 281), or more as needed, room temperature

HOURS

1. Line asparagus up on a cutting board with the tops even. Cut off tough bottom ends. Lay a large tea towel on the counter.

2. Half fill a very large skillet with salted water and bring to at boil over high heat. Add the baking soda. Add the asparagus and arrange in a single layer (or as close to a single layer as possible). Bring the water back to a boil and cook the asparagus for 2 to 4 minutes, depending on size, or just until crisp-tender. Do not overcook.

3. Using a kitchen tongs, arrange the asparagus in a single layer on the tea towel. When cool, transfer to a serving platter.

SERVE

AFTER THE FIRST COURSE

4. Drizzle the asparagus with the Lemon–Shallot Vinaigrette. Taste and adjust salt and pepper as needed. Serve at room temperature.

Tip!

You can also dress the asparagus with Essential Vinaigrette (p. 279), Truffle Vinaigrette (p. 280), or Beurre Blanc (p. 282). If using beurre blanc, serve the asparagus hot.

Scalloped Potatoes with Onions, Tomatoes, Anchovies, and Fresh Herbs

Yield: 12 side-dish servings

4 cups thinly sliced onions

¼ cup plus 1 tablespoon extra virgin olive oil, divided

3 pounds ripe tomatoes, cut into a rough ½-inch dice

½ teaspoon fine sea salt

12 oil-packed anchovies, drained, oil reserved, and roughly chopped

4 large cloves garlic, chopped

½ cup julienned fresh basil

½ teaspoon dried thyme

⅓ teaspoon freshly ground black pepper

Reserved anchovy oil plus extra virgin olive oil to equal ¼ cup

4 pounds Yukon gold potatoes, sliced ⅛-inch thick

½ cup grated Gruyère or Italian Parmesan cheese

1. In a large skillet set over medium heat, cook the onions with the ¼ cup olive oil, stirring frequently, until tender and beginning to color.

2. Remove from the heat, add the tomatoes and salt, and toss. Set aside.

3. Mash together the anchovies, garlic, herbs, pepper, and the ¼ cup of the anchovy–olive oil mixture. Set aside.

4. Grease a 12-inch ×17-inch ceramic gratin dish (or use 2 smaller ones) and spread ¼ of the tomato–onion mixture evenly over the bottom.

5. Arrange ½ of the potato slices evenly on top followed by ½ of the anchovy mixture.

6. Spread ½ of the remaining tomatoes and onions on top of that followed by the remaining potatoes and then the last of the anchovy mixture.

7. Top with remaining tomatoes and onions. Sprinkle with the cheese and drizzle with the remaining 1 tablespoon of olive oil. Cover and refrigerate if not baking right away. (This will keep in the refrigerator for up to 24 hours.)

If you want to make the entire Scalloped Potatoes recipe in one day, you can assemble it up to 4 hours before baking and it set aside at room temperature.

CONTINUED

Scalloped Potatoes with Onions, Tomatoes, Anchovies, and Fresh Herbs

CONTINUED

6½ HOURS

8. Remove the gratin dish from the refrigerator.

4½ HOURS

9. Preheat oven to 400°F.

4 HOURS

10. Bake, uncovered, for about 50 minutes, or until the potatoes are tender (test with a small knife) and have absorbed all of the juices from the tomatoes. If the gratin is browning too quickly, cover loosely with a sheet of aluminum foil. Set aside if not serving right away.

SERVE

11. If reheating, cover the gratin dish loosely with a sheet of aluminum foil and transfer to a 350°F oven for 15 to 25 minutes, or until the potatoes reach the desired temperature.

AFTER THE FIRST COURSE

12. When done, remove from the oven. Serve hot, warm, or at room temperature.

Individual Chocolate–Espresso Soufflés

Yield: 12 servings

6–8 tablespoons unsalted butter, for preparing molds

Granulated sugar, for preparing molds

12 ounces best-quality semisweet chocolate, coarsely chopped

¾ cup whole milk, room temperature

¾ cup plus 6 tablespoons granulated sugar, divided

3 tablespoons instant espresso powder

9 large egg yolks

12 large egg whites, room temperature

1½ teaspoons cream of tartar

Large pinch fine sea salt

Sweetened whipped cream or softened ice cream, for serving

1 DAY

1. Generously butter 12 (12-ounce or 1½-cup) ramekins or soufflé molds. Then use the sugar to coat. Set aside or refrigerate.

2. To make the soufflé base, melt the chocolate in a double boiler set over low heat or a metal bowl set over simmering water for 3 to 4 minutes, or until melted.

3. Whisk in the milk followed by the ¾ cup of sugar and the espresso powder until smooth. Remove from heat.

4. Whisk in the yolks, 1 at a time. Make sure no traces of yolk remain visible. Leave in the pan and cover with plastic wrap, making sure it touches the surface of the chocolate mixture, and refrigerate.

2 HOURS

5. Remove the soufflé base from the refrigerator.

SERVE

AFTER THE FIRST COURSE

6. Preheat the oven to 400°F.

AFTER THE MAIN COURSE

7. Stirring constantly, reheat the soufflé base to lukewarm over very low heat.

CONTINUED

Tip!

Many ingredients in this book are specified "room temperature" and it is also suggested that many dishes be served at room temperature as they taste much better that way than straight from the fridge. However, room temperature implies about 70°F even if you are cooking in a swelteringly hot kitchen in the tropics.

Individual Chocolate–Espresso Soufflés

CONTINUED

8. Using a stand mixer fitted with the whisk attachment or an electric handheld set on low speed, beat the room temperature egg whites with the salt for 1 minute, or until frothy. Add the cream of tartar and increase the speed to medium–low. Mix—continuing to slowly increase the mixer speed to medium and then medium–high. When the whites are opaque and beginning to stiffen, very gradually add the remaining 6 tablespoons of sugar while gradually increasing the speed to high and beat until the egg whites hold soft peaks but are not yet stiff.

9. Stir ¼ of the beaten whites into the soufflé base to lighten it and then transfer the mixture to a large bowl. Gently fold in the re-maining whites. Be very careful—for the best rise and the fluffiest texture you want to keep as much air in your soufflé mixture as possible.

10. Place the prepared ramekins on a large sheet pan and use a ladle or a large metal measuring cup to evenly divide the batter among them.

11. Place the sheet pan on the center rack of the oven. Immediately reduce the oven temperature to 375°F and bake for 20 to 25 min-utes or until a toothpick inserted into the middle of 1 of the soufflés comes out clean. If you like your soufflés creamy at the center as I do, remove them from the oven a bit sooner.

12. Serve immediately with the sweetened whipped cream or soft-ened ice cream.

Coconut Layer Cake

Yield: 12–14 servings

For the Batter

1½ cups granulated sugar, divided

2¼ cups sifted cake flour

1 tablespoon baking powder

1 teaspoon plus pinch fine sea salt, divided

½ cup neutral vegetable oil, such as canola

5 large egg yolks

½ cup freshly squeezed lemon juice

¼ cup freshly squeezed orange juice

1 teaspoon best-quality pure vanilla extract

8 large egg whites, room temperature

1½ teaspoons cream of tartar

For the Filling

5½ ounces instant vanilla pudding mix

1¼ cups whole milk

1 (7-ounce) package shredded sweet-ened coconut

2 cups heavy cream, very cold, whipped to soft peaks

For the Icing

2⅔ cups plus 4 teaspoons granulated sugar

½ cup cold water

4 large egg whites, room temperature

2 tablespoons light corn syrup

½ teaspoon cream of tartar

2 teaspoons best-quality pure vanilla extract

2 cups sweetened shredded coconut

1. Preheat the oven to 325°F. Grease and flour a 10-inch tube pan and set aside.

2. *Start the Batter:* Sift 1 cup of the sugar, the flour, the baking powder, and 1 teaspoon of the salt together into a large bowl or the bowl of a stand mixer fitted with the whisk attachment.

3. Set the stand or handheld mixer on low speed and add the oil, yolks, lemon and orange juices, and vanilla in that order. Mix until smooth, scraping down the sides of the bowl once or twice, and set aside.

4. In a separate bowl, use the handheld mixer set on low speed to beat the room temperature egg whites with the remaining pinch of salt for 1 minute, or until frothy. Add the cream of tartar and increase the speed to medium–low. Mix—continuing to slowly increase the mixer speed to medium and then medium–high—until the egg whites hold soft peaks but are not yet stiff.

5. Stir ¼ of the whipped whites into the flour mixture. Then, using a large rubber spatula, slowly and very gently fold the lightened flour mixture into the remaining whites until just homogenous. Do not overfold.

Fresh-squeezed citrus juices freeze perfectly for many months but begin to lose flavor if refrigerated for longer than 24 hours.

CONTINUED

Coconut Layer Cake for Easter

CONTINUED

6. Pour the batter into the prepared pan, smoothing the top with the rubber spatula. Rap once on your work surface to eliminate air bubbles.

7. Bake for 1 hour, or until the cake is golden and a toothpick inserted into the center comes out clean. Do not underbake.

8. Transfer the cake to a wire rack and let cool completely. Run a sharp knife around the outer and interior edges to loosen and remove from the pan.

9. *Make the Filling:* Stir together the instant pudding mix, milk, and shredded coconut in a medium bowl. Gently fold in the whipped cream and set aside.

10. Using a large knife, split the cake horizontally into 3 layers. The final cake will be upside down and the largest layer will be on the bottom.

11. Lay the bottom layer of the cake on a large cake plate. Spread ½ of the filling on top. Then add the second layer of cake and spread on the rest of the filling. Top with the third cake layer. Cover or wrap and refrigerate. (The cake will keep in the refrigerator at this point for up to 24 hours.)

12. *Start the Icing:* Place all the icing ingredients, except the vanilla and the coconut, in the top of a double boiler or in a metal bowl set over a pan of simmering water. Beat with a handheld electric mixer or a whisk until combined.

13. Still over simmering water, continue to beat with a hand held mixer on medium–high, for 7 minutes. Remove from the heat.

14. Using a stand mixer fitted with the whisk attachment or an electric handheld mixer set on high, beat until completely cool. When cool, add the vanilla and beat.

15. Spread the icing over the top and sides of cake. Pat the coconut over the icing. Cover and refrigerate. (This iced cake will keep in the refrigerator for up to 24 hours.)

16. Remove the cake from the refrigerator.

SERVE

AFTER THE MAIN COURSE

17. Slice at the table and serve.

This recipe comes from my
college roommate's mother.
Decades later, it's still my
favorite layer cake.

THANKSGIVING

DINNER FOR TWELVE

DISH	BEGIN PREP	PAGE
ENTRÉE		
Roast Turkey with Pan Gravy	3 days ahead	240
ON THE SIDE		
Cornbread Stuffing with Wilted Greens, Chorizo, and Roasted Garlic	3 days ahead	243
Cranberry–Tangerine Relish	1 week ahead	246
Grated Sweet Potato–Ginger Gratin	1 day ahead	247
Mushy Peas	3 days ahead	176
Mixed Green Salad	3 days ahead	248
DESSERT		
Pumpkin Crème Caramel	3 days ahead	249
Candied Pecan Tart	3 days ahead	251

Thanksgiving is essentially about people coming together to enjoy one another and a great meal. It's a day that does not involve gift giving, Easter baskets, fireworks, jack-o'-lanterns, or too much candy. And I find the absence of political and religious overtones to be a huge plus as well. For these reasons, among others, it's my favorite holiday.

For most people, the third Thursday in November is a happy time defined by a groaning board of sumptuous food. The following menu is no exception. I also love the fact that Thanksgiving is the one day of the year where potluck requests are the norm rather than the exception. As the host, you're on overload, so if you can foist part of the work off on others with impunity, why not? Parcel out the side dish and dessert recipes to the better cooks among the invitees and gleefully delete them from your to-do list. Alternatively—and if you feel you can gracefully accept whatever shows up—assign general recipe categories, such as salads, sides, condiments, desserts, to those who are game.

My Thanksgivings are always grand buffets preceded by cocktails, light nibbles, and/or Gravlax (p. 130). If, however, you're a stickler for a first course, serve the Arugula Salad with Green Apples (p. 143), the Wilted Spinach Salad (p. 171), or my go-to holiday fave: Mixed Lettuce Salad with Pears, Tarragon and Pomegranate–Hazelnut Vinaigrette (p. 258). They're not too heavy, and guests should still have an appetite when the main event rolls around.

At Thanksgiving, I generally serve traditional dishes, gently tweaked to provide interest and variety. I dry brine my Roast Turkey (p. 240) for maximum flavor and succulence and enhance basic Pan Gravy (p. 242) with tomato paste and cognac. I also lighten my Stuffing (p. 243) by replacing about a third of the bread with roasted vegetables and wilted greens, and I've added hefty doses of chorizo and smoked paprika to this one for extra pizzazz. Cranberry Relish (p. 246), adapted from a Laura Zarubin recipe, remains distinctively fresh and bright. The unusually short cooking time combined with the additions of tangerine juice and both fresh and candied ginger results in the best "cranberry sauce" I know.

If candied yams define your holiday, serve them by all means. Having eaten the dish a few too many times myself, I now opt for the spice-and-duck-fat-enhanced Sweet Potato–Ginger Gratin (p. 247) that master chef Jeremiah Tower taught me several years ago when we were cohosting Thanksgiving dinner. It's less sweet and a long-overdue, sophisticated alternative to marshmallow-laden yams. If you like your sweet potatoes simple and straightforward, substitute yams for the Yukon golds in the Quick Roast from Chapter 1 (p. 30). It's delicious and couldn't be easier, especially as the vegetables can be roasted earlier in the day and then reheated in time to serve.

A while back, I realized that frozen peas were a godsend and not just the item previously employed to lessen pain when I couldn't find an ice pack. They are now the one vegetable I actually prefer to buy frozen (if not taking garden peas straight from the vine to pot to table), especially since they're inexpensive and available everywhere, all year 'round. They bring a cheery touch of spring green to your table, even in the colder months, and Mushy Peas (p. 176)—my favorite pea dish of all time—is the perfect side dish to do just that at Thanksgiving.

When it comes to the turkey, a heritage or pasture-raised bird is optimal (but remember to plan ahead, as you'll probably have to order in advance from your butcher or online). In addition to brining (not requisite but suggested), you'll achieve extra-juicy white meat by roasting the bird breast-side down for the first two hours in the oven. And remember, for maximum succulence and to avoid a dry bird, the finished turkey will need to rest for at least 30 minutes before slicing.

A final suggestion: Enlist someone else to carve. This 11th-hour job is not for you, since you will be plenty busy scurrying around with your own last-minute chores.

Many—myself included—view dessert as the jewel in Thanksgiving's crown, and I believe that any serious holiday buffet requires several. If you feel overwhelmed, it's easy to purchase desserts or delegate them to others. If, however, you plan to prepare only one sweet treat yourself, make sure it's the Candied Pecan Tart (p. 251). The recipe is adapted from a drop-dead delicious walnut tart I used to adore at March, Wayne Nish's now-closed restaurant on Manhattan's Sutton Place. Unlike traditional pecan pies, it is almost pure nuts and contains no starchy filler. If pecans aren't your thing, try hazelnuts, almonds, or a nut mixture.

I can't resist a good crème caramel and look forward to this rich pumpkin version (p. 249) every November. The inclusion of pumpkin purée provides an ideal excuse to serve it at Thanksgiving.

If you're so inclined, complete the dessert buffet with an Apple Galette (p. 68) or easy streusel tart, Baked Alaska (p. 87), *Fané* (p. 177), Lemon Bombe (p. 101), Chocolate Mousse (p. 40), and/or the Devil's Food Cake from the Christmas menu (p. 264). I usually make the Vanilla Ice Cream Mold—also from the Christmas menu—as well to serve instead of plain vanilla ice cream or whipped cream with the Candied Pecan Tart and any other pies or cakes I add to the buffet.

THAWING YOUR TURKEY

If you weren't able to plan ahead and are stuck with a frozen turkey, remember that it must be thawed before roasting. For the best results, follow one of these methods:

1. Refrigerator Thawing

Thaw, breast side up, in an unopened wrapper on a tray in the fridge.

Allow at least 1 day of thawing for every 4 pounds.

2. Cold Water Thawing

Thaw, breast side down, in an unopened wrapper with enough cold water to cover your turkey completely.

Change water every 30 minutes to keep the turkey chilled.

Estimate a minimum thawing time of 30 minutes per pound.

ORDER OF PREPARATION

START

1 WEEK

1. Complete Steps 1 and 2 for the Cranberry–Tangerine Relish (p. 246). Cool, cover, and refrigerate.

3 DAYS

1. Complete Steps 1 and 2 for the Roast Turkey (p. 240), wrap, and refrigerate.

2. Complete Step 1 for the Crème Caramel (p. 249). Cool and store at room temperature.

3. Make the Cornbread (p. 245) for the Cornbread Stuffing (p. 243). Store, uncovered, at room temperature to become a bit stale.

4. Make the vinaigrette (p. 279) for the Mixed Green Salad (p. 248) and refrigerate.

5. Complete the Sweet Pie Crust (p. 293) for the Pecan Tart (p. 251), wrap, and store at room temperature.

2 DAYS

1. Complete Step 3 for the Turkey.

2. Make the Tart (Steps 1 through 4). Cool, wrap, and store at room temperature.

3. Complete Steps 1 and 2 for the Pan Gravy (p. 242). Cool, cover, and refrigerate.

4. Complete Steps 1 through 4 for the Stuffing. Cool, cover, and refrigerate.

1 DAY

1. Complete Step 1 for the Gratin (p. 247). Cover and refrigerate.

2. Complete Steps 2 through 5 for the Crème Caramel. Cool, cover, and refrigerate.

3. Complete Step 4 for the Turkey.

10 HOURS

1. Remove the Turkey from the refrigerator (Step 5).

6 HOURS

1. Preheat the oven to 500°F.

2. While the oven preheats, complete Steps 7 through 11 for the Turkey.

5½ HOURS

1. Complete Step 12 for the Turkey.

4 HOURS

1. Complete Step 13 for the Turkey.

2. Remove the Stuffing from the refrigerator (Step 5).

3½ HOURS

1. Complete Step 14 for the Turkey.

3 HOURS

1. Remove the Gratin from the refrigerator (Step 2).

2. Complete Steps 1 through 3 for the Mushy Peas (p. 176). Cool, cover, and set aside.

2½ HOURS

1. Complete Steps 15 for the Turkey.

2. Remove the vinaigrette for the Salad from the refrigerator.

1½ HOURS

1. While the Turkey is resting, complete Step 16.

2. Remove the Relish from the refrigerator (Step 3).

3. With racks adjusted the top and center positions, preheat the oven to 375°F.

50 MINS

1. Complete Step 7 for the Stuffing.
2. Complete Step 4 for the Gratin.
3. Complete Step 3 for the Gravy and set aside.

25 MINS

1. Complete Step 5 for the Gratin.

10 MINS

1. Complete Step 8 for the Stuffing and set aside.
2. Complete Step 4 for the Gravy.
3. Complete Step 1 for the Salad and set aside.

5 MINS

1. Complete Step 6 for the Gratin.

SERVE

1. Complete the Peas (Step 4) and the Relish (Step 4).
2. Complete Step 7 for the Gratin.
3. If reheating the Tart, reduce the oven temperature to 350°F.
4. Complete the Salad (Step 2) and place on the buffet.
5. Complete the Turkey (Step 17) and place on the buffet with the Gravy.
6. Place the Peas, Stuffing, Gratin, and Relish on the buffet.

AFTER THE MAIN COURSE

7. If reheating the Tart, complete Step 6.
8. Complete the Crème Caramel (Step 6).
9. Serve the Crème Caramel, Pecan Tart, and any optional desserts with the ice cream.

GET A HEAD START!

The cornbread for the **Stuffing** can be made in advance and frozen for at least 4 months.

The **Cranberry–Tangerine Relish** can be made at least 3 months ahead and refrigerated.

Make and refrigerate the vinaigrette for the **Mixed Green Salad** up to 2 weeks in advance.

The crust for the **Pecan Tart** can be made and frozen—prebaked or raw—at least 4 months in advance. Make the entire dessert, cool, wrap in foil, and store at room temperature for at least 4 days or freeze for at least 3 months. If frozen, thaw and reheat (to recrisp the crust) before serving. If refrigerated, you should also recrisp the crust before serving.

Roast Turkey with Pan Gravy

Yield: 12–14 main-course servings

To properly roast a turkey, you will need a roasting pan large enough to hold it, cheesecloth, an instant-read thermometer, and a bulb baster.

5 cloves garlic, minced

¼ cup kosher salt

2 tablespoons whole coriander seeds, crushed

2 tablespoons freshly ground black pepper

5 bay leaves, crumbled, divided

1 tablespoon granulated or brown sugar

1 tablespoon ground fennel

2 teaspoons dried thyme

1 (18–20 pound) fresh heritage or free-range turkey, rinsed in cool water and dried well

6 large carrots, trimmed, peeled, and coarsely chopped

6 ribs celery, trimmed, peeled, and coarsely chopped

2 large onions, trimmed and coarsely chopped

4 cloves garlic, coarsely chopped

½ bunch fresh thyme or 1 tablespoon dried thyme

½ cup chopped fresh Italian parsley and/or parsley stems

8–10 slices white bread (optional)

2 cups (4 sticks) unsalted butter

1 cup Madeira or port, divided

6 cups chicken or turkey stock, or more as needed, divided

1 recipe Pan Gravy (recipe follows), for serving

1. Mix the minced garlic, kosher salt, coriander seeds, pepper, 4 of the bay leaves, brown sugar, fennel, and dried thyme together.

2. Rub the mixture all over the outside of the turkey, inside the cavities, and under the skin where possible. Wrap the bird in a large unscented plastic bag, place in a large bowl, and refrigerate.

3. Turn the bag over and brine for 24 hours more.

4. Remove the bowl from the refrigerator, wipe the turkey with a damp cloth, and dry well. Place the turkey on a plate and return to the refrigerator, uncovered. Allow to air dry in the refrigerator.

5. Remove the turkey from the refrigerator.

6 HOURS

6. Preheat the oven to 500°F.

7. While the oven preheats, combine the carrots, celery, onions, chopped garlic, remaining bay leaf, fresh thyme, and parsley in a large bowl. Strew ¾ of the vegetable–herb mixture over the bottom of a large roasting pan. Rub the remaining vegetable–herb mixture around inside the turkey.

8. Place a rack in the pan on top of the vegetables and place the turkey, breast-side down, on the rack. To prevent rack marks, you can place the slices of bread on the rack under the turkey.

9. In a small saucepan set over medium heat, melt the butter with ½ cup of the Madeira. When the butter is melted, remove from the heat.

10. Pour 2 cups of the stock and the remaining ½ cup of Madeira into the bottom of the roasting pan over the vegetables.

11. Dip a large double thickness of cheesecloth in the melted butter mixture and drape it over the turkey. Reserve the remaining mixture in its pan.

Roasting will take approximately 3½–4 hours or about 11 minutes per pound.

5½ HOURS

12. Transfer the turkey in the oven and immediately reduce the oven temperature to 400°F. Roast for 1½ hours, basting every 20 to 25 minutes with pan drippings. As liquid evaporates, add the remaining stock to the drippings to dilute the fat and keep the vegetables from burning. If you run out of stock, continue with water.

4 HOURS

13. Reduce the oven temperature to 350°F and roast 30 minutes more.

3½ HOURS

14. Discard the cheesecloth. Turn the turkey breast side up, dip a fresh double thickness of cheesecloth in the melted butter mixture (remelt over medium heat, if necessary), and place it over the breast. If there is no butter left, dip the cheesecloth in the pan drippings. Continue to roast and baste for 1 hour more.

2½ HOURS

15. Begin to test for doneness by inserting an instant-read thermometer into the center of a thigh, making sure not to touch the bone. Continue roasting, basting, adding stock or water, and testing in the same manner until the thermometer registers 160°F. (This could take up to 1 hour more.) When done, transfer the turkey to a large cutting board, loosely tent with foil, and let rest at least 30 minutes and up to 2 hours.

CONTINUED

PAN GRAVY VARIATIONS

Mushroom: Add 1 pound of chopped, butter-sautéed mushrooms (white button, portobello, cremini, chanterelle, morel, or a mixture) to the finished gravy.

Truffle: Replace the 1 stick of unsalted butter with ¼ pound of Truffle Butter (p. 274). Add 2 extra tablespoons of Truffle Butter to the finished gravy, if desired.

Cream: Replace the 2 tablespoons of cognac with heavy cream or add the cream in addition to the alcohol.

Giblet: Add 1 cup chopped cooked giblets to the finished gravy.

Fresh Herb: Stir 4 tablespoons of chopped fresh sage, parsley, chives, or a combination into the finished gravy or into any of the variations.

Onion: Add 2 large chopped and caramelized onions to the finished gravy.

Roast Turkey with Pan Gravy

CONTINUED

16. While the turkey rests, pour the pan juices into a large Pyrex measuring cup or jar. Freeze or refrigerate. After 30 minutes, remove and discard the fat that has risen to the surface. Reserve the defatted juices for the Pan Gravy recipe.

17. Carve the turkey. Arrange the carved turkey on a large platter and, if desired, drizzle with some of the Pan Gravy. Transfer the rest of the gravy to a gravy boat and place on the buffet along with the turkey.

Pan Gravy

Yield: 3 cups

8 tablespoons (1 stick) unsalted butter or rendered chicken, duck, or turkey fat
1 medium onion, finely chopped
1–2 cloves garlic, thinly sliced
¼ cup all-purpose flour
1 teaspoon fine sea salt, or to taste

½ teaspoon freshly ground black pepper, or to taste
2½ cups reserved defatted turkey drippings mixed with chicken or turkey stock, plus more as stock as needed*
2 tablespoons double concentrated tomato paste
2 tablespoons cognac, port, or Madeira

1. Cook the butter, onion, and garlic in a large saucepan set over medium–low heat for 15 minutes, or until the onions are light gold.

2. Sprinkle the flour over the vegetables. Add the salt and pepper and stir to combine. Cook, stirring constantly, for 2 to 3 minutes. Cool, cover the pan, and refrigerate.

3. Remove the vegetable mixture from the refrigerator and reheat over medium–low heat. Whisk in the hot stock mixture, tomato paste, and cognac, and cook, stirring, for 4 to 5 minutes, or until thickened. The gravy should be the consistency of heavy cream. Add more stock if it's too thick. Taste and adjust the seasoning as needed. Set aside.

4. Reheat the gravy over low heat, taking care that it does not come above a simmer. Remove from the heat and cover to keep warm if not using right away.

* If the drippings are extremely salty, use less drippings and more stock.

Cornbread Stuffing with Wilted Greens, Chorizo, and Roasted Garlic

Yield: 12–14 side-dish servings

20–30 whole cloves garlic, peeled

3 medium onions, cut into 1-inch dice

2 large celeriac (celery root), peeled and cut into ½-inch dice

1 cup (16 tablespoons) extra virgin olive oil, divided

¾ cups chicken or turkey stock, plus more as needed

1 pound thickly sliced bacon, cut cross-wise into ½-inch strips

¾ pound chorizo, very thinly sliced

1 large onion, roughly chopped

2½ teaspoons smoked Spanish paprika, plus more to taste

6 large bunches chard, rinsed, trimmed, and cut into horizontal ½-inch ribbons

3 recipes Cornbread (recipe follows), stale and crumbled

10 cups stale white bread crumbs, plus more or minus enough to equal 28 cups when combined with the crumbled cornbread

Fine sea salt and freshly ground black pepper, to taste

1. Preheat the oven to 425°F.

2. On a sheet pan or in a large, shallow roasting pan, toss the garlic, diced onions, and celeriac with 10 tablespoons of the olive oil. Roast, tossing occasionally, for 30 to 45 minutes, or until caramelized and tender. When done, remove from the oven and stir the stock into the vegetables, scraping up any bits on the bottom of the pan. Set aside.

3. Place the bacon in a large casserole or Dutch oven and cook over medium–low heat for 5 to 8 minutes, or until about ½ the fat is rendered. Raise the heat to medium–high, add the remaining 6 tablespoons of olive oil and the chorizo, and cook, stirring frequently, for 2 to 4 minutes, or until the chorizo is lightly colored. Add the chopped onion and smoked paprika and cook for 5 minutes, or until the onion begins to color. Raise the heat to high, add the chard, and cook, tossing frequently, for 5 to 8 minutes, or until the chard is wilted and tender.

4. Remove from the heat and toss in the cornbread and white breadcrumbs and the roasted vegetables. Taste and adjust salt, pepper, and smoked paprika as needed and toss. Do not pack down. If too dry, add more stock. Cool, cover, and refrigerate. (You do not need to refrigerate if baking right away.)

The stuffing can also be baked in 2 very large gratin dishes covered with foil. The advantage here is that they will take only about 20 minutes to cook.

CONTINUED

Cornbread Stuffing with Wilted Greens, Chorizo, and Roasted Garlic

CONTINUED

 4 HOURS
5. Remove from refrigerator.

 1½ HOURS
6. With a rack adjusted to the center position, preheat the oven to 375°F.

 50 MINS
7. Bake, covered with foil, for about 40 minutes, or until piping hot.

 10 MINS
8. When done, remove from the oven and set aside or keep in a turned off oven with the door ajar for up to 20 minutes.

 SERVE
9. Remove the foil and serve hot or very warm from the casserole.

Cornbread

Yield: 8 servings

1¾ cups stoneground cornmeal (white or yellow)

1 tablespoon granulated sugar

1 teaspoon baking powder

1 teaspoon baking soda

1 teaspoon fine sea salt

2 large eggs, lightly beaten, room temperature

2 cups buttermilk, room temperature

1 tablespoon unsalted butter or bacon fat

Leftovers are good wrapped in foil and re-warmed in a 300°F oven.

3 DAYS

1. With a rack adjusted to the highest position, preheat the oven to 450°F.

2. Whisk the cornmeal, sugar, baking powder, baking soda, and salt together in a large bowl.

3. In another bowl, whisk the eggs together with the buttermilk.

4. Add the buttermilk mixture to the dry ingredients and whisk just until combined.

5. Place the fat in a heavy 9-inch cast iron skillet (in a pinch, use an 8-inch square baking pan) and transfer to the oven. When the fat melts and begins to smoke, quickly pour in the batter and return to the oven.

6. Bake for 20 to 25 minutes, or until the top is brown and a tooth-pick inserted in the center comes out clean. Cool on a wire rack if not serving right away.

If not using this cornbread for the stuffing, cut into wedges and serve immediately. Alternatively, cool on a wire rack and wrap in foil. Store at room temperature for 1 day, in the fridge for 3 days, or freeze for up to 4 months.

Cranberry–Tangerine Relish

Yield: 1½ quarts

2 cups firmly packed dark brown sugar

1½ cups water

1½ cups freshly squeezed tangerine juice

1 cup granulated sugar

1 cup candied ginger, cut into ⅛-inch dice

¼ cup apple cider vinegar

5 tablespoons grated fresh ginger

1 (4-inch) cinnamon stick

Pinch fine sea salt

2½ pounds fresh cranberries

If you don't have access to tangerines, use freshly squeezed orange juice instead.

1 WEEK

1. Combine everything, except the cranberries, in a large saucepan set over medium heat. Partially cover, bring to a simmer, and then cook for 10 minutes.

2. Add the cranberries and bring to a boil. Reduce the heat to medium–low and simmer for 8 minutes. Remove from the heat. Remove and discard the cinnamon stick. Cool completely. Cover and refrigerate if not using within a few hours. (The relish will keep in the refrigerator for at least 3 months.)

1½ HOURS

3. Remove from the refrigerator.

SERVE

4. Transfer to a serving bowl and serve at room temperature.

Grated Sweet Potato–Ginger Gratin

Yield: 12 side-dish servings

6 pounds sweet potatoes or yams, peeled and coarsely grated

10 cloves garlic, grated or finely minced

5–6 tablespoons extra virgin olive oil

3 tablespoons all-purpose flour

3 tablespoons freshly grated ginger

1 tablespoon ground cardamom

Fine sea salt and freshly ground black pepper, to taste

8 tablespoons duck fat, chicken fat, or butter

¾ cup white bread crumbs mixed with 5 tablespoons melted unsalted butter

¼ cup chopped fresh Italian parsley

1. Toss the sweet potatoes, garlic, oil, flour, ginger, cardamom, salt, and pepper, together in a large gratin dish. Spread evenly but don't compact. Put several dollops of the fat or butter on top, evenly spaced. Cover tightly with foil and refrigerate. (This will keep at room temperature for up to 3 hours.)

2. Remove the gratin dish from the refrigerator.

3. With a rack adjusted to the top position, preheat the oven to 375°F.

4. Bake, still covered, for 25 minutes.

5. Uncover and toss. Recover and bake for 20 minutes more, or until tender.

6. Remove the foil and raise the oven temperature to 475°F. Sprinkle the breadcrumb–butter mixture over the potatoes and place on the top rack of the oven. Alternatively, run under the broiler to brown. Bake or broil for a few minutes, or until golden. Watch carefully so the topping doesn't burn.

7. Remove from the oven and set aside or leave in the turned off oven with the door ajar to stay warm. Serve hot or very warm from the gratin dish.

Mixed Green Salad

Yield: 12 servings

If you prefer, add butter lettuce, romaine, and/or mâche to the mix or add or substitute greens of your choice.

4 Belgian endives

2 radicchios, very roughly chopped

1 large frisée, very roughly chopped or torn into bite-sized pieces

3 bulbs fennel, thinly sliced

8 cups baby arugula

1 recipe for vinaigrette of choice (p. 279)

1. Thinly slice the endives. Transfer to a large salad bowl along with the radicchios, frisée, fennel, and arugula. Set aside.

2. Toss with enough vinaigrette to moisten and flavor. Taste and adjust the seasoning.

3. Serve right away.

Pumpkin Crème Caramel

Yield: 12 servings

1 cup granulated sugar, for caramelizing the dish

¼ cup water, for caramelizing the dish

¾ cup granulated sugar, divided

2 teaspoons ground ginger

2 teaspoons ground cinnamon

Large pinch fine sea salt

2 cups canned pumpkin purée

10 large eggs, room temperature and lightly beaten

3 cups evaporated milk

6 tablespoons water

5 tablespoons dark rum

1 tablespoon best-quality pure vanilla extract

3 DAYS

1. Melt the 1 cup of sugar with the ¼ cup of water in a medium saucepan set over low heat until a dark caramel forms. Pour immediately into a rectangular or oval 8-inch ×16-inch ceramic gratin dish or low baking dish, tilting quickly to coat bottom of the dish evenly before the caramel hardens. Set aside to cool and store at room temperature.

1 DAY

2. Preheat the oven to 350°F.

3. Using a stand mixer fitted with the paddle attachment or an electric handheld mixer set on low speed, combine the ¾ cup of sugar, the ginger, the cinnamon, and the salt. Add the pumpkin purée and eggs and raise speed to medium. Add the evaporated milk, water, rum, and vanilla. Mix well and pour into the caramelized gratin dish.

4. Carefully place the gratin dish inside a larger baking dish and transfer to the oven. Pour boiling water into the larger baking dish to come half way up the sides of the crème caramel dish (a bain-marie). Bake about 1¼ hours, or just until a knife inserted into center comes out clean. Don't overcook.

5. Let cool. When completely cool, cover, and refrigerate. (This will keep for up to 2 days in the refrigerator.)

SERVE

AFTER FINISHING THE MAIN COURSE

6. When ready to serve, run a spatula around the edges of the custard and invert onto a serving dish, pouring accumulated caramel syrup on top. Serve lukewarm, cold, or at room temperature.

Candied Pecan Tart

Yield: 12 small servings

1 pound pecan halves or pieces
4 tablespoons unsalted butter
6 tablespoons dark brown sugar
1 tablespoon granulated sugar
Large pinch fine sea salt
3 tablespoons fragrant honey

6 tablespoons heavy cream
1 prebaked Sweet Pie Crust (p. 293) or (10-inch) store-bought prebaked pie crust
Store-bought best-quality vanilla ice cream, for serving (optional)

2 DAYS

1. Preheat the oven to 350°F.

2. Place pecans on a sheet pan and toast for 10 minutes, or until very hot. Be careful they don't burn.

3. Meanwhile, in a large saucepan set over medium heat, melt the butter with the brown and granulated sugars and salt. Add the honey and simmer for 5 minutes, or until lightly caramelized or a candy thermometer registers 250°F. Remove from the heat. Add the cream and the still-hot nuts. Stir well. If necessary, return to low heat to reliquify and combine.

4. Pour the nut mixture into the prebaked pie crust, even it out, and bake for 15 to 20 minutes, or until the center bubbles a bit. Let rest for 20 minutes before serving or cool completely, wrap in foil, and store at room temperature.

SERVE

5. If reheating , preheat the oven to 350°F.

AFTER FINISHING THE MAIN COURSE

6. If reheating, bake for about 5 minutes.

7. Serve warm or at room temperature with the vanilla ice cream, if using.

Other than many fresh fruit pies, most pies can be assembled 24 hours in advance and stashed in the fridge to be baked off when needed. This is also true for lasagnas and other baked pastas, many of which can even be frozen for 3 months—and then thawed—before baking.

This pie divides into 12 very small pieces. However, with ice cream and crème caramel—let alone samplings of other buffet desserts—this should be plenty. If, however, this is the only dessert you are serving, for 12 people you might consider doubling the recipe and baking 2 pies.

CHRISTMAS

DINNER FOR TWELVE

DISH	BEGIN PREP	PAGE
FIRST COURSE		
Mixed Lettuce Salad with Pears, Tarragon, and Pomegranate–Hazelnut Vinaigrette	1 week ahead	258
ENTRÉE		
Prime Rib Roast with Pan Juices and Horseradish Cream Sauce	4 days ahead	259
ON THE SIDE		
Fresh-Herbed Popovers	45 mins ahead	261
Creamed Spinach Gratin	1 day ahead	262
Caramelized Cauliflower with Crispy Capers	6½ ahead	263
Wheel of Stilton and a Bowl of Fresh Pears with a Selection of Breads and Crackers (optional)		
DESSERT		
Devil's Food Layer Cake with Double Fudge Frosting	1 week ahead	264
Vanilla Ice Cream Mold	1 week ahead	

This quintessential Christmas dinner kicks off with a gorgeous Mixed Lettuce Salad (p. 258) that is my go-to starter for the entire winter season. Lettuces in all shades of green are set off by pomegranate seeds glistening like rubies. Toasted hazelnuts, ripe pears, and a tangy vinaigrette guarantee more than just good looks. This is the best kind of holiday starter, satisfying but leaving an appetite for the feast to follow. When in a more casual mood (or when running low on plates!), I sometimes omit the first course altogether and place the salad on the main buffet instead. When a more substantial starter or a lunch main course is called for, add bite-sized pieces of poultry or shrimp. In any case, the salad is a winner— versatile and, with seasonal adaptations, useful all year long.

If you're not hosting Christmas dinner, create the same menu for New Year's Eve or New Year's Day instead. To ring in the new year, however, serve Champagne—or even a Cava or Prosecco cocktail—before dinner along with the best caviar you can afford. For much less money—and only a little bit more work—make and serve Gravlax (p. 130) instead.

The salad, beef, sides, desserts, and an optional cheese course should be more than enough food for even a football team, but if for some reason you want more, include the Pan-Roast of Root Vegetables (p. 67). It's quick and easy and will certainly put the kibosh on any residual hunger.

Prime Rib (p. 259) for Christmas dinner is traditional, tasty, and always welcome. And miraculously, the timing in the recipe works for any size roast, so depending on the size of your party, you can scale up or down without having to rethink. For those who want a change of pace, however, the Mustard-Coated Leg of Lamb (p. 225) from the Easter menu is appropriate—and delicious—here as well.

There are recipes for three delectable sides to offer with the meat. If three is more than you can manage, omit one. But don't omit the Popovers (p. 261). As amusing as they are scrumptious, popovers have always gone hand in hand with roast beef. Though I should be used to the process by now, I'm still awed each time the baking batter swells and "pops over" the top of the muffin tin to form oversized, moist, and enticingly eggy creations. Fresh herbs enliven this version, but leave them out if you prefer or add coarsely grated cheese and/or crumbled bacon instead.

Enhancing the Caramelized Cauliflower (p. 263) with a scattering of crispy capers raises the dish far above any reasonable expectations for a this humble vegetable. Another huge plus: this meltingly tender pan-roast—like so many recipes in this book—can be made earlier in the day and served at room temperature or reheated briefly in a hot oven.

The Creamed Spinach Gratin (p. 262) is my redo of a *New York Times* recipe I've been making for 30 years and ideal for entertaining, as it can be prepared a couple of days in advance and refrigerated until needed. With hints of nutmeg, garlic, and sage, and lots of onion, butter, and cream cheese, it's voluptuously hedonistic. However, if a less rich veggie sounds somewhat saner, a double recipe of Mushy Peas (p. 176) from the Candlelight Soirée menu slips into this menu seamlessly.

A wheel of perfectly aged Stilton, the richest and creamiest of all the blue cheeses, is always an integral part of my annual Christmas festivities. Though hardly requisite, I serve it right before offering the dessert buffet or as a buffet component along with pears, a basket of interesting breads and crackers, and a bottle of Bordeaux or a good port. Some people prefer celery sticks, but I find the floral sweetness of a perfectly ripe pear to be the ideal match for Stilton's salty pungency, peppery veining, and buttery fullness. For spring dinners or Easter lunch, omit it as without the cold weather appeal, it is overly heavy, and the gesture falls flat.

For those of you who love a decadently dark chocolate layer cake, the Devil's Food Cake (p. 264) is as good as it gets. Like the Coconut Cake in the Easter menu—and in a very American sort of way—a devil's food cake derives much of its bang from the frosting. This cake recipe comes from Ruth Reichl, who frosts her creation with Marshmallow Icing (p. 232). However, for the richest, most chocolaty version of the classic, I prefer a dark, fudgy frosting instead—although I sometimes go overboard and fill the cake with fudge and slather the Marshmallow Icing on the top and sides.

Like most cake layers, these can be made in advance and frozen. Assemble and ice the cake up to 3 days before needed and store at room temperature.

Hard as it is for me to fathom, I do know that some people are not addicted to chocolate and some don't even like it. If you fall into one of those sad categories, never fear. There are a number of other desserts that will also brilliantly culminate this special meal. Try the Apple Galette (p. 68), Raspberry–Nectarine Tart (p. 79) (but use my suggestions for apple or pear), Coconut Layer Cake (p. 231), or the Candied Pecan Tart (p. 251) among others. Any one or a combination of these cakes and pies is great accompanied by the Vanilla Ice Cream Mold. So many desserts cry out for à la mode and this "bombe" is genius. It takes just moments to smash softened vanilla ice cream into a metal bowl and pop it in the freezer where it can wait for many weeks before consuming. Once unmolded, it's infinitely more impressive and hostess-friendly than ice cream spooned from cartons or dumped into a serving bowl last minute.

Remember, as with Thanksgiving, guests love to bring desserts to Christmas dinner. So if you're feeling overwhelmed—or even just a bit tired or lazy—get other people to bring the cakes and pies. But do provide ice cream or whipped cream.

Need a meatless main dish for your holiday gala? Try the Cioppino (p. 85) from Chapter 2. It is ideal for those of you who—like the Italians—choose to eat seafood on Christmas, but it's genius for everyone else as well. The casual fish stew contrasts nicely with the rich turkey, goose, lamb, or prime rib most probably scheduled for Christmas dinner.

If there are vegetarians in your mix, consider the Baked Pasta with Asparagus (p. 139) as a holiday main course accompanied by a green salad. Start the meal with a beautifully garnished Tomato–Cumin Soup (p. 74), and follow with a wheel of Stilton and ripe pears. Even the most discriminating diners—vegetarian or otherwise—will feel celebrated and certainly won't go home hungry.

ORDER OF PREPARATION

START

1 WEEK

1. Transfer softened vanilla ice cream into a metal bowl or mold and place in the freezer.

2. Make the Pomegranate–Hazelnut Vinaigrette for the Mixed Lettuce Salad (p. 258) and refrigerate.

3. Complete Steps 1 through 6 for the Devil's Food Cake (p. 264). Cool, wrap, and freeze.

4 DAYS

1. Make the Horseradish Cream Sauce (p. 260). Cover and refrigerate.

2 DAYS

1. Place a serving platter in the freezer for at least 15 minutes.

2. Rest the ice cream mold in a basin of very hot water for 15 seconds and then immediately invert onto the cold platter. Cover tightly with foil and return to the freezer.

1 DAY

1. Complete Steps 1 through 5 for the Spinach Gratin (p. 262). Cool, cover, and refrigerate.

2. Complete Step 1 for the Prime Rib (p. 259). Cover and refrigerate.

3. Complete Steps 7 through 11 for the Cake, cover, and store at room temperature.

9 HOURS

1. Remove the Prime Rib from the refrigerator (Step 2).

6½ HOURS

1. Preheat the oven to 350°F.

2. Complete Steps 2 through 5 for the Cauliflower (p. 263) and set aside.

5 HOURS

1. With a rack adjusted to the second lowest position, raise the oven temperature to 375°F.

2. Complete Step 4 for the Prime Rib.

4 HOURS

1. Complete Step 5 for the Prime Rib. Do not open the oven.

2. Remove the Gratin from the refrigerator (Step 6).

3. Remove the Stilton and the pears from the refrigerator, if using.

2 HOURS

1. Complete Step 6 for the Prime Rib.

2. Remove the Pomegranate–Hazelnut Vinaigrette from the refrigerator.

3. Remove the Horseradish Sauce from the refrigerator.

75 MINS

1. Complete Steps 7 and 8 for the Prime Rib.

45 MINS

1. With racks adjusted to the top and bottom positions, raise the oven temperature to 450°F.

2. While the oven comes to temperature, complete Steps 2 through 6 for the Popovers (p. 261). Then complete Step 7.

10 MINS

1. Reduce the oven temperature to 350°F and complete Step 8 for the Popovers and Step 8 the Gratin.

SERVE

1. Make the Mixed Lettuce Salad and serve.

2. When done, remove the Popovers (Step 9) and Gratin (Step 9) from the oven. One or both may finish before the end of the First Course.

3. If reheating the Cauliflower, make sure the oven is at 350°F.

AFTER THE FIRST COURSE

4. If reheating the Cauliflower, complete Step 7.

5. Complete the Prime Rib (Step 9) and serve with the Horseradish Sauce, Popovers, Spinach, and Cauliflower.

AFTER FINISHING THE MAIN COURSE

6. Remove the unmolded ice cream from the freezer to soften.

7. Complete the Cake (Step 12).

8. Place the Cake, Ice Cream Mold, and if including, the Stilton and pears on the buffet.

GET A HEAD START!

The vinaigrette for the **Mixed Lettuce Salad** can be made up to 2 weeks in advance and refrigerated. The nuts can be toasted 1 week in advance and stored, covered, in the refrigerator.

The **Horseradish Sauce** can be made up to 4 days in advance and refrigerated.

The **Popover** batter can be made up to 2 days ahead and refrigerated. Remove it from the fridge 2 hours before baking and give it a quick whisk just before making the popovers.

The **Creamed Spinach Gratin** can be made through Step 5 up to 2 days ahead and refrigerated.

The layers for the **Devil's Food Cake** can be made up to 2 months ahead and frozen. The entire dessert can be made up to 3 days in advance and stored at room temperature.

You can transfer the **vanilla ice cream** to the mold and freeze for at least 2 weeks.

Mixed Lettuce Salad with Pears, Tarragon, and Pomegranate– Hazelnut Vinaigrette

Yield: 12 first-course servings

You can replace the hazelnuts with another nut of your choice. Just be sure to swap out the hazelnut oil in the vinaigrette for an oil that matches the nut.

12 handfuls baby arugula

2 medium heads frisée

2 small fennel bulbs, trimmed and julienned

2 Belgian endives, sliced crosswise

2 pears or apples, very thinly sliced

⅔ cup coarsely chopped, toasted, and skinned hazelnuts

Seeds from 1 large pomegranate

Leaves from ½ bunch fresh tarragon

1 recipe Pomegranate–Hazelnut Vinaigrette (recipe follows), room temperature

You can remove the seeds from the pomegranates up to 3 days in advance and refrigerate in a covered container until needed.

SERVE

1. Toss all the salad ingredients in a large salad bowl with enough of the Pomegranate–Hazelnut Vinaigrette to moisten and flavor. Taste and adjust the seasoning as needed.

2. Serve.

Pomegranate–Hazelnut Vinaigrette

Yield: About 1½ cups

If you've bought your hazelnuts with their skins still on, you can skin and toast them at the same time. Spread the nuts in a single layer on a sheet pan, place in the center of a 350°F oven and bake for about 10 minutes, or until the skins begin to blister. While still hot, wrap the nuts in a kitchen towel and let them steam for 1 minute. Use the towel to rub off the loose skins, but don't worry about those that don't come off. Cool completely.

¾ cup extra virgin olive oil

¼ cup red wine vinegar

4 tablespoons hazelnut oil

3 tablespoons sherry or balsamic vinegar

2 teaspoons pomegranate molasses (optional but suggested)

1 large shallot, minced or very thinly sliced

1 clove garlic, minced

1–2 sprigs fresh thyme

Fine sea salt and freshly ground black pepper, to taste

1 WEEK

1. Place all vinaigrette ingredients in a lidded jar and shake vigorously until well combined. Set aside for at least 1 hour to let flavors marry. Taste and adjust the seasoning as needed.

2. Use right away or refrigerate for up to 2 weeks. Bring to room temperature and reshake the jar before using.

Prime Rib Roast with Pan Juices and Horseradish Cream Sauce

Yield: 12 generous main-course servings

1 (12-pound) well-marbled, dry-aged, bone-in prime rib roast*

3 tablespoons kosher salt, or more to taste

2 tablespoons freshly ground black pepper, or more to taste

1–2 teaspoons dried thyme

15 cloves garlic, cut vertically into 2 or 3 slices each

1 recipe Horseradish Sauce (recipe follows), room temperature, for serving

> This roast feeds 12, but you can make a smaller or bigger roast using the exact same recipe and timing. It's miraculous and foolproof.

1. Place the prime rib in a low-sided roasting pan just large enough to hold it comfortably. Combine the salt, pepper, and thyme and liberally rub the seasoning all over the roast. Using a small, sharp knife, make small slits in the fatty part of the meat and between the ribs. Stick the garlic slices in all the slits. If you need to, make additional cuts until you've used up all the garlic. Cover and refrigerate overnight.

2. Remove the prime rib from the refrigerator.

3. With a rack adjusted to the second lowest position, preheat the oven to 375°F.

4. Roast for 45 minutes.

5. Turn the oven off, but *do not open it*. Leave the meat in the turned off oven for at least 2 hours.

6. Without opening the oven, turn the temperature back to 375°F and cook the prime rib for 45 more minutes.

CONTINUED

* Be sure to ask the butcher to crack between the bones for easier carving. Otherwise, you won't be able to cut the ribs apart.

Prime Rib Roast with Pan Juices and Horseradish Cream Sauce

CONTINUED

Even better than an instant-read thermometer is a digital thermometer that you can leave in the meat while it cooks. You read the temperature outside the oven and you know exactly what is going on inside. In Step 7, you'll know when the meat is done without having to open the door and check.

75 MINS

7. Open the oven and begin checking the prime rib's temperature with an instant-read thermometer. It should register 118°F to 120°F. To keep the heat from escaping, do this as quickly as possible and don't keep the oven door open while you do it.

8. When it reaches temperature, remove the prime rib from oven and let it rest for at least 30 and up to 90 minutes. Resting is *very* important, as it allows the meat to finish cooking and the juices to redistribute.

SERVE

AFTER THE FIRST COURSE

9. Carve and serve from the cutting board (the meat will stay warmer) or transfer to a warm (if possible) serving platter and serve with the pan juices and the Horseradish Sauce.

Horseradish Cream Sauce

Yield: About 2 cups

If fresh horseradish is unavailable, use drained bottled white horseradish for this sauce instead.

9 tablespoons freshly grated horseradish
½ cup Hellman's or Basic Mayonnaise (p. 275)

1 cup crème fraîche or sour cream
Fine sea salt and freshly ground black pepper, to taste

4 DAYS

1. Combine all the ingredients in a small serving bowl, cover, and refrigerate. Bring to room temperature, taste, and adjust seasoning before serving.

Fresh-Herbed Popovers

Yield: 12–16 side-dish servings

8 large eggs, room temperature

3 cups milk, lukewarm

1¼ teaspoons fine sea salt

3 cups all-purpose flour

6 tablespoons unsalted butter, melted

½ cup fresh Italian parsley, basil, tarragon, chervil, chives, or a mixture

⅓ cup chopped shallot (optional)

45 MINS

1. With a rack adjusted to the bottom position, preheat the oven to 450°F. (The top of the fully risen popovers should come about midway up the oven. You don't want the tops of the popovers to be too close to the top of the oven and burn.)

2. While the oven preheats, place the eggs in a bowl of hot water. After 10 minutes, crack them into a large bowl.

3. Thoroughly and generously grease a standard or nonstick metal 12-cup muffin pan with olive oil, meat grease, or butter, covering the area between the cups as well as the cups themselves. Set aside. Make sure the oven is up to temperature before you continue with the popover batter.

4. Whisk the milk and salt into the eggs until well combined.

5. Add the flour, all at once, and whisk until frothy. There should be no large lumps in the batter but small ones are fine.

6. Add the melted butter, the fresh herbs and, if using, the shallot. Whisk just to combine.

7. Pour the batter into the prepared muffin cups, filling them almost full. Bake for 20 minutes without opening the oven door.

10 MINS

8. Reduce the heat to 350°F and bake for an additional 10 to 20 minutes, until the popovers are deep, golden brown. If they seem to be browning too quickly, lay a piece of aluminum foil loosely over the top.

SERVE

9. Remove from the oven and immediately stick the tip of a knife into the top of each popover to release steam and help prevent sogginess. Transfer to a breadbasket.

AFTER THE FIRST COURSE

10. Serve right away or set aside until ready to serve.

If you have two ovens, use 2 standard or nonstick 12-cup metal muffin pans but only fill every other cup. This will allow the popovers more room to potentially grow larger and become more regularly shaped.

I like to use a stand mixer fitted with the whisk attachment or an electric handheld mixer to make the batter. Whisk at high speed for 20 seconds. Stop, scrape the sides of the bowl, and whisk for an additional 20 to 30 seconds at high speed, until frothy.

Creamed Spinach Gratin

Yield: 12 side-dish servings

6 (10-ounce) packages frozen spinach, thawed

1 cup (2 sticks) unsalted butter, divided

1 large onion, finely chopped

4 cloves garlic, minced

¼ teaspoon freshly grated nutmeg

Fine sea salt and freshly ground black pepper, to taste

2 (8-ounce) packages cream cheese, cut into small pieces, room temperature

1½ cups ¼-inch cubes crustless stale white bread

1 teaspoon ground sage or 1 tablespoon julienned fresh sage leaves

1. Squeeze the water out of the thawed spinach and set aside.

2. In a large skillet set over medium heat, sauté the onion with 1 stick of the butter until it begins to color. Add the garlic, nutmeg, salt, pepper, and spinach and sauté 2 to 3 minutes, stirring occasionally, until very hot.

3. Stir in the cream cheese until melted and well combined. Transfer the mixture to a large gratin dish.

4. Melt the remaining 1 stick of butter in a sauté pan set over medium heat. Toss with the bread cubes and sage. Sprinkle this mixture over the spinach.

5. Set aside. When completely cool, cover, and refrigerate.

6. Remove the gratin from the refrigerator.

7. With a rack adjusted to the top position, preheat the oven to 350°F. (The oven will be at 450°F for the popovers if you are following the Order of Preparation chart. This is fine, as the temperature is reduced to 350°F when it's time to put in the gratin.)

8. Bake for 20 to 30 minutes, or until hot, bubbly, and lightly browned. Watch carefully and if browning too quickly, cover loosely with a piece of aluminum foil.

SERVE

9. Remove from the oven and set aside or leave in the turned off oven with the door ajar to stay warm.

AFTER FIRST COURSE

10. Serve hot or warm from the gratin dish.

Caramelized Cauliflower with Crispy Capers

Yield: 12 side-dish servings

3 large heads cauliflower, trimmed, room temperature

1½ cups extra virgin olive oil

4 tablespoons anchovy paste, or to taste

Fine sea salt and freshly ground black pepper, to taste

1 cup large capers, rinsed in cool water and well drained

6½ HOURS

1. Preheat the oven to 350°F.

2. While the oven preheats, with the help of a sharp, heavy knife, cut and break the cauliflower into large florets and chunks. Set aside.

3. Whisk the oil and anchovy paste together in a small skillet. Transfer ¾ of the mixture to the bowl with the cauliflower, season generously with salt and pepper and toss well. Place the cauliflower florets and chunks in a single layer on 2 or 3 sheet pans. Drizzle with any oil left in the bowl.

4. Bake, tossing occasionally, for 30 to 40 minutes, or until tender and a bit caramelized.

5. Add the capers to the remaining oil mixture in the skillet and warm over low heat. Stir and pour over the cauliflower. Bake, stirring once or twice, for 5 more minutes. Remove from the oven and set aside.

SERVE

6. If serving warm, preheat the oven to 350°F.

AFTER THE FIRST COURSE

7. If serving warm, bake for 5 to 10 minutes.

8. Transfer to a serving bowl and serve warm or at room temperature.

Devil's Food Layer Cake with Double Fudge Frosting

Yield: 12 generous servings

For the Batter

1 cup whole milk

¾ cup unsweetened cocoa powder

⅓ cup granulated sugar

1 cup (2 sticks) unsalted butter, room temperature

1 cup dark brown sugar

3 eggs, room temperature

1 cup sour cream, room temperature

1 teaspoon best-quality pure vanilla extract

2 cups sifted cake flour

1½ teaspoons baking soda

⅛ teaspoon fine sea salt

For the Frosting

6 squares (6 ounces) unsweetened chocolate

¾ cup (1½ sticks) unsalted butter

1½ pounds (1½ boxes) sifted confectioners' sugar

Pinch fine sea salt

¾ cup whole milk

1 tablespoon best-quality pure vanilla extract

When combining dry ingredients to add to a batter, I like to sift them onto a sheet of waxed paper or parchment paper and then fold and lift the paper to add to the batter.

SIFTING FLOUR

"2 cups flour, sifted" means you measure before sifting.

"2 cups sifted flour" means you sift before measuring.

Hard as it is to believe, it does make a difference!

1. Preheat oven to 350°F.

2. *Start the Batter:* Generously grease and flour 2 (9-inch) layer cake pans and set aside.

3. Bring the milk to a simmer in a small saucepan set over medium heat. Remove from the heat and whisk the cocoa and then the sugar into the warm milk. Set aside.

4. Using a stand mixer fitted with the paddle attachment or an electric handheld mixer set on medium–high speed, cream the butter with the brown sugar. Add the eggs, sour cream, and vanilla. Beat, occasionally scraping down the sides of the bowl with a rubber spatula, for 3 to 5 minutes, or until light and fluffy. Reduce to low speed, add the cocoa mixture, and beat until combined.

5. Sift the flour, baking soda, and salt together. With the motor off, add to the creamed butter mixture. Beat on low speed until just combined. Do not overbeat.

6. Turn into the prepared pans and bake for 25 to 30 minutes, or until the cake layers shrink slightly from sides of pans and spring back when touched gently in the center. Cool on a wire rack for 3 to 4 minutes, then invert onto the wire rack to cool completely. Individually wrap the cake layers in aluminum foil and, if not using within 3 days, freeze until needed.

7. If frozen, remove the cake layers from the freezer and set aside for at least 2 hours.

8. *Start the Frosting:* Melt the chocolate together with the butter, stirring frequently, over very low heat. Remove from heat just before completely melted and set aside.

9. Using a stand mixer fitted with the paddle attachment or an electric handheld mixer set on low speed, beat the sugar, salt, milk, and vanilla. Add the hot chocolate mixture and beat on low speed over ice water until the frosting has reached a spreadable consistency. Alternatively, skipping the ice water is fine, but the cooling will take longer.

10. Place one thawed cake layer on a serving platter and cover with ¼ of the frosting. Top with the second layer and spread the remaining frosting over the top and sides of cake.

11. Store, covered, at room temperature until ready to serve or for up to 3 days.

AFTER THE MAIN COURSE

12. Place the cake on the buffet. Slice and serve as needed.

SERVE

CAKE FLOUR

It's easy to make your own cake flour. Sift 5¼ cups of all-purpose flour together with ¾ cup of cornstarch 6 times. You will have approximately 6 cups of cake flour. You can scale up or down depending on the recipe. I like to make extra and keep it in a canister for the next cake.

Tip!

This may be too much frosting, but having to skimp is no fun. Use a lot—it tastes much better. If you really have extra, freeze it (though for better or worse, sometimes I just finish it off with a spoon).

Tip!

This cake is also delicious with the icing from the Coconut Cake (p. 232). Make it the same, but omit the shredded coconut. My favorite alternative is to double-frost, first with the chocolate fudge frosting and then, once it has hardened, with the white icing on top. Or make a ¼ recipe of one frosting for the filing and ¾ of the other to ice the cake.

CHAPTER 6
ASSETS

Kitchen Staples
p. 268

Kitchen Extras
p. 270

Make-Ahead Recipes
p. 272

Critical Condiments & Marinades
p. 273

Delicious Dressings
p. 279

Savory Sauce Essentials
p. 282

Simple Stocks
p. 285

Noteworthy Nibbles
p. 289

Something Sweet
p. 293

We all approach cooking in our own ways, but it's safe to say that among the various methods we employ, similarities are more common than differences. It's also safe to say that pretty much everyone recognizes the efficiencies and benefits of a well-stocked kitchen. Recognition, however, does not equal putting into practice.

On the other hand, "well-stocked" means different things to different people. If you make dinner every night, it makes sense to have all sorts of perishables—fresh vegetables; delicate herbs, lettuces, and berries; fresh fish, meat, and poultry; and salad makings—on hand in addition to the basics. If you cook only occasionally, these ingredients would probably spoil before you got around to using them, and your kitchen staple list should only include items with long shelf or refrigerator lives.

If Mexican, Asian, Indian, African, or Middle Eastern meals are your thing, your pantry will look quite different from someone who only cooks "American." The same holds true if you or a family member is vegan, vegetarian, kosher, allergy-ridden, or has another dietary restriction. In this chapter, I address general kitchen staples and culinary assets and assume you will adjust for personal needs and preferences.

When entertaining, no matter how full your pantry, fridge, and freezer, you'll probably still need to stop at the market for an item or two to complete most meals. Whether a fragile frisée, a super fresh Burrata, or the perfect baguette, there will almost certainly be something to buy before setting dinner on the table. Taking the lists below into consideration, you'll have pantry, fridge, and freezer items on hand and thus keep last-minute purchases to a minimum. You'll do a lot less list making and errand running when you could be home with your feet up. With even just some of these ingredients at the ready, you can put together casual meals for yourself and your family without any last minute shopping at all.

Kitchen Staples

I keep citrus fruits, garlic, shallots, and onions in a basket in the pantry. However, if you don't use them regularly, are going out of town, or have surplus, I suggest the refrigerator.

PANTRY

Baking powder
Baking soda
Bay leaves, dried
Cayenne pepper, ground
Chocolate chips, semisweet
Chocolate, unsweetened and semisweet
Cinnamon, ground and sticks
Coriander seed, whole and ground
Cream of tartar
Cumin seed, whole and ground
Fennel seed, whole and ground
Flour, all-purpose and whole-wheat
Garlic
Ginger, powdered
Honey
Hot sauce, such as Tabasco
Lemons

Limes
Meringue shells (p. 294)
Mustard, Dijon and grainy
My pepper mix (p. 273)
Oil, extra virgin olive
Oil, neutral, such as canola
Onions, red and yellow
Peppercorns, black
Rosemary, dried
Salt, fine sea and kosher
Shallots
Soy sauce
Sugar; granulated, confectioners', and brown
Thyme, dried
Vanilla extract, best-quality and pure
Vinegar; Balsamic, sherry, white wine, red wine, and rice

REFRIGERATOR

Apples
Apricots
Arugula
Avocados
Bell peppers
Berries, varieties of choice
Broccoli
Butter, unsalted and/or salted
Cabbage, white and/or red
Carrots
Cauliflower
Celery
Cherries
Eggs
Endive, Belgian
Fennel, bulb
Figs
Hot peppers, such as jalapeño, serrano, scotch bonnet, and Thai bird

Lettuces
Mangoes
Milk, whole, skim, or 2%
Nectarines
Nuts; walnuts, pecans, almonds, hazelnuts, pine nuts, peanuts, and/or other
Orange juice
Oranges, navel
Parmesan, Italian
Peaches
Pears
Plums
Pomegranates
Potatoes
Scallions
Sweet potatoes
Tomatoes
Turnips

Use fresh herbs, like this cilantro, to brighten up any dish.

FRESH HERBS

Basil	Oregano
Chives	Parsley, Italian
Cilantro	Rosemary
Dill	Sage
Marjoram	Tarragon
Mint	Thyme

FREEZER

Bacon	Pancetta
Chicken, breasts and thighs, with or without bones	Peas, boxed or bagged
	Puff pastry, store-bought
Chorizo	Raspberries, bagged
Corn, boxed or bagged	Sausage, varieties of choice
Ice cream, flavors of choice	Sorbets, flavors of choice
Ice cream, super-premium vanilla	Stock, chicken (p. 288)
Onions, pearl, boxed or bagged	Stock, fish (p. 285)
Orange juice concentrate	

Of course, it's great if you can grow your own herbs. I used to have a real garden and envy those of you who still do. Now instead, I grow a plethora of herbs on my Manhattan fire escape in summer and try (with mixed success) to keep pots of rosemary, thyme, parsley, and chives alive on my windowsill all winter.

Kitchen Extras

If you have room to store them, buying nonperishable ingredients in bulk saves both time and money. I find it reassuring to know that I have sugars, flours, pastas, tomato paste, canned tomatoes, vinegars, mustards, and a number of other bottled sauces and condiments stashed away for the long haul. Oils keep quite a while in the pantry, but for real longevity, store the ones you use less often—such as citrus, nut, and truffle oils—in the fridge. Olives, nuts, maple syrup, and most grains last many months when refrigerated. Butter too, though I like to freeze the surplus if I don't plan to use it within a few weeks. In addition to buying in bulk, one big grocery trip per week—rather than several small ones—can save hours wasted on multiple last-minute jaunts to the market.

PANTRY

Amaretti

Anchovies

Capers

Coconut milk

Coffee, instant espresso powder

Corn meal

Couscous

Dried fruit, such as raisins, currants, apricots, prunes, and dates

Ginger, candied

Jam, flavors of choice

Maple syrup, best-quality

Pasta, dried

Peppercorns, pink

Polenta, instant

Quinoa

Red pepper, crushed

Rice; long grain white or brown, wild, and/or risotto rice, such as Arborio or Carnaroli

Soup bases, such as Better than Bouillon or Minor's

Tomato paste, double-concentrate

Tomatoes, canned whole and chopped San Marzano

BONUS ITEMS FOR THE PANTRY

Ancho chili powder

Anchovy paste

Asian noodles

Beans, dried varieties of choice

Bread crumbs

Chinese chili garlic paste

Cocoa powder, unsweetened dark, such as Valrhona

Crackers, varieties of choice

Croutons

Espresso powder, instant Medaglia d'Oro or El Pico

Fish sauce, Thai or Vietnamese

Hoisin sauce

Kecap manis

Lentils

Marmalade, orange and/or lemon

Mushrooms, dried varieties of choice

Praline and/or caramelized nuts (p. 302)

Rice papers, round or square

Saffron threads

Vanilla sugar (p. 293)

Vinegar, sherry

Wasabi paste

REFRIGERATOR

Blue cheese, such as Roquefort, Gorgonzola, or Danish blue
Caramel sauce (p. 303)
Chocolate sauce (p. 302)
Cream, heavy
Feta or ricotta salata
Garlic oil (p. 273)
Ginger, fresh
Goat cheese (chèvre)
Gruyère
Horseradish, bottled or fresh
Lemongrass, fresh
Lemons, Moroccan preserved (p. 276)
Mayonnaise, basic and flavored (p. 275), and Hellman's
Oil, black and/or white truffle
Oil, dark sesame
Oil, hazelnut and/or walnut
Oil, lemon and/or orange
Peanut butter
Raspberry sauce (p. 303)
Salami, varieties of choice
Salmon, smoked
Sour cream or crème fraîche
Tahini
Vinaigrette, basic (p. 279) plus varieties of choice
Yogurt, plain

ALCOHOL

Brandy, Cognac, and/or Armagnac
Pernod
Port
Rum, dark
Sherry
Wine, red and white

FREEZER

Beurre blanc (p. 282)
Beurres composés (p. 274), varieties of choice
Biscotti, chocolate–ginger (p. 298)
Biscuits, cheddar and chive (p. 52)
Bread, Irish brown (p. 132)
Cake layer, for baked Alaska (p. 89)
Cake layers, for coconut cake (p. 231)
Cake layers, devil's food (p. 264)
Cakes, molten mini chocolate (p. 31)
Cookie dough, chocolate chip (p. 300)
Crostata crust, savory (p. 122)
Lemon curd (p. 304)
Marinades (p. 277), varieties of choice
Pasta, baked with asparagus (p. 139)
Pesto (p. 284)
Pie crust, sweet (p. 293)
Pie, Key lime (p. 53)
Raspberry–Port sauce (p. 172)
Shortbread coins (p. 295), flavors of choice
Soup, tomato–cumin (p. 74)
Stock (p. 285)
Tomato sauce (p. 283)

Tip!

Eat fish and shellfish within a couple of days of purchase. Meat and poultry can be kept three to five days in the fridge. Freeze if using later in the week. Another trick is to buy a variety of vegetables and use the more perishable ones—green beans, spinach, sugar snaps and snow peas—first and save root vegetables, tomatoes, peppers, kale, chard, chicories, and members of the cabbage family—including Brussels sprouts, cauliflower, and all forms of broccoli—for later in the week. Frozen vegetables are a good end-of-week option as well. And most salad greens and fresh herbs should keep 5 to 7 days if wrapped loosely in damp paper towels, placed in unsealed plastic bags, and refrigerated. Consider a vegetarian dinner or two at week's end.

Tip!

You can extend freezer life by many months and avoid freezer burn by freezing food in Pyrex containers or a double layer of foil rather than in the more porous plastic containers and baggies.

Make-Ahead Recipes

To elevate a last-minute, makeshift dinner to the talk of the town, in addition to my normal staples, I stash special goodies—reduction sauces, beurres blancs, flavored butters, homemade marinades and glazes, soups, baked pastas, ice creams, ice cream bases, and ice cream pies, lemon curd, dessert bombes, and pie crusts—in the freezer and garlic oil; chocolate, raspberry, and caramel sauces; meringue shells; and spice mixes in the pantry and fridge. And when I remember, I freeze marinated and butterflied lamb or some chicken pieces to pull out in the event that unexpected guests arrive at 6:00 p.m. in search of dinner. In the following pages, I offer recipes for some of my best go-to assets.

I personally enjoy spending a weekend or the occasional evening or Sunday afternoon producing and stockpiling these tidbits. If you're into that sort of thing, it can be a fun activity to undertake with a few friends, a bit like making Christmas cookies or hosting a Tupperware party. But if stocking up for a rainy day is not how you choose to spend your free time, you can skip the homemade items and use purchased assets only.

Scope out local gourmet shops, and you'll be set to pop in last minute the next time you need a fancy mustard, artisanal loaf, cocktail nibble, or even a cold vegetable, pasta, or grain salad to fill out a meal. A good knowledge of potential suppliers is its own priceless asset. And while you're at it, find out if your fishmonger will poach a salmon, open oysters, or steam lobster, crab, and shrimp for you. Does he carry top-of-the-line smoked salmon, and if not, who does? Where can you find the best selection of other smoked fish (a smoked fish platter makes a divine brunch main course or dinner party starter)? And who in your neighborhood sells the finest charcuterie and the best cheeses? Of course, with a bit of planning, online buy-aheads become instant new best friends. Start exploring the vast array of food items—exotic spices, specialty chocolates, and unusual honeys, olives, nut oils, and much more—available at your fingertips.

CRITICAL CONDIMENTS & MARINADES

My Pepper Mix

I discovered this pepper mix about 10 years ago, and it's enlivened my cooking ever since. Make it in large batches to keep in a canister for topping off the peppermill when needed. Optimally, mix several varieties of black pepper instead of using just one. Basic Malabar or Tellicherry is just fine alone, but adding Sarawak, Black Lampong, Madagascar, Vietnamese, and/or Kampot peppercorns, is mind-blowing.

3 parts black peppercorns
1 part white peppercorns

Allspice, to taste
Whole coriander seed, to taste

1. Stir the spices together and transfer to a pepper mill. Stored in a peppermill or a covered container, this mix will easily keep for up to 1 year.

Garlic Oil

Yield: 2 cups

Garlic oil is great tossed with pasta, added to salad dressings, spread on garlic toast, sautéed with vegetables, or rubbed on fish, chicken, or meat before grilling. Garlic oil is probably the most useful ingredient in my kitchen after salt and pepper, and it only takes about 3 minutes to make. If too garlicky for your intended purpose, dilute with more olive oil before using.

10 cloves garlic, peeled

2 cups extra virgin olive oil, plus more if needed

1. In the bowl of a food processor or in a blender, purée the garlic and the oil together until smooth. Taste and adjust the oil as needed.

2. Transfer to a covered container and refrigerate. This garlic oil will keep in the refrigerator for at least 2 months.

Tip!

A cellophane bag of this mix tied with a ribbon is an always appreciated hostess gift.

Fresh Herb Butter

Beurre composé (compound butter) is flavored butter that is lightly enhanced but still recognizable, and I love it. This fresh herb variety is my favorite of these special butters, which take less than five minutes to blend and roll into logs that can be stored in the refrigerator for weeks and in the freezer for months. Simply slice as needed and melt over meats, fish, poultry, or vegetables for an instant sauce. Try one of the variations below, and then go to town with whatever is in season or in your pantry.

1 cup (2 sticks) unsalted butter
⅓ packed cup fresh herbs, such as tarragon, chives, parsley, and/or basil
1 teaspoon fine sea salt, or to taste

½ teaspoon freshly ground black pepper, or to taste
1 clove garlic (optional)
1 small shallot, halved

1. Put all the ingredients in the bowl of a food processor and pulse until combined. Using a rubber spatula, spread the butter in a strip across a large sheet of waxed paper or plastic wrap, leaving 1 to 2 inches at each end.

2. Roll the waxed paper around the butter and then roll back and forth to form a cylinder, 1 inch to 1½ inches in diameter, that is smooth and equal in size from end to end.

3. Twist the waxed paper at both ends of the butter cylinder to close. Refrigerate for at least 1 hour, or until needed. Compound butter will keep in the refrigerator at least 2 weeks. For longer storage, wrap well in aluminum foil and freeze for up to 6 months

These bold butters aggressively boost flavor when swirled into soups, stews, or more complex sauces last minute. Pasta, rice, and grains are equally enhanced; and any *beurre composé* atop a baked potato is food for the gods.

VARIATIONS

Anchovy Butter: Use 2 sticks unsalted butter, 12 to 18 anchovy fillets, 2 teaspoons freshly squeezed lemon juice, ¼ teaspoon fine sea salt, and 1 teaspoon freshly ground black pepper.

Curry Butter: Use 2 sticks unsalted butter, 1 tablespoon curry powder, 1 teaspoon fine sea salt, and ½ teaspoon freshly ground pepper. 1 clove garlic, and/or 1 shallot can be added if desired.

Truffle Butter: Use 2 sticks unsalted butter, 1 to 4 ounces fresh black truffles, 1 teaspoon fine sea salt, and ½ teaspoon freshly ground black pepper, or to taste.

Basic Mayonnaise

Yield: about 1¾–2 cups

Homemade mayo beats Hellman's hands down and takes just five minutes to prepare. Up the ante dramatically by making one of the flavored variations. Feeling extravagant? Stir caviar or chopped truffles into the basic mayo. Sublime. With approximately 100 calories per tablespoon, mayonnaise is not diet food, but the delicious calories are jam-packed with flavor and greatly enhance everything they come in contact with—from a basic BLT to lavish meat, poultry, fish, and vegetable creations.

All ingredients must be at room temperature

1 large egg

1½ tablespoons freshly squeezed lemon juice, plus more to taste

2 teaspoons Dijon mustard

1 teaspoon fine sea salt, plus more to taste

¼ teaspoon freshly ground black or white pepper

1¼ cups oil—half neutral vegetable oil (such as canola) and half extra virgin olive oil

1. Combine the egg, lemon juice, mustard, salt, and pepper in blender or food processor.

2. Mix the oils together and, with the motor running, add the mixed oils in driblets.

3. When about ¼ of the oil mixture has been added, add the rest in a very slow stream.

4. Taste and adjust the salt, pepper, and lemon juice as needed.

VARIATIONS

Garlic Mayonnaise: Add 1 large clove of garlic to the initial ingredients.

Ginger–Garlic Mayonnaise: Add 1 inch of peeled fresh ginger and 1 large clove of garlic to the initial ingredients.

Tartar Sauce: Prepare Basic Mayonnaise, then mix in ½ cup finely minced cornichons, ¼ cup Champagne or white wine vinegar, ¼ cup minced capers, 1 tablespoon grainy mustard, and fine sea salt and freshly ground black pepper, to taste.

Curry Mayonnaise: Prepare Basic Mayonnaise, then mix in 1 to 3 teaspoons curry powder.

Fresh Herb Mayonnaise: Prepare Basic Mayonnaise, then stir in 1 cup chopped fresh herbs, such as chives, Italian parsley, tarragon, basil, cilantro, or mint. If using fresh oregano, thyme, marjoram, or rosemary, 2 tablespoons should be enough.

Tip!

Be sure to use very fresh organic eggs. Raw egg is not recommended for infants, the elderly, pregnant women, and people with weakened immune systems. To avoid any risk of salmonella, use pasteurized eggs.

Fresh Mango and Mint Salsa

Yield: 8 servings

Sweet and hot at the same time—and fresh and tropical as well—this easy-to-make salsa is the perfect summer accompaniment for grilled chicken, fish, shellfish, or pork.

3 large hard-ripe mangoes, peeled and cut into ½ inch dice

1 hot red pepper (jalapeño, scotch bonnet, or serrano), ribs and seeds removed and very finely minced or cut in big slices

1 medium red onion, halved and cut into paper-thin half rings

½–¾ cup fresh mint leaves, julienned

Freshly squeezed juice of 2 limes

Fine sea salt and freshly ground black pepper, to taste

1. Mix all the ingredients together and set aside for at least 1 hour and up to 3 hours at room temperature.

2. If using slices of hot pepper, remove them before serving.

3. This salsa keeps up to 2 days in the refrigerator, but it's best eaten within 3 hours of preparing.

Moroccan Preserved Lemons

Yield: 48 wedges

These preserved lemons are one of my favorite refrigerator assets, and I use them frequently. Even a teaspoon or two of the juice alone works wonders to brighten up a salad dressing, mayonnaise, sauce, or soup. I preserve limes and oranges in the same way, as they too are great additions to many savory dishes.

6 large lemons

⅔ cup kosher salt

1 tablespoon fennel seeds (optional)

1 tablespoon coriander seeds (optional)

1 cinnamon stick (optional)

1 tablespoon black peppercorns (optional)

1 crumbled bay leaf (optional)

1–1½ cups freshly squeezed lemon juice

2 tablespoons extra virgin olive oil

1. Blanch the lemons in a large pot of boiling water for 5 minutes, then drain.

2. When cool enough to handle, cut each lemon into 8 wedges. Remove and discard the visible seeds.

3. Toss the lemons with the kosher salt. If using, add one or more of the optional spices and toss. Tightly pack the lemons, along with the salt and spices, into a 6-cup jar with a tight-fitting lid.

4. Add enough of the lemon juice to cover the lemons.

5. Seal the jar and let the lemons stand at room temperature for 5 days, shaking gently once a day.

6. Uncover, pour the oil on top of the lemons, recover, and refrigerate. These preserved lemons will keep in the refrigerator for at least 1 year.

Basic Marinade for Lamb, Chicken, and Steak

Yield: approximately 3 cups

This makes enough marinade for 4 to 6 pounds of meat, although it can be scaled up. Marinate (in the refrigerator and turning occasionally) for at least 12 hours, although 24 to 48 hours is better. To marinate lamb or chicken instead of steak, add 2 tablespoons fresh or 2 teaspoons dried rosemary.

2 cups thinly sliced onions

⅔ cup extra virgin olive oil

¼ cup chopped fresh Italian parsley

3 tablespoons freshly squeezed lemon juice

2 tablespoons chopped fresh thyme or 2 teaspoons dried thyme

1 teaspoon fine sea salt, plus more to taste

1 teaspoon freshly ground black pepper, plus more to taste

3 crumbled bay leaves

3 cloves garlic, thinly sliced

1. Mix the marinade ingredients together in a covered container. Refrigerate for up to a week. (This marinade cannot be frozen.)

Asian Marinade for Chicken Pieces or Steak

Yield: approximately 1 cup

This makes enough marinade for 4 to 6 pounds of meat. Marinate in the fridge, turning occasionally, for at least 12 hours, although 24 to 48 hours is better.

10 tablespoons soy sauce

¼ cup dark sesame oil

4 teaspoons granulated sugar

8 whole scallions (white and green parts), roughly chopped

6 garlic cloves, minced

1 (2-inch) piece fresh peeled ginger, minced

Freshly ground black pepper, to taste

1. Shake the marinade ingredients together in a lidded jar. Refrigerate for up to 2 weeks or freeze for up to 6 months.

Basic Marinade for Shrimp, Scallops, and Fish

Yield: approximately ¾ cup

This makes enough marinade for about 6 pounds of seafood or fish. It can also be used with chicken. For lamb, replace the tarragon and basil with 2 tablespoons dried rosemary.

½ cup extra virgin olive oil

3 tablespoons fresh tarragon, 3 tablespoons fresh basil, or ½ teaspoon dried thyme

3 tablespoons chopped fresh Italian parsley

1–2 teaspoons freshly ground black pepper

1 whole (8 wedges) Moroccan Preserved Lemon (p. 276), rinsed and diced (optional)

3 cloves garlic

1 medium red or yellow onion or 2 large shallots, cut into chunks

Freshly grated zest of 1 large lemon

1. Put all of the ingredients in the bowl of a food processor and pulse several times to combine. Marinade should remain somewhat chunky.

2. Transfer to a covered container and refrigerate for up to 1 week. (This marinade should not be frozen.)

DELICIOUS DRESSINGS

The Essential Vinaigrette

Yield: About 1 cup

I don't understand why anyone would buy bottled salad dressing when it takes just minutes to prepare vinaigrette in your own kitchen. And while this basic oil–vinegar emulsion is a classic match for green salads, everything from asparagus, haricots verts, and grain salads to chicken, fish, and seafood benefits from its bright tang. If you remember the general ratio of 3 or 4 (depending on the strength of the acid you use and how acidic you like your dressing) parts oil to 1 part acid (vinegar or citrus juices), you'll never again need a recipe! Just add salt and pepper and emulsify by whisking, shaking in a jar, or blending in a food processor.

¾ cup extra virgin olive oil

¼ cup red or white wine vinegar

1 tablespoon Dijon mustard

¼ teaspoon fine sea salt

⅛ teaspoon freshly ground black pepper

1 medium shallot or ½ small red onion, finely minced

1. Place all vinaigrette ingredients in a lidded jar and shake vigorously until well combined. Set aside for at least 1 hour to let flavors marry. Taste and adjust the seasoning as needed.

2. Use right away or refrigerate for up to 2 weeks. Bring to room temperature and reshake the jar before using.

VARIATION

Balsamic Vinaigrette: Substitute balsamic vinegar for the red or white vinegar.

Tip!

It has been said that the two biggest mistakes when making a salad are under-tossing and under-salting. One famous chef swore that a green salad should be tossed 100 times!

Walnut, Hazelnut, or Pecan Vinaigrette

Yield: ¾–1 cup

When dressing a salad with a nut vinaigrette, it's fun to include toasted nuts along with the lettuces. Just be sure the nuts match the oil. Crumbled goat cheese, feta, and ricotta salata are tasty additions as well.

½ cup walnut, hazelnut ,or pecan oil
2 tablespoons Sherry or balsamic vinegar
1 tablespoon grainy mustard

¼ teaspoon fine sea salt
¼ teaspoon freshly ground black pepper
1 small to medium shallot, finely minced
1 large clove garlic, finely minced

1. Place all vinaigrette ingredients in a lidded jar and shake vigorously until well combined. Set aside for at least 1 hour to let flavors marry. Taste and adjust the seasoning as needed.

2. Use right away or refrigerate for up to 2 weeks. Bring to room temperature and reshake the jar before using.

Truffle Vinaigrette

Yield: ¾–1 cup

Truffle oil is the simplest and least expensive way to add the special tuber's uniquely pungent taste and aroma to a vinaigrette. If you can gild the lily with truffle salt, so much the better. This dressing animates a green salad, but it will embolden vegetable, pasta, and rice salads as well and works wonders drizzled over grilled swordfish, roast cod, or almost any chicken breast preparation.

½ cup extra virgin olive oil
2 tablespoons red wine vinegar
2 tablespoons best-quality white or black truffle oil
Scant ½ teaspoon fine sea salt or truffle salt

Scant ¼ teaspoon freshly ground black pepper
1 small to medium shallot, finely minced
1 large clove garlic, finely minced

1. Place all vinaigrette ingredients in a lidded jar and shake vigorously until well combined. Set aside for at least 1 hour to let flavors marry. Taste and adjust the seasoning as needed.

2. Use right away or refrigerate for up to 2 weeks. Bring to room temperature and reshake the jar before using.

Lemon–Shallot Vinaigrette

Yield: ¾–1 cup

It's just common sense that heavier salads stand up to heavier dressings while a delicate lettuce—such as mâche or Boston—is often best paired with a light oil and lemon juice vinaigrette, like this one.

3 tablespoons freshly squeezed lemon juice

1 small to medium shallot, finely minced

1 large clove garlic, finely minced

Scant ½ teaspoon fine sea salt

Scant ¼ teaspoon freshly ground black pepper

½ cup extra virgin olive oil

1. Place all vinaigrette ingredients in a lidded jar and shake vigorously until well combined. Set aside for at least 1 hour to let the flavors marry. Taste and adjust the seasoning as needed.

2. Use right away or refrigerate for up to 2 weeks. Bring to room temperature and reshake the jar before using.

SAVORY SAUCE ESSENTIALS

Beurre Blanc

Yield: Approximately 1¼ cups

Once you've got the basics down, go wild. Play around with flavored vinegars or stir in fresh herbs. You can even make a beurre rouge by substituting red wine and red-wine vinegar for white. Whatever you do, remember that you're working with very few ingredients: Begin with a good wine and the best butter you can afford.

This bright, delicate, and versatile French sauce pairs particularly well with seafood, poultry, and vegetables. Made correctly, it's light, airy, and just thick enough to cling to the dish it adorns. The main points to remember while making it are to never let the sauce get too hot and to not add the butter too quickly. Control the temperature by taking the pan on and off the heat. And if you over-reduce in Step 1, be sure to add some water back in. A certain amount of liquid is necessary for emulsification.

3 shallots, finely minced
1 cup dry white wine
6 tablespoons white wine vinegar
2 tablespoons heavy cream
1 cup (2 sticks) best-quality unsalted butter, very cold and cut into ½-inch slices

Scant ¼ teaspoon fine sea salt, or to taste
Generous pinch freshly ground white pepper (in a pinch, black pepper may be substituted)
Freshly squeezed lemon juice, to taste

1. Combine the shallots, wine, and vinegar in a nonreactive saucepan over high heat and reduce to 2 tablespoons. Watch carefully. If over-reduced, add a little water back in.

2. Add the cream to the reduction. Once the liquid simmers, remove the pan from the heat and whisk in a few pieces of butter, 1 at a time.

3. Reduce the heat to the lowest setting possible. Return the pan to the heat and continue whisking in the butter—1 piece at a time—allowing each piece to just melt into the sauce before adding the next. Be sure that the sauce does not go above a low simmer and comes absolutely nowhere near boiling. Control is gained by occasionally removing the pan from the heat.

4. Once all the butter has been added and the sauce is smooth, remove the pan from the heat and season with the salt, white pepper, and lemon juice. Whisk until well blended.

5. Store finished beurre blanc over warm water, in a bain-marie, or in a thermos until ready to serve. For longer storage, cool, cover and refrigerate for up to 5 days or freeze for up to 4 months. Thaw before reheating. To reheat, cut into chunks or spoon into a medium saucepan set over very low heat. Stir constantly until sauce is very warm but not hot. It should come nowhere near simmering.

Quick Tomato Sauce

Yield: Approximately 3½–4 cups

Why buy premade tomato sauce when this homemade version—picked up from a Roman friend—is infinitely tastier and can be thrown together in about 15 minutes? And it uses canned tomatoes rather than fresh, so make it all year long. And while you're at it, make extra, as it freezes for up to a year.

3 tablespoons extra virgin olive oil

1 large onion, chopped

1 large pinch crushed red pepper

2 (28-ounce) cans chopped San Marzano tomatoes

6 large cloves garlic, minced

2 teaspoons fine sea salt, plus more to taste

Large pinch granulated sugar

½ teaspoon balsamic vinegar, plus more to taste

Freshly ground black pepper, to taste

½ cup chopped fresh basil

1. In a large skillet set over medium heat, sauté the oil, onion, and crushed red pepper until the onion is golden.

2. Add the remaining ingredients, except the basil, raise the heat to high, and cook, stirring constantly, for 5 to 10 minutes, or until enough liquid has evaporated to result in a thick, flavorful sauce.

3. Add the basil. Taste and adjust salt, pepper, and balsamic as needed. Serve right away or cool and refrigerate for up to 2 weeks or freeze for up to 1 year.

My Favorite Pesto

Yield: Approximately 1¾ cups

If you prefer traditional pesto, simply omit the additions from this recipe.

This particular pesto is so good that I sometimes sneak off and eat it by the spoonful like soup. The inclusion of walnuts and cream sets it apart from (and in my mind improves upon) the recipes for the basic sauce.

2 packed cups fresh basil leaves
½ packed cup roughly chopped fresh Italian parsley
½ cup toasted pine nuts
1 tablespoon toasted walnut pieces (optional)

2 large cloves garlic
½ cup extra virgin olive oil
½ cup grated Italian Parmesan cheese
¼ teaspoon fine sea salt, or more to taste
4 tablespoons light cream (optional)

1. Using a food processor, purée the basil, parsley, pine nuts, walnuts, if using, garlic, and oil to a smooth paste.

2. Add the Parmesan, salt, and cream, if using, and pulse to blend completely.

3. Serve right away or refrigerate under a thin layer of olive oil or with plastic wrap touching the surface of the sauce. This pesto will keep in the refrigerator for up to 3 days or in the freezer for up to 3 months.

My Favorite BBQ Sauce

Yield: Approximately 10–12 cups

I admit that this sauce may require a major shopping expedition. However, once you have the ingredients, 20 minutes start to finish will get you enough of the best BBQ sauce on the planet to last you a lifetime—or at least for quite a while.

2 cups catsup
2 (12-ounce) bottles Heinz Chili Sauce
1 cup dark molasses
1 cup apple cider vinegar
1 teaspoon Tabasco sauce
2 tablespoons minced garlic, or to taste
1 cup dark brown sugar
½ teaspoon allspice
½ teaspoon cinnamon
½ teaspoon mace
1 teaspoon freshly ground black pepper
1 tablespoon madras or West Indian curry powder

2 teaspoons chili powder
2 teaspoons paprika
1 tablespoon instant espresso coffee powder
1 tablespoon bottled horseradish
1 tablespoon powdered ginger
1 tablespoon powdered mustard
2 teaspoons Chinese chili garlic paste
1 (10-ounce) jar mango, Major Grey's, or other chutney, puréed if at all lumpy
¼ cup concentrated tomato paste
Few drops of liquid smoke (optional)

1. Place all the ingredients in a large saucepan, and simmer, stirring frequently, over medium–low heat for 20 minutes. Cool completely.

2. Pour into lidded jars and refrigerate. This sauce will keep in the refrigerator for at least 1 year.

SIMPLE STOCKS

Known to many cooks as *fonds de cuisine* (the foundations of the kitchen), stocks are the liquids in which meat, poultry, or fish bones—along with other flavorful ingredients—have simmered to extract their flavor. Whether homemade or store-bought, stocks are prerequisite to preparing a great number of soups and an even greater number sauces. They are essential to a number of recipes in this book, and in most other cookbooks as well.

Many of the best home cooks I know—people who find preparing a pie crust, meringue, or Béarnaise sauce to be child's play—are stymied by stock-making. They shouldn't be. There is really nothing to it; and if you remember to simmer rather than boil and not to leave for vacation with the stock still simmering, virtually nothing will go wrong. Yes, a stock takes several hours to complete, but only about 15 minutes of that time are you actively doing anything. After that, you can stick the pot on a back burner and virtually forget about it.

To make basic meat, poultry, or fish stock, here's what you do:

Place the meat, fish, or poultry bones (with or without some of the protein itself) in a stockpot or saucepan—the size will depend on the amount of stock you plan to make. If making meat broth, brown the meat and bones on a sheet pan in a 400°F oven for about 45 minutes, or until caramelized, before adding them to the pot. For both chicken and fish stock, browning is optional.

Next add an abundance of onions, garlic, carrots, and celery and lots of fresh parsley, a crumbled bay leaf or two, and fresh or dried thyme. For deeper flavor, sauté the vegetables in the stockpot with a couple tablespoons of olive oil before adding the bones.

Cover the contents of the pan with cool water by one to two inches and simmer over medium–low heat until the broth is pleasantly and delicately flavored—6 to 10 hours for meat (the longer the better), about 4 hours for chicken, and about 1 hour for fish.

Use a skimmer or large spoon to remove and discard all the fat and

When I make fish stock, though not absolutely necessary, I do make sure to sauté the vegetables—and the fish bones along with them—before proceeding with the recipe. Because fish stock only cooks for an hour, this quick extra step will add important flavor.

scum that rises to the top during cooking. Do this as you go along or all at once at the end. If you choose to skim as you go, set the stock-pot about one-third off the burner with the lid askew, exposing the contents of the pot that are off the heat. The stock, simmering on the warmer side only, will push the fats and scum to the other side, making them easy to remove as the stock simmers.

If planning to refrigerate rather than use right away, you can skip the skimming. Once cold, the fat will rise to the top and form a seal that lifts off easily. When the stock is finished simmering, strain, cool, and defat. If not using right away, refrigerate for up to 3 days or freeze for up to 1 year.

When making stock, it is *very* important that the liquid *simmers* rather than boils. Boiling causes rendered fat to be emulsified into the liquid rather than rising to the top. However, if the stock does boil and the fat becomes cloudy, an old restaurant trick will save the day: Throw several ice cubes into the impaired stock and slowly, slowly bring the liquid back to a simmer. Like magic, the fat will separate out, come to the top, and you'll be back in business.

It's far beyond the call of duty to make your own stock every time you plan to make soup or a sauce. I make large batches occasionally to keep frozen in useable quantities. There's no need to thaw a full gallon if you only need a cup or two.

To save space in the freezer, reduce the finished (and defatted) stock to a concentrate and add water when ready to use. The reconstituting proportions don't have to be exact, but the rule is to add back in about as much water as you removed. Let's say you've reduced 1 gallon (16 cups) of stock to 1 cup of concentrate. You've removed about 15 cups of water, so that's the ratio you'll use when it comes time to reconstitute it. If a recipe calls for 1 cup of stock, you would use ½ tablespoon of stock and 1 scant cup (about 15½ tablespoons) of water. However, I usually like more flavor, so I tend to use two or three times as much reduction as needed.

During stock-making, liquid will evaporate and the stock will automatically become more concentrated. If you want a concentrated

Another advantage of homemade stock is that it's your creation, so add and subtract vegetables and aromatics as you see fit. Additional fresh or dried herbs, fresh or dried mushrooms, dried chilies, fresh fennel, scallions, and leeks, are all options, depending how you plan to use the stock. To make stock for Asian recipes, for example, replace the carrots, celery, parsley, bay leaf, and thyme with several slices of unpeeled ginger.

Do not salt your stock as you want maximum flexibility vis-à-vis salti-ness later on when you are incorporating it into a sauce, soup or stew.

stock, add just enough water to keep the bones barely covered. For basic, non-concentrated stock, periodically replace all the water that has evaporated.

You can also purchase, rather than make, stock. Supermarkets abound in products called anything from stock to broth to consommé, and they come canned, bottled, frozen, cubed, and granulated. Although some are acceptable, most are too salty, too weak, or just taste wrong. The best way to find out which will work is to buy several and taste them. In a pinch, most can be improved upon by simmering for 30 to 45 minutes with some or all of the following: a chopped carrot, onion, celery stalk, garlic clove, crumbled bay leaf, and/or a few peppercorns.

Recently, however, my good friend, Alex Hitz, introduced me to a richer, more flavorful option. Soup bases (concentrated pastes made primarily from meat, seafood, or vegetables) were previously relegated to professional chefs and restaurant kitchens, but they're now available online and in some supermarkets. While not as good as homemade, they are infinitely better than anything else you can buy. Alex uses Better Than Bouillon. Minor's is also excellent but a bit harder to find.

I hope this short introduction to stocks persuades you to give stock-making a try. If you're not yet ready to explore uncharted territory without a map, I've included a very basic chicken stock recipe to suggest approximate proportions and the lay of the land. You should soon be making basic stocks plus your own variations and improvisations from scratch and without recipes.

Have fun!

Reducing is the process of thickening and intensifying the flavor of a liquid by simmering or boiling. Place the liquid—stock, fruit or vegetable juices, wine, vinegar, or sauce—in a heavy saucepan and set, uncovered, over medium high heat. Boil or simmer, stirring frequently, until the desired volume is reached by evaporation.

Very Basic Chicken Stock

Yield: About 2½ quarts stock

You can purchase chicken pieces to make stock, use leftover chicken or even use rinsed chicken bones right off people's plates. I realize the latter sounds seriously unappealing, but remember, the bones will be in boiling liquid for many hours. Any conceivable germs will be long gone after that. For deeper flavor, brown the chicken parts in a 400°F oven for 45 minutes or until caramelized.

Approximately 5 pounds assorted skinless chicken parts (backs, necks, legs, wings, and/or bones or cut up carcasses)

3 large carrots, peeled if not organic and chopped into 2-inch lengths

3 celery stalks, chopped into 2-inch lengths

3 medium onions, unpeeled and quartered

1 head garlic, halved crosswise

1 large bay leaf, crumbled

3 sprigs fresh thyme or ¼ teaspoon dried thyme

10 sprigs fresh Italian parsley, including stems

1 teaspoon whole black peppercorns

1. Place the chicken parts in a stockpot just large enough to hold them with about 3 inches of room above (an 8- to 10-quart pot should do) and add enough water to cover by 1 to 2 inches (about 3 quarts).

2. Bring to a boil over medium–high heat. Use a ladle to skim the impurities and fat that rise to the top and discard.

3. Add the vegetables, bay leaf, thyme, parsley, and peppercorns and reduce the heat to low, keeping the mixture at a bare simmer (bubbles should just gently break the surface). Cook, skimming frequently, for at least 4 hours and up to 6 hours.

4. Strain through a fine-mesh sieve into a bowl or another pot, pressing on and then discarding solids.

5. Let cool completely (in an ice-water bath, if desired) before transferring to covered containers. Refrigerate at least 8 hours to allow the fat to accumulate at the top; lift off and discard fat before using, reducing, or storing.

6. Refrigerate for up to 3 days or freeze for up to 1 year.

NOTEWORTHY NIBBLES

Gourmet Trail Mix

Yield: 6 cups

This is my take on a great cocktail nibble I sampled over 15 years ago at Chef Daniel Boulud's flagship restaurant, Daniel. It's healthy and tasty and keeps in the fridge almost indefinitely. Make sure not to undersalt.

3 cups mixed dried fruit, such as cranberries, raisins, cherries, coarsely
chopped mango, peaches, apricots,
and/or pear

3 cups mixed roasted and salted nuts,
such as hazelnuts, pistachios, peanuts,
cashews, pecans, and/or almonds

1–2 teaspoons fine sea salt, or more to
taste

1. Mix all the ingredients together in a large bowl. The final mix should be on the salty side.

2. Transfer to a covered container and refrigerate. This mix will keep in the refrigerator for up to 4 months. Bring to room temperature before serving.

Parmesan–Rosemary Coins

Yield: Approximately 40 shortbread coins

Savory shortbreads, such as this one, are ideal with cocktails or a glass of bubbly. A fancy Italian fashion designer once purchased several pounds of these Parmesan–Rosemary Coins from me and carried them—wrapped in a pashmina—back to Milan to offer at her fashion show along with Prosecco served from her collection of mismatched cut crystal glasses. She wrote me later that they were a huge hit!

2 cups all-purpose flour

4 ounces (about 1 cup) toasted walnuts,
chopped

2 tablespoons finely minced fresh
rosemary

1 teaspoon fine sea salt

⅛ teaspoon freshly ground black pepper

Pinch cayenne pepper

1 cup (2 sticks) unsalted butter, room
temperature

½ pound freshly grated Italian Parmesan
cheese, room temperature

1. Mix everything, except the butter and the cheese, together in a medium bowl and set aside.

CONTINUED

2. Using a stand mixer fitted with the paddle attachment or an electric hand-held mixer set on medium–high speed, beat the butter for 3 minutes, or until light and fluffy. Add the cheese and mix until well combined. Scrape down the sides of the bowl with a metal spatula.

3. Add the dry ingredients and mix on low speed just until combined.

4. Divide the dough into 4 or 5 pieces and roll each piece into a log about 1½ inches in diameter. Lightly flouring your hands and the work surface will help. If the dough is too warm to do this easily, refrigerate for about 30 minutes, or until it is easy to work with.

5. Wrap each log in plastic wrap and refrigerate for at least 1 hour and up to 3 days (or wrap the logs in foil and freeze for up to 6 months).

6. Preheat the oven to 350°F. Cut the logs into ⅜-inch slices and place on cookie sheets lined with parchment paper. If frozen, thaw until the logs are sliceable.

7. Bake for 12 to 15 minutes, or until golden. Transfer the coins to wire racks. When completely cool, store in covered containers for up to 2 days, refrigerate for up to 1 week, or freeze for up to 6 months.

Curry Coins

Yield: Approximately 75 shortbread coins

This recipe has been featured in various publications over the years, and for a while I even packaged these shortbreads and sold them commercially! You can slice the little biscuits thicker if you prefer. Just bake them a few minutes longer.

1½ cups (3 sticks) unsalted butter, room temperature
⅔ cup granulated sugar
3 cups all-purpose flour
2¼ teaspoons curry powder
1½ teaspoons sweet paprika powder

1½ teaspoons turmeric powder
1 teaspoon fine sea salt
½ teaspoon chili powder
¼ teaspoon ground cayenne pepper
¼ teaspoon freshly ground black pepper

1. Using a stand mixed fitted with the paddle attachment or an electric hand-held mixer set on high speed, cream the butter and the sugar for 5 minutes, or until light and fluffy. Scrape down occasionally with a rubber spatula.

2. Sift the flour together with all the spices into a medium bowl.

3. Add the dry ingredients to the butter mixture and beat on low speed until just combined, scraping the sides of the bowl as necessary.

4. Roll the dough into logs 1 to 1¼ inches in diameter and 6 to 8 inches long. Lightly flouring your hands and the work surface can help. If the dough is too warm to do this easily, refrigerate for about 30 minutes or until it is easy to work with.

5. Wrap the logs in plastic wrap and refrigerate for at least 1 hour and up to 3 days (or wrap the logs in foil and freeze for up to 6 months).

6. Preheat the oven to 350°F. Cut the logs into ⅛- to ³⁄₁₆-inch slices and place on cookie sheets lined with parchment paper.

7. Bake for 10 to 15 minutes, or until lightly colored. Transfer the coins to wire racks. When completely cool, store in a covered container for 1 week or freeze for up to 6 months.

Truffled Almonds

Yield: 1 pound

Recently I've seen one version or another of these nuts advertised for sale, but when I initially created them for Petrossian over 10 years ago, I don't think there were any others on the market. They're easy to make and one of the least expensive truly luxe items that I can think of. If you can't find truffle salt, fine sea salt can be substituted, but the nuts will be a bit less truffley.

1 pound blanched almonds
2–3 tablespoons black or white truffle oil
1–2 teaspoons truffle salt, or to taste

1. Preheat the oven to 350°F.

2. Place the almonds on a sheet pan in 1 layer. Bake, stirring once or twice, for 10 minutes, or until very lightly colored. Watch carefully so the nuts don't burn.

3. Remove the sheet pan from the oven and immediately toss the almonds with the truffle oil and truffle salt.

4. When completely cool, store the nuts in a covered container and refrigerate. They will keep in the refrigerator for at least 3 months. Bring to room temperature before serving with champagne or cocktails.

Marinated Olives

Yield: 1 pound olives

This simple process takes no time and dramatically improves store-bought olives for snacking or serving with cocktails.

1 pound Kalamata and/or Cerignola olives, rinsed in cool water and dried well

2 long, thin pieces of lemon peel removed with a vegetable peeler, yellow part only

3 cloves garlic, coarsely chopped

½ teaspoon dried thyme or 2 teaspoons fresh thyme

1 large shallot, thinly sliced or chopped

2 crushed juniper berries

Extra virgin olive oil, to cover

1. Mix all the ingredients together in a lidded container. Be sure the oil covers the olives. If it doesn't, add a little more.

2. Cover and refrigerate for 1 week, although you can eat the olives sooner. Covered with oil, the olives will keep in the refrigerator for at least 3 months.

3. To serve, bring to room temperature and drain the excess oil back into the container.

SOMETHING SWEET

Vanilla Sugar

Yield: 6 cups

Just recently, I saw vanilla sugar selling for $3 an ounce. Make it yourself—to sprinkle on shortbread cookies, sweet pastry, and meringue or to add to sweet sauces, compotes, jellies, and jams as well as to cake, cookie, pancake, and waffle batters—and rather than $3 an ounce, it will cost you $3 a pound or less.

6 cups granulated sugar   2 vanilla beans

1. Pour the sugar into a covered container.

2. Slice the vanilla beans in half lengthwise. Use a small knife to scrape the black gooey interior (the seeds) into the sugar. Stir and then bury the bean pod halves in the sugar. Cover the jar and let stand for at least 1 week and stir before using. The vanilla sugar will keep indefinitely in your pantry.

> **Tip!**
> You can also reuse left-over vanilla pods (from this or another recipe) to make more vanilla sugar. If previously used for steeping in a liquid—as for an ice cream base or custard—be sure to rinse and dry them well before using to make vanilla sugar.

Sweet Pie Crust

Yield: 1 pie crust

This is my favorite sweet dough recipe for pies, tarts, and crostatas. Make the dough, roll it out, and refrigerate or freeze it raw for future use. Or, when you require a prebaked crust, follow the instructions below for baking. You can also freeze prebaked crusts, but keep in mind that they are more fragile and take up more room in the freezer than rolled out raw ones. On the other hand, they do allow you to avoid the hassle of blind baking last-minute.

2 cups all-purpose flour
¼ cup granulated sugar
½ teaspoon fine sea salt

½ cup (1 stick) plus 6 tablespoons very cold unsalted butter, cut into pieces
4 tablespoons ice water
Beans or rice, for blind baking

1. Combine flour, sugar, and salt in a food processor. Add the butter and pulse until pea-size clumps form. With the food processor off, pour 3½ tablespoons of the ice water evenly over the mixture. Pulse until no dry patches remain, taking care that the dough does not form a ball. Grab a handful of dough and squeeze. If the dough will not cohere, add the remaining ½ tablespoon of water and pulse to incorporate. Remove the dough from food processor and form into a ball.

CONTINUED

If you're worried about your pie crust sagging or shrinking, add a large pinch of baking powder to the dough to help the crust expand into the pie pan.

2. Flatten the ball into a disk on a large piece of parchment paper. Place a second piece of parchment paper on top and using a rolling pin, roll into a 13-inch to 14-inch circle. At this point, you can wrap the crust in foil and refrigerator for up to 3 days or freeze for up to 6 months.

3. Fit the dough into a 10-inch fluted tart pan with a removable bottom. To form a thick and sturdy edge, fold the excess dough inward and press against the sides of the tart pan and trim away excess dough. Refrigerate the unbaked crust at least 1 hour or up to 3 days or freeze, well wrapped in foil, for up to 6 months before baking.

4. Once the crust has rested, adjust a rack to the lower third position, and preheat the oven to 400°F. Cover the crust with a sheet of aluminum foil large enough to loosely fold the edges of the foil over edges of the crust. Fill with raw dried beans, rice, or pie weights, and bake for 15 to 20 minutes, or until the dough is no longer shiny (peek under the foil to check).

Brushing an uncooked pie crust with beaten egg—whole egg, yolks, or whites—before pouring in the filling will create a moisture barrier between the crust, and the filling and help keep the crust from getting soggy.

5. Remove the crust from oven. Discard the foil (the cooled beans or rice can be re-used as pie weights) and prick the crust all over with a fork. Return the crust to the oven and bake for 5 to 10 minutes, or until deeply golden Remove from oven and let cool. (If planning to rebake with pie filling, bake only until just beginning to color, as the crust will continue cooking during the second baking.)

6. Store the prebaked crust, well wrapped, in the freezer for at least 3 months or at room temperature for up to 1 week. If filling and rebaking, the crust will recrisp as it bakes. If filling and not baking again, recrisp in a 350°F oven for 5 minutes and cool before using.

Meringue Shell

Yield: 1 meringue shell

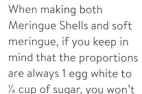

When making both Meringue Shells and soft meringue, if you keep in mind that the proportions are always 1 egg white to ¼ cup of sugar, you won't need a recipe.

4 egg whites, room temperature
Pinch fine sea salt
½ teaspoon cream of tartar

1 cup granulated sugar
½ teaspoon best-quality pure vanilla extract

1. Preheat the oven to 250°F. Draw a 10-inch circle on a piece of parchment paper. Turn the paper over and place on a cookie sheet.

2. Using a stand mixer fitted with the whisk attachment or an electric hand-held set on low speed, beat the room temperature egg whites with the salt for 1 minute, or until frothy. Add the cream of tartar and increase the speed to medium–low. Mix—continuing to slowly increase the mixer speed to medium and then medium–high—until very soft peaks form.

3. With the motor running, add the sugar very, very slowly and, once all the sugar has been added, raise the speed to high, add the vanilla, and beat for 2 to 5 minutes more, or until the meringue is very stiff and glossy.

4. Spoon the meringue onto the traced circle and smooth with a spatula. Shape the meringue a bit like a shallow bowl or soup plate.

5. Place the meringue on the bottom rack of the oven and reduce the temperature to 150°F. Bake for 6 hours and then turn off the oven. Leave the meringue in the closed oven for at least 4 hours or, preferably, overnight. Remove from the oven, cool, and store—in a safe place as meringues are fragile—at room temperature, well-wrapped in foil, for up to 4 months.

It is useful to remember that 8 egg whites equal 1 cup.

Basic Shortbread with Variations

Yield: Approximately 200 (1½-inch round) cookies

This makes enough basic shortbread dough for a huge number of cookies. The exact number will depend on the size. If there is too much dough to use at one time (there probably will be), you can freeze the surplus in one or in multiple packages. Thaw in the fridge before using.

2 cups (4 sticks) unsalted butter, room temperature
1 cup granulated sugar
½ teaspoon fine sea salt

1 large egg, room temperature
2 teaspoons best-quality pure vanilla extract
5 cups sifted all-purpose flour

1. Using a stand mixer fitted with the paddle attachment or an electric hand-held mixer set on medium–high speed, cream the butter, sugar, and salt for 3 to 5 minutes, or until light and fluffy.

2. Add the egg and the vanilla and beat 3 minutes more, scraping down the sides of the bowl once or twice with a rubber spatula.

3. With motor off, add the flour.

4. With the mixer on low speed, mix until just combined.

5. Roll the dough into logs 1½ inches in diameter and 8 inches to 10 inches long. Lightly flouring your hands and the work surface can help. If the dough is too warm to do this easily, refrigerate for about 30 minutes or until it is easy to work with.

6. Wrap the logs in plastic wrap and refrigerate at least 3 hours and up to 3 days (or wrap the logs in foil and freeze for up to 6 months).

Basic shortbread dough is a perfect excuse to get out your cookie cutters! At holiday time, cover fanciful shapes with multi-colored icings and fancy sprinkles.

To avoid flour flying everywhere, add all the flour with the motor turned off, then cover the top of the mixer bowl with a large tea towel for the first few seconds of beating.

CONTINUED

7. Preheat the oven to 350°F. Cut the logs into ⅛-inch to ½-inch slices (depending on how thick you want your cookies) and place on cookie sheets lined with parchment paper.

8. Bake for 10 to 20 minutes, or until slightly colored (timing will depend on the thickness of the cookies). Transfer the cookies to wire racks. When completely cool, store in a covered container for 1 to 2 weeks or freeze for up to 6 months.

As for the variations, the candied ginger is my favorite, but the elegant espresso version is divine with an after-dinner coffee or a cappuccino. And any variety is great solo or added to a cookie platter!

VARIATIONS

Espresso: Replace 10 tablespoons of the flour with 10 tablespoons of finely ground espresso. Use only 1 teaspoon of vanilla extract.

Anise: Add 3 tablespoons of toasted whole anise seed and 1 teaspoon of ground anise seed to the flour. Replace the vanilla with 2 teaspoons of Pernod or another anise-flavored liquor.

Citrus: Add the freshly grated zest of 3 oranges, 4 lemons, or 6 limes and 1 teaspoon of a matching citrus extract. Omit the vanilla.

Ginger: Use only a ½ teaspoon of vanilla and add 2 tablespoons of ground ginger and 1 cup of very finely minced candied ginger.

Chocolate–Chocolate Shortbread

Yield: 35–45 cookies

These cookies are adapted from a Pierre Hermé recipe via Dorie Greenspan. They are soft and chewy—so not technically shortbread—and the best chocolate cookies I know. Because the combination of chocolate and salt is a fave, I've added extra salt. For the original, less salty version, use ¼ rather than ½ teaspoon.

1¼ cups all-purpose flour
⅓ cup Dutch-process cocoa powder
½ teaspoon baking soda
½ teaspoon fine sea salt
½ cup (1 stick) plus 3 tablespoons unsalted butter, room temperature
⅔ cup densely packed dark brown sugar

¼ cup granulated sugar
1 teaspoon best-quality pure vanilla extract
5 ounces best-quality bittersweet or semisweet chocolate, chopped into bits (best-quality semisweet chocolate chips can be substituted)

1. Sift together the flour, cocoa powder, baking soda, and salt.

2. Using a stand mixer fitted with the paddle attachment or an electric handheld mixer set on medium–high speed, cream the butter with the brown and granulated sugars for 3 to 5 minutes, or until creamy.

3. Add the vanilla and beat for 1 to 2 more minutes. Reduce the speed to low, add the dry ingredients and chocolate bits, and mix until just combined. Don't be concerned if the dough looks a little crumbly. For the best texture, work the dough as little as possible once the flour is added.

4. Turn the dough out onto a work surface, gather it together, and divide it in half. Working with one half at a time, shape the dough into logs that are 1½ inches in diameter. Lightly flouring your hands and the work surface will help.

5. Wrap the logs in plastic wrap and refrigerate them for at least 3 hours. (The dough can be refrigerated for up to 3 days or frozen for up to 4 months. If you've frozen the dough, you needn't defrost it completely before baking, but you will need to bake the frozen dough 1 minute longer.)

6. Preheat the oven to 325°F. Line 2 cookie sheets with parchment paper and set aside.

7. Working with a sharp knife, slice the logs into rounds about ⅓-inch thick. (If the cookies break apart when slicing, just squeeze the broken bits back together.) Place on the prepared cookie sheets, leaving at least ¾ of an inch between cookies.

8. Bake 1 sheet at a time for 13 minutes. The cookies won't look done and will not be firm, but that is the way they should be. Let cool on the cookie sheets. Stored in a covered container, the cookies will keep up to 3 days. They can be frozen for up to 1 month.

If you bake the cookies a few minutes longer, when cool, they will end up more like traditional shortbreads—crisp rather than soft and chewy—and can be stored longer, for 2 to 3 weeks, at room temperature.

Peppermint Bark

Yield: 2½ pounds bark

This is virtually the same bark (actually I think it's better) that you can order online for $20 to $30 per pound. It makes an ideal Christmas gift or stocking stuffer, though I'm addicted all year long. Coarsely chopped and served over vanilla or peppermint ice cream, it's to die for. A drizzle of Bitter Chocolate Sauce (p. 302) sends the sundae over the top.

1½ pounds Guittard or other best-quality semisweet chocolate chips or chopped semisweet chocolate

½ pound Guittard or other best-quality white chocolate chips or chopped white chocolate

½ teaspoon peppermint extract

1–2 cups peppermint candy canes, cut into approximate ½-inch pieces

1. Preheat the oven to 250°F and line a 9-inch × 13-inch pan with parchment paper, letting the paper hang over the sides for easy removal. Set aside.

CONTINUED

2. Shake or spread the chocolate chips into an even layer on the parchment paper. Place in the oven for 5 minutes, or until almost melted. Remove from oven, smooth with an offset spatula or knife. Set aside.

3. Melt the white chocolate chips in a double boiler or in a metal bowl set over simmering water (don't let bottom of the bowl touch water), until almost melted. Remove the bowl from the water, add the peppermint extract, and stir until completely melted.

4. Pour melted white chocolate over the still slightly soft chocolate layer and, working quickly, spread to cover. The 2 chocolates may "marble" a bit. If you prefer that they don't, chill chocolate layer before adding the white chocolate. However, if the first layer is too hard, the layers don't properly adhere and sometimes separate when cut into pieces.

5. While the white chocolate is still warm, evenly sprinkle with the candy canes and then use your hands to press the candy into the chocolate.

6. Chill for 30 to 60 minutes, or until both layers are firm. Lift paper out of pan and place on a cutting board.

7. The easiest way to "cut" the bark is to insert the tip of a large heavy knife and apply pressure. The bark will immediately begin to break up. Repeat until the pieces are the desired size.

8. Place the candy in a covered container. Store at room temperature for up to 1 week or in the refrigerator for up to 2 months.

Chocolate–Ginger Biscotti

Yield: About 36 biscotti

I created these biscotti years ago for the original Dean & Deluca grocery store. That gig is long over, but I'm still making the biscotti and everyone still loves them. The combination of dark chocolate and chewy, sweet, and spicy candied ginger is hard to beat.

1 cup granulated sugar

5½ tablespoons unsalted butter, room temperature

2 large whole eggs, room temperature

¼ teaspoon best-quality pure vanilla extract

3 ounces candied ginger, chopped

2½ ounces bittersweet or semisweet chocolate, chopped

2 ounces toasted unsalted macadamia or cashew nuts, coarsely chopped

½ teaspoon baking powder

¼ teaspoon powdered ginger

¼ teaspoon fine sea salt

2⅓ cups all-purpose flour

3 tablespoons unsweetened cocoa powder

7 ounces semisweet chocolate (optional)

2 teaspoons neutral oil, such as canola (optional)

1. Preheat the oven to 350°F.

2. Using a stand mixer fitted with the paddle attachment or an electric handheld mixer set on medium speed, cream the sugar and butter for 3 to 5 minutes, or until light and fluffy.

3. Add the eggs and vanilla and beat 5 minutes more, scraping down the sides of the bowl occasionally with a rubber spatula.

4. Mix the chopped ginger, chopped chocolate, and nuts together in a small bowl. Add them to the batter and beat until combined.

5. Sift the baking powder, powdered ginger, salt, flour, and cocoa powder together onto a piece of waxed paper and gradually add to the batter while beating on low speed. Beat until just combined.

6. Divide the batter into quarters and roll into logs about 1½ inches in diameter. Lightly flouring your hands and the work surface will help, as the dough is sticky.

7. Place the logs at least 2 inches apart on cookie sheets lined with parchment paper and bake for 20 minutes.

8. Remove from the oven. When cool, cut the logs into ½-inch slices and place them back on the cookie sheets. Bake for 5 minutes on each side and transfer to wire racks to cool.

9. Optionally, once the biscotti are completely cool, melt the semisweet chocolate with the oil in a small saucepan set over low heat. One at a time, dip a flat side of each of the biscotti into the chocolate and place on wax paper–lined cookie sheets. Refrigerate until the chocolate is hard.

10. Store in airtight cans for up to 4 weeks at room temperature or in the refrigerator or freezer for at least 4 months.

VARIATION

Orange–Hazelnut Biscotti: Omit both gingers and replace with 1 tablespoon grated orange zest. Use hazelnuts instead of the macadamias or cashews. And add ¼ cup of raisins or currants along with the chopped chocolate.

Tiny Chocolate Chip Cookies

Yield: At least 200 tiny cookies

This is truly a case of less is more. These tiny, bite-sized cookies are infinitely better than the large ones. Or maybe it's a case of more is more as they are incredibly chocolaty with proportionately 4 times as many chocolate chips as in normal Toll House cookies. Remember: It's easier to form the cookies if the dough is very cold; refrigerate for several hours or freeze for an hour or two.

2¼ cups all-purpose flour

1¼ teaspoons fine sea salt

1 teaspoon baking soda

1 cup (2 sticks) unsalted butter, room temperature

1 cup densely packed dark brown sugar

½ cup granulated sugar

1 teaspoon best-quality pure vanilla extract

2 large eggs, room temperature

8 cups (4 [12-ounce] packages) semi-sweet chocolate chips

1. Preheat the oven to 375°F.

2. Sift the flour, salt, and baking soda together onto a piece of waxed paper. Set aside.

3. Using a stand mixer fitted with the paddle attachment or an electric handheld mixer set on medium–high speed, cream the butter and brown and granulated sugars for 3 to 5 minutes, or until light and fluffy. Scrape down the sides of the bowl. Add the vanilla extract and then the eggs and continue to mix about 3 to 5 minutes more, or until fluffy.

4. Add the sifted dry ingredients and the chips and beat on low speed until just combined, scraping down the sides of the bowl as needed.

5. Using a table knife, scoop up small bits of batter—a teaspoon or less per cookie—and place about ½ inch apart on cookie sheets lined with parchment paper. Be sure to include at least 2 or 3 chocolate chips in each cookie cookie. Bake for about 8 minutes, or until golden. Transfer to wire racks to cool.

6. When completely cool, store in a covered container for up to 2 weeks or freeze for up to 6 months.

Sour Cream Coffee Cake

Yield: Approximately 10 servings

I've been making my grandmother's sour cream coffee cake since I was in high school, and on Sunday morning, it's still my favorite treat along with the *New York Times* and a cup of coffee. It's also a great snack and in a pinch, a passable dessert. And it's just the right place to try out your first batch of Vanilla Sugar (p. 293).

For the Topping:

½ cup plus 2 tablespoons granulated sugar

1 tablespoon ground cinnamon

1¼ cups lightly toasted walnuts or pecans, broken into pieces or very roughly chopped

For the Batter

1 cup (2 sticks) unsalted butter, room temperature

1½ cups granulated sugar

3 large eggs, room temperature

1 teaspoon best-quality pure vanilla extract

1 cup sour cream, room temperature

2½ cups sifted cake flour

2½ teaspoons baking powder

½ teaspoon baking soda

½ teaspoon fine sea salt

1. Preheat the oven to 325°F. Grease and flour a 10-inch springform pan and set aside. Mix the topping ingredients together and set aside.

2. Using a stand mixed fitted with the paddle attachment or an electric handheld mixer set on medium–high speed, cream the butter and sugar for 3 to 5 minutes, or until light and fluffy. Add the eggs, 1 at a time, and beat well, scraping down the sides of the bowl as needed.

3. Add the vanilla and then the sour cream. Beat well.

4. Sift the remaining dry ingredients together and then add to the batter. Mix just until combined.

5. Pour half the batter into the prepared pan and smooth. Sprinkle with ½ of the topping. Repeat with the rest of the batter and then the remaining topping.

6. Bake for 40 to 45 minutes, or until a toothpick inserted in the center of the cake comes out clean. Transfer to a wire rack. When the cake is cool, remove it from the pan. Wrap in foil and store at room temperature for up to 24 hours, in the fridge for up to 3 days. or in the freezer for at least 4 months. Serve at room temperature or slightly warmed.

Nut Praline

Yield: About 3 cups

This recipe can be scaled up or down as needed.

1 cup granulated sugar
Large pinch fine sea salt
2 tablespoons water

2 cups toasted walnuts, pecans, skinned hazelnuts, blanched almonds, peanuts, or cashews

1. Lightly grease a sheet pan and set aside.

2. Cook the sugar, salt, and water in a heavy medium saucepan set over medium heat, stirring with a fork, until the sugar dissolves. Stop stirring and, still over the heat, instead swirl the pan occasionally until the caramel is deep gold. Remove from the heat and add nuts, stirring until coated well.

3. Immediately pour the mixture onto the prepared pan and allow to cool completely, at least 30 minutes.

4. Remove the praline from pan (by turning it upside down and hitting it on the counter) and break into pieces.

5. Praline may be eaten as candy or chopped to use as a dessert topping. Store at room temperature for up to 1 week or freeze for at least 6 months.

Bitter Chocolate Sauce

Yield: 1⅓ cups

Drizzle this sauce on grilled fruit—pineapple, peach, or nectarine slices—as well as on ice cream sundaes!

I've been making Andre Soltner's Bitter Chocolate Sauce for years. Though rich, deeply chocolaty, and to die for, compared to caramel and fudge sauces, it's diet food as its major ingredient is water!

1 cup water
¾ cup granulated sugar

½ cup unsweetened cocoa powder
2 tablespoons unsalted butter, cut into pieces

1. Whisk together the water, sugar, and cocoa powder in a medium saucepan.

2. Place the saucepan over medium heat and, bring the mixture to the boil while whisking constantly. Allow to boil gently for 2 minutes while continuing to whisk.

3. Add the butter. Continue to whisk constantly and allow to boil for 3 minutes more. Remove from the heat.

4. Use right away or store. The sauce can be served hot or cold. It can be stored in a covered container in the refrigerator for at least 4 months or frozen for at least 1 year. Reheat over very low heat, stirring frequently, before serving.

Raspberry Sauce

Yield: Approximately 2 strained cups or 3 unstrained cups

2 (10-ounce) bags frozen raspberries, preferably thawed

½ cup granulated sugar, or more to taste

Pinch fine sea salt

Freshly grated zest and freshly squeezed juice of 1 lemon

1. Put all ingredients in a medium saucepan set over medium heat and boil gently, stirring frequently, until the raspberries have lost their shape completely and the sauce tastes good, about 5 minutes. Remove from the heat. Strain if desired.

2. Once cool, taste and adjust lemon and sugar as needed.

3. Cover and refrigerate. The raspberry sauce will keep for at least 2 months. Serve at room temperature.

Caramel Sauce

Yield: Approximately 2 cups

1 cup granulated sugar

½ cup apple cider or water

Large pinch of fine sea salt

⅓ cup heavy cream

4 tablespoons unsalted butter (optional)

1 teaspoon best-quality pure vanilla extract

1. Place the sugar and cider in a medium saucepan set over medium heat and bring to a boil, stirring until sugar dissolves. Simmer for 10 minutes, or until the sauce turns deep amber. Add the salt and slowly add the cream. Sauce may seize up, but leave it on the heat, stirring, and it will turn back into a liquid. Stir until smooth. For a richer sauce, stir in the butter.

2. Remove from the heat. When slightly cooled, stir in the vanilla. Cool completely, cover, and refrigerate. This sauce will keep in the refrigerator for at least 3 months or in the freezer almost indefinitely. Reheat before serving.

Lemon Curd

Yield: Approximately 4 cups

You can make other types of curds by replacing the lemon and juice and zest with either oranges (zest of 4 and juice of 3) or limes (zest of 10 and juice of 8).

2 cups granulated sugar
Freshly grated zest of 6 lemons
10 egg yolks

3 whole eggs
Freshly squeezed juice of 4 lemons
1 cup plus 2 tablespoons heavy cream

1. Stir the sugar together with lemon zest in a large bowl or the bowl of a stand mixer.

2. Using a stand mixed fitted with the paddle attachment or an electric hand-held mixer set on medium–high speed, beat the lemon–sugar with the egg yolks and whole eggs for 3 to 5 minutes, or until light, fluffy and pale yellow, scraping down the sides of the bowl as needed. Stir in the lemon juice.

3. In a large saucepan, heat the cream until it just begins to simmer. While whisking the egg mixture, pour the hot cream into the bowl in a slow stream.

4. Pour the mixture back into the saucepan and bring to a gentle boil over medium heat, stirring constantly. Boil for about 3 minutes, or until very thick and somewhat darkened in color. Pour back into the bowl. Cover with plastic wrap touching the surface of the hot curd, cool, and then refrigerate for at least 6 hours, or until set. The lemon curd will keep in the refrigerator for at least 2 weeks or in the freezer for up to a year.

ACKNOWLEDGEMENTS

Many people have helped me with this book, some with hands-on assistance and some—family members, friends, and students—have listened and offered appreciated encouragement during what turned out to be a process that took much longer than expected. To mention everyone by name is nearly impossible, but a huge thanks to all of you—and hopefully you know who you are! Special thanks to:

Doug Seibold, who gave me this opportunity, and to his entire team at Agate, who were generous with their time and effort as well as flexible and accommodating.

Jessica Easto, my editor whose patience, conscientiousness, good advice, and tireless hours of editing and re-editing were far beyond the call of duty.

Lisa Queen, my agent, and her colleague Sophia Seidner, first for believing so strongly in me and in this book and also for tireless work, ongoing excellent advice, and common sense—and for being readily available when called on.

Gary Duff and Julia Becker for photography. Gary fastidiously photographed the chapter openers and Julia is responsible for additional images. And thanks to both of you for moral support and handholding as well!

Eric Boman for his brilliance in general and brilliant eye in particular.

Alex Kerry who, almost 20 years ago, first suggested that I teach cooking classes. She put a group of friends together that—with the subsequent subgroups, offshoots, and word of mouth add-ons—comprises my student body to this day.

INDEX

Note: Recipes are indicated by **bold** page numbers.

A

Adobo mayonnaise, 37
Advance preparation
    advantages and principles of, 1–7
    tips for, 272
Alcohol
    pantry items, 271
    see also Cognac; Rum
Almonds
    Arugula Salad with Marcona, 141–142, **143**
    Marzipan Cake, 109–110, **114–115**
    Truffled, **291**
Anchovy fillets
    Anchovy Butter, **274**
    Favorite Caesar Salad, 81–83, **84**
    Green Goddess Dressing, **158**
Anise seed
    Moroccan Spice-Crusted Leg of Lamb, 70–73, **75**
    Shortbread Variations, **296**
Apples
    Arugula Salad with Almonds and, 141–142, **143**
    Galette with Rum-Raisin Ice Cream, 59, 61–63, **68–69**
Arugula
    Grilled Seafood and Chorizo Salad, 109–110, **111**
    Mixed Green Salad, 235–239, **248**
    Mixed Lettuce Salad, 253–257, **258**
    Salad with Green Apples and Almonds, 141–142, **143**
Asian dried shrimp
    Lemongrass Bisque and, 179–181, **182–183**
Asian Marinade for Chicken Pieces or Steak, **277**
Asian Salsa Salad, 91–93, **98**
Asparagus
    Green Vegetable Ragout, 13–15, **16**
    Grilled Mimosa, 191–193, **194**
    Lemon–Shallot Vinaigrette with, 219–223, **226**
    Pasta with Green Peas and, 135–137, **139**
Avocados
    Green Goddess Dressing, **158**
    Guacamole Salad, 33–35, **36**

B

Bacon
    Cornbread Stuffing, 235–239, **243–245**
    Soft-Shell Crab Sandwiches, 155–156, **157–158**
    Spinach Salad, 167–170, **171**
    Warm Green Bean Salad with, 117–119, **123**
Baked Alaska, 81–83, **87–89**
Balsamic Vinaigrette, 279
    Marjoram–Balsamic Vinaigrette, **138**
Bananas Foster, 13–15, **21**
Basil
    Corn Salad with Sun-Dried Tomatoes and, 43–45, **51**
    Pesto, **284**
    Tomato–Caper Salsa, **19**
    Tomato Sauce, **283**
    Wild Rice Salad, 91–93, **100**
BBQ Sauce, **284**
Béarnaise Mayonnaise, 25, **29**
    Rib-Eye Steaks with, 23–26, **28–29**
Beef
    about: resting of after cooking, 65
    Asian Marinade for, **277**
    Marinade for Tougher Cuts of, **277**
    Prime Rib Roast with Horseradish Cream Sauce, 253–257, **259–260**
    Rib-Eye Steaks with Béarnaise Mayonnaise, 23–26, **28–29**
    Shanghai Short Ribs, 179–181, **184–185**
Beets, Roasted with Carrots, **77**
Belgian endive
    Mixed Green Salad, 235–239, **248**
    Mixed Lettuce Salad, 253–257, **258**
    Salad of Mixed Baby Greens, 59, 61–63, **63**
Bell peppers
    Roast of Root Vegetables and, 59, 61–63, **67**
    Stir-Fried Vegetables, **183**
Beurre Blanc, **282**
Beurre composé (compound butter), **274**
Biscotti
    Chocolate–Ginger, **298–299**
    Orange–Hazelnut, **299**
Biscuits, Cheddar and Chive, 43–45, **52**
Bitter Chocolate Sauce, **302**
    Fané, 167–170, **177**
Black Lentil and Moroccan Preserved Lemon Salad with Roasted Beets and Carrots, 70–73, **76–77**

Bok choy, in Stir-Fried Vegetables, **183**
Boozy Bananas Foster, 13–15, **21**
Broccoli, in Potato and Garlic Smash, 13–15, **20**
Brownies, Golden Coconut–Chocolate Chunk, 125–128, **133**
Butter
    about: storing of, 270
    Beurre Blanc, **282**
    Fresh Herb, **274**
Buttermilk
    Cornbread, **245**
    Crème fraîche, **31**
    Irish Brown Bread, 125–128, **132**
    Soft-Shell Crab Sandwiches with Dressing, 155–156, **157–158**

C

Cabbage
    Gingered, and Tomato Slaw, 155–156, **159**
    Sweet 'n' Spicy Salad, 179–181, **187**
    Vietnamese Summer Rolls, 91–93, **94–95**
Caesar Salad, 81–83, **84**
Cakes
    Caramelized Plum and Rosemary Polenta Pound Cake, 201–202, 204, **210–211**
    Coconut, 219–223, **231–232**
    Coffee Ice Cream Baked Alaska, 81–83, **87–89**
    Devil's Food, 253–257, **264–265**
    Venetian Polenta, 141–142, **145**
Calamari, in Grilled Seafood and Chorizo Salad, 109–110, **111**
Capers
    Asparagus Mimosa, 191–193, **194**
    Caramelized Cauliflower with Crispy, 253–257, **263**
    Tomato– Salsa, **19**
Caramel Sauce, **303**
    Fané, 167–170, **177**
Carrots
    Chicken Stock, **288**
    Duck Magrets, 167–170, **172–173**
    Roasted Beets and, **77**
    Root Vegetables and Bell Peppers, 59, 61–63, **67**
Cauliflower
    Caramelized, with Crispy Capers, 253–257, **263**

Roasted, and Watercress Salad, 125–128, **129**

Celeriac
  Cornbread Stuffing, 235–239, **243–245**
  Root Vegetables and Bell Peppers, 59, 61–63, **67**

Celery
  Chicken Stock, **288**
  Green Pea and Celery Soup, 219–223, **224**
  Tomato–Cumin Soup, 70–73, **74**

Chard, in Cornbread Stuffing with Wilted Greens, 235–239, **243–245**

Cheddar and Chive Biscuits, 43–45, **52**

Chicken
  about: resting of after cooking, 65
  Asian Marinade for, **277**
  Basic Marinade for, **277**
  Roast, with 40 Cloves of Garlic, 59, 61–63, **64–65**
  Sweet 'n' Hot Malaysian, 91–93, **96–97**

Chicken Stock
  Basic, **288**
  Tomato–Cumin Soup, 70–73, **74**

Chili garlic paste
  Favorite BBQ Sauce, **284**
  Sweet and Spicy Chili Dipping Sauce, **95**

Chili peppers
  Chipotle-Citrus Turkey Paillards, 33–35, **37**
  Rice Casserole with Cheese and, 33–35, **39**
  Stir-Fried Vegetables, **183**
  Sweet 'n' Spicy Cabbage Salad, 179–181, **187**

Chives
  Cheddar and Chive Biscuits, 43–45, **52**
  Corn Salad with Sun-Dried Tomatoes and Herbs, 43–45, **51**
  Tomato–Cumin Soup, 70–73, **74**

Chocolate
  Chocolate Chip Cookies, **300**
  –Chocolate Shortbread, **296–297**
  –Espresso Soufflés, 219–223, **229–230**
  Fané, 167–170, **177**
  –Ginger Biscotti, **298–299**
  Golden Coconut– Brownies, 125–128, **133**
  Mexican Mousse, 33–35, **40**
  Molten Chocolate Cakes, 23–26, **31**
  Peppermint Bark, **297–298**

Chorizo
  Cornbread Stuffing with, 235–239, **243–245**
  Seafood Salad with, 109–110, **111**

Cilantro
  Asian Salsa Salad, 91–93, **98**

-Citrus Turkey Paillards, 33–35, **37**
Guacamole Salad, 33–35, **36**
Mango and Plum Salsa with, 33–35, **38**
-Mint Pesto, **49**
Rice Casserole, 33–35, **39**
Stir-Fried Vegetables, **183**
Sweet 'n' Spicy Cabbage Salad, 179–181, **187**
Tomato–Cumin Soup, 70–73, **74**
Vietnamese Summer Rolls, 91–93, **94–95**
Yogurt Soup, 43–45, **46**

Cioppino with Crusty Toasts and Garlic Mayonnaise, 81–83, **85–86**

Clams, in Cioppino, 81–83, **85–86**

Cocoa powder
  Bitter Chocolate Sauce, **302**
  Chocolate–Chocolate Shortbread, **296–297**

Coconut
  –Chocolate Chunk Brownies, 125–128, **133**
  Layer Cake, 219–223, **231–232**

Cod, with Tomato–Caper Salsa, 13–15, **18–19**

Coffee Cake, Sour Cream, **301**

Coffee Ice Cream Baked Alaska, 81–83, **87–89**

Cognac
  Duck Magrets, 167–170, **172–173**
  Mexican Chocolate Mousse, 33–35, **40**
  Pan Gravy, 235–239, **242**
  Plum and Rosemary Polenta Pound Cake, 201–202, 204, **210–211**
  Venetian Polenta Cake, 141–142, **145**

"Coins"
  Curry, **290–291**
  Parmesan–Rosemary, **289–290**

Condiments, **273–277**

Cookies, **295–296**
  Chocolate Chip, **300**
  Chocolate–Chocolate Shortbread, **296–297**

Cooking class favorite meals, 54–57
  recipes, 58–101

Cornbread, **245**
  Cornbread Stuffing, 235–239, **243–245**

Cornmeal
  Caramelized Plum and Rosemary Polenta Pound Cake, 201–202, 204, **210–211**
  Corn Pudding, 191–193, **197**
  Soft-Shell Crab Sandwiches, 155–156, **157–158**
  Venetian Polenta Cake, 141–142, **145**

Corn
  Pudding, 191–193, **197**

Salad with Sun-Dried Tomatoes and Herbs, 43–45, **51**

Country Toasts, 59, 61–63, **66**

Cranberry–Tangerine Relish, 235–239, **246**

Crème Caramel, Pumpkin, 235–239, **249**

Crème Fraîche
  about: making, **31**
  Ginger-Caramelized Pears with Vanilla, 179–181, **188**
  Horseradish Cream Sauce, **260**
  Molten Chocolate Cakes, 23–26, **31**

Crostata Crust, **122**

Cucumbers
  Wasabi Rémoulade with Radish and, **185**
  Yogurt Soup with, 43–45, **46**

Cumin
  Moroccan Spice-Crusted Leg of Lamb, 70–73, **75**
  Sweet 'n' Hot Malaysian Chicken, 91–93, **96–97**
  Tomato–Cumin Soup, 70–73, **74**
  Yogurt Soup with Herbs, Cucumber, Feta and, 43–45, **46**

Curds, Lemon and variations, **304**

Curry powder
  BBQ Sauce, **284**
  Curry Butter, **274**
  Curry Coins, **290–291**
  Curry Mayonnaise, **275**

D

Dates, in Spinach Salad with Bacon, 167–170, **171**

Daytime entertaining meals, 102–107
  recipes, 108–159

Delmonico Potatoes Gratin, 201–202, 204, **208–209**

Desserts
  Frozen Lemon Meringue Bombe, 91–93, **101**
  Raspberry–Nectarine Streusel Tart, 70–73, **79**
  see also Cakes; Cookies; Ice Cream

Devil's Food Layer Cake, 253–257, **264–265**

Dill
  Homemade Gravlax, 125–128, **130–131**
  Roast Potato and Feta Frittata with, 147–149, **150**

Dinner for 8 meals, 162–165
  recipes, 166–211

Dinner in a Flash meals, 8–11
  recipes, 12–53

Dressing, Sweet 'n' Spicy, **187**. *See also* Vinaigrettes

Duck Magrets with Raspberry–Port Sauce, 167–170, **172–173**

E

Eggs

about: cup equivalents of whites, 295; folding whipped, 175; room temperature, 150; separating of, 174; whipping whites, 88

Basic Mayonnaise, **275**

Béarnaise Mayonnaise, **29**

Cheese, Garlic, and Herb Soufflé, 167–170, **174–175**

Chocolate–Espresso Soufflés, 219–223, **229–230**

Espresso coffee

BBQ Sauce, **284**

Chocolate– Soufflés, 219–223, **229–230**

Mexican Chocolate Mousse, 33–35, **40**

Shortbread Variations, **296**

F

Fané, 167–170, **177**

Fennel bulbs

Arugula Salad, 141–142, **143**

Chicken with 40 Cloves of Garlic, 59, 61–63, **64–65**

Mixed Green Salad, 235–239, **248**

Mixed Lettuce Salad, 253–257, **258**

Pork Loin with Caramelized, 201–202, 204, **206–207**

Spinach Salad, 167–170, **171**

Tomato–Caper Salsa, **19**

Fennel seeds

Malaysian Chicken, 91–93, **96–97**

Moroccan Preserved Lemons, **276–277**

Feta cheese

Potato Frittata, 147–149, **150**

Spinach Salad, 167–170, **171**

Yogurt Soup with, 43–45, **46**

Figs, Pork Loin with Caramelized, 201–202, 204, **206–207**

Fish

about: roasting of, 14; storing of, 271

Basic Marinade for, **278**

see also specific fish and shellfish

Flour

about: making cake flour, 265; making self-rising flour, 132

Fricassee of Mixed Mushrooms and Fresh Herbs, 23–26, **27**

Frisée

Arugula Salad, 141–142, **143**

Mixed Baby Greens, 59, 61–63, **63**

Mixed Lettuce Salad, 253–257, **258**

Frittata, Roast Potato and Feta, 147–149, **150**

Frozen Lemon Meringue Bombe, 91–93, **101**

G

Garlic

Cheese, Garlic, and Herb Soufflé, 167–170, **174–175**

Cornbread Stuffing with Wilted Greens, Chorizo, and Roasted, 235–239, **243–245**

Garlic Oil, **273**

Ginger–Garlic Mayonnaise, **275**

Potato, Veggie, and Garlic Smash, 13–15, **20**

Roast Chicken with 40 Cloves of, 59, 61–63, **64–65**

Garlic Mayonnaise, **275**

Cioppino with Crusty Toasts and, 81–83, **85–86**

Get a Head Start boxes, about, 6

Ginger

Asian Marinade for Chicken Pieces or Steak, **277**

BBQ Sauce, **284**

Cabbage and Tomato Slaw, 155–156, **159**

-Caramelized Pears with Vanilla Crème Fraîche, 179–181, **188**

Chocolate– Biscotti, **298–299**

Cranberry–Tangerine Relish, 235–239, **246**

Shanghai Beef Short Ribs, 179–181, **184–185**

Shortbread Variations, **296**

Shrimp and Lemongrass Bisque, 179–181, **182–183**

Sweet 'n' Hot Malaysian Chicken, 91–93, **96–97**

Sweet Potato– Gratin, 235–239, **247**

Vinaigrette, **100**

Ginger–Garlic Mayonnaise, **275**

Whiskey-Marinated Salmon with, 191–193, **195**

Goat cheese, Caramelized Onion Crostata and, 117–119, **121–122**

Gratins

Creamed Spinach, 253–257, **262**

Delmonico Potato, 201–202, 204, **208–209**

Sweet Potato–Ginger, 235–239, **247**

Gravlax with Sweet Mustard–Dill Sauce, 125–128

Gravy

Pan, for Roast Turkey, 235–239, **242**

variations, **242**

Green beans

Green Vegetable Ragout, 13–15, **16**

Warm, and Bacon Salad with Vinaigrette, 117–119, **123**

Green Goddess Dressing, **158**

Green Pea, Lettuce, and Celery Soup, 219–223, **224**

Green Vegetable Ragout, 13–15, **16**

Gruyère cheese

Cauliflower and Watercress Salad with, 125–128, **129**

Cheese, Garlic, and Herb Soufflé, 167–170, **174–175**

Delmonico Potatoes Gratin, 201–202, 204, **208–209**

Guacamole Salad, 33–35, **36**

H

Haricot verts, in Green Vegetable Ragout, 13–15, **16**

Hazelnut Vinaigrette, **280**

Mixed Lettuce Salad with, 253–257, **258**

Herbs

Country Toasts, 59, 61–63, **66**

Fricassee of Mixed Mushrooms and, 23–26, **27**

Herb Butter, **274**

Herb Mayonnaise, **275**

Pan Gravy, **242**

Scalloped Potatoes with, 219–223, **227–228**

see also specific herbs

Holiday meals, 212–217

recipes, 218–265

Horseradish Cream Sauce, **260**

I

Ice cream

Boozy Bananas Foster, 13–15, **21**

Coffee Ice Cream Baked Alaska, 81–83, **87–89**

Fané, 167–170, **177**

Mini Molten Chocolate Cakes, 23–26, **31**

Mixed Berry Pavlova, 191–193, **198**

Raspberry–Nectarine Streusel Tart with, 70–73, **79**

Rum-Raisin, **69**

store-bought with *Amaretti* and Bitter Chocolate Sauce, 118

Irish Brown Bread, 125–128, **132**

J

Jack cheese, Rice Casserole with, 33–35, **39**

Jalapeño peppers
    Guacamole Salad, 33–35, **36**
    Malaysian Chicken, 91–93, **96–97**
    Mango and Mint Salsa, **276**
    Mango and Plum Salsa, 33–35, **38**
Jicama, in Asian Salsa Salad, 91–93, **98**
Juniper berries, in Marinated Olives, **292**

K

Kale Purée, **152**
    Creamy Green Polenta, 147–149, **151**
Ketjap manis, in Sweet 'n' Hot Malaysian
        Chicken, 91–93, **96–97**
Key Lime Pie, 43–45, **53**
Kitchen staples, tools, and extras, 267
    alcohol, 271
    buying in bulk and storing of, 270
    freezer, 6–7, 269, 271
    herbs, 269
    microplane graters, 98
    nonstick pans, 28
    pantry, 268, 270
    refrigerator, 268, 271

L

Lamb
    Butterflied Moroccan Spice-Crusted
        Leg of Lamb, 70–73, **75**
    Marinade for, **277**
    Mustard-Coated, 219–223, **225**
Lemon Curd, **304**
    Frozen Lemon Meringue Bombe,
        91–93, **101**
Lemongrass
    Shanghai Beef Short Ribs, 179–181,
        184–185
    Shrimp Bisque and, 179–181, **182–183**
    Sweet 'n' Spicy Dressing, **187**
Lemons and lemon juice
    about: extract of, 98
    Black Lentil and Moroccan Preserved
        Lemon Salad, 70–73, **76–77**
    Lemon Curd, **304**
Lemon–Shallot Vinaigrette, **281**
    Arugula Salad with Green Apples and
        Marcona Almonds, 141–142, **143**
    Asparagus with, 219–223, **226**
    Grilled Seafood and Chorizo Salad
        with, 109–110, **111**
Lentils, Black, and Moroccan Preserved
        Lemon Salad, 70–73, **76–77**
Lettuce, in Green Pea and Celery Soup
        and, 219–223, **224**. *See also* Salads
Limes and lime juice
    about: extract of, 98
    Key Lime Pie, 43–45, **53**

M

Mangoes
    Asian Salsa Salad, 91–93, **98**
    Mango and Mint Salsa, **276**
    Mango and Plum Salsa, 33–35, **38**
    Sweet 'n' Spicy Cabbage Salad,
        179–181, **187**
Marinades
    Asian, for Chicken or Steak, **277**
    Basic, for Lamb, Chicken, Steak, **277**
    Basic, for Shrimp, Scallops, Fish, **278**
Marinated Olives, **292**
Marjoram–Balsamic Vinaigrette, **138**
Marzipan
    Marzipan Cake with Mixed Berries,
        109–110, **114–115**
Mascarpone cheese, in Creamy Green
        Polenta, 147–149, **151–152**
Mayonnaise
    about: flavoring of, 25; repairing
        breakage of, 29; temperature of
        ingredients for, 29
    Adobo, 37
    Basic, and variations, **275**
    Béarnaise, 25, **29**
    Gingered Cabbage and Tomato Slaw,
        155–156, **159**
    Horseradish Cream Sauce, **260**
    Wasabi Rémoulade, **185**
Meringue Shell, **294–295**
    Fané, 167–170, **177**
    Frozen Lemon Meringue Bombe,
        91–93, **101**
    Mixed Berry Pavlova, 191–193, **198**
Mexican Chocolate Mousse, 33–35, **40**
Mint
    Asian Salsa Salad, 91–93, **98**
    Cilantro– Pesto, 49
    Lentil and Moroccan Preserved Lemon
        Salad, 70–73, **76–77**
    Mango and Mint Salsa, **276**
    Mango and Plum Salsa, 33–35, **38**
    Salad of Mixed Baby Greens, 59, 61–63,
        63
    Sweet 'n' Spicy Cabbage Salad,
        179–181, **187**
    Vietnamese Summer Rolls, 91–93,
        94–95
    Wild Rice Salad, 91–93, **100**
    Yogurt Soup, 43–45, **46**
Molten Chocolate Cakes, 23–26, **31**
Monkfish, in Cioppino, 81–83, **85–86**
Moroccan Preserved Lemons, **276–277**
    Salad with Roasted Beets and Carrots,
        70–73, **76–77**
Moroccan Spice-Crusted Leg of Lamb,
        70–73, **75**

Mousse, Rich and Easy Mexican
        Chocolate, 33–35, **40**
Mushrooms
    Fricassee of, with Herbs, 23–26, **27**
    Pan Gravy, **242**
    Risotto, 141–142, **144**
    Stir-Fried Vegetables, **183**
Mushy Peas, 167–170, **176**
Mussels, in Cioppino, 81–83, **85–86**
Mustard-Coated Leg of Lamb, 219–223,
        225

N

Nectarines, Raspberry– Streusel Tart,
        70–73, **79**
Nuts
    about: toasting of, 114
    Gourmet Trail Mix, **289**
    Nut Praline, **302**
    Scones with Crème Fraîche and Jam,
        147–149, **153**
    Sweet 'n' Spicy Cabbage Salad,
        179–181, **187**
    see also specific nuts

O

Oats, in Irish Brown Bread, 125–128, **132**
Oils, storing of, 270
Olives, Marinated, **292**
Onions
    Caramelized Onion and Goat Cheese
        Crostata, 117–119, **121–122**
    Chicken Stock, **288**
    Pork Loin, 201–202, 204, **206–207**
    Red Onion Confit, 191–193, **196**
    Roast of Potatoes and Red, 23–26, **30**
    Scalloped Potatoes with, 219–223,
        227–228
Oranges and orange juice
    about: extract of, 98
    Cilantro–Mint Pesto, **49**
    Orange–Hazelnut Biscotti, **299**
Order of Preparation charts, about, 5–6

P

Parmesan cheese
    Arugula Salad, 141–142, **143**
    Creamy Green Polenta, 147–149,
        151–152
    Delmonico Potatoes Gratin, 201–202,
        204, **208–209**
    Favorite Caesar Salad, 81–83, **84**
    Pesto, **284**
    –Rosemary Coins, **289–290**

Parsnips, in Roast of Root Vegetables, 59, 61–63, **67**

Pasta with Asparagus, Green Peas, and Lemon, 135–137, **139**

Peanuts, in Wild Rice Salad, 91–93, **100**

Pears
    Ginger-Caramelized, with Crème Fraîche, 179–181, **188**
    Mixed Lettuce Salad with, 253–257, **258**
    Salad of Mixed Baby Greens with, 59, 61–63, **63**

Peas
    Baked Pasta with Asparagus, Lemon and, 135–137, **139**
    Green Vegetable Ragout, 13–15, **16**
    Lettuce and Celery Soup and, 219–223, **224**
    Mushy, 167–170, **176**

Pecan Tart, 235–239, **251**

Pecan Vinaigrette, **280**

Peppermint Bark, **297–298**

Pepper Mix, **273**

Peppers, hot, 38. *See also* Chili peppers; Jalapeño peppers

Pesto
    Cilantro–Mint, **49**
    Favorite, **284**

Pies
    about: preventing soggy crust, 294
    Key Lime, 43–45, **53**
    Sweet Crust for, **293–294**

Pineapple, in Asian Salsa Salad, 91–93, **98**

Plums
    Caramelized, and Rosemary Polenta Pound Cake, 201–202, 204, **210–211**
    Mango Salsa and, 33–35, **38**
    Prepared, **211**

Polenta
    about: instant, 151
    Caramelized Plum and Rosemary Pound Cake, 201–202, 204, **210–211**
    Creamy Green, 147–149, **151–152**
    Pan-Fried Mixed Pepper, 109–110, **112–113**
    Venetian Cake with Dried Fruit and Cognac, 141–142, **145**

Pomegranate, in Mixed Lettuce Salad with Vinaigrette, 253–257, **258**

Popovers, Fresh-Herbed, 253–257, **261**

Pork
    about: resting of after cooking, 65
    Loin with Figs and Fennel, 201–202, 204, **206–207**

Potatoes
    Delmonico Gratin, 201–202, 204, **208–209**
    Potato, Veggie, and Garlic Smash, 13–15, **20**
    Roast, and Feta Frittata, 147–149, **150**
    Roast of Red Onions and, 23–26, **30**
    Scalloped, with Onions, Tomatoes, Anchovies, and Herbs, 219–223, **227–228**

Puff Pastry
    about: egg wash for, 69; using frozen, 61
    Caramelized Apple Galette, 59, 61–63, **68–69**

Pumpkin Crème Caramel, 235–239, **249**

R

Radicchio, in Mixed Green Salad, 235–239, **248**

Radishes, Wasabi Rémoulade with Cucumber and, **185**

Raisins
    Arugula Salad, 141–142, **143**
    Rum-Raisin Ice Cream, **69**

Raspberries
    Almond Marzipan Cake with, 109–110, **114–115**
    Duck Magrets with –Port Sauce, 167–170, **172–173**
    Mixed Berry Pavlova, 191–193, **198**
    –Nectarine Streusel Tart, 70–73, **79**
    Raspberry Sauce, **303**

Red Onion Confit, 191–193, **196**

Rice
    Casserole with Cheese and Chilies, 33–35, **39**
    Mushroom Risotto, 141–142, **144**
    Vietnamese Summer Rolls, 91–93, **94–95**
    Wild, Salad with Ginger Vinaigrette, 91–93, **100**

Risotto, Mixed Mushroom, 141–142, **144**

Root Vegetables and Bell Peppers, Roasted, 59, 61–63, **67**

Roquefort cheese, Salad of Mixed Baby Greens with Pears and, 59, 61–63, **63**

Rosemary
    Caramelized Plum and Rosemary Polenta Pound Cake, 201–202, 204, **210–211**
    Mustard-Coated Leg of Lamb, 219–223, **225**
    Parmesan– Coins, **289–290**
    Roast of Potatoes and Red Onions, 23–26, **30**

Rum
    Boozy Bananas Foster, 13–15, **21**
    Pumpkin Crème Caramel, 235–239, **249**
    Rum-Raisin Ice Cream, **69**

S

Salads
    Arugula, 141–142, **143**
    Asian Salsa, 91–93, **98**
    Black Lentil and Moroccan Preserved Lemon, 70–73, **76–77**
    Caesar, 81–83, **84**
    Guacamole, 33–35, **36**
    Mixed Baby Greens, 59, 61–63, **63**
    Mixed Green, 235–239, **248**
    Mixed Lettuce with Pears, 253–257, **258**
    Wild Rice, with Ginger Vinaigrette, 91–93, **100**

Salmon
    Homemade Gravlax with Sweet Mustard–Dill Sauce, 125–128, **130–131**
    Whiskey-Marinated, with Ginger–Garlic Mayonnaise, 191–193, **195**

Salsa
    Mango and Mint, **276**
    Mango and Plum, 33–35, **38**
    Tomato–Caper, **19**

Sandwiches
    about: tips for, 107
    Soft-Shell Crab, 155–156, **157–158**

Sauces
    BBQ, **284**
    Beurre Blanc, **282**
    Bitter Chocolate, **302**
    Caramel, **303**
    Horseradish Cream, **260**
    Raspberry, **303**
    Sweet and Spicy Chili Dipping, **95**
    Tartar, **275**
    Tomato, **283**
    see also Pesto

Scallions
    Potato and Feta Frittata with, 147–149, **150**
    Stir-Fried Vegetables, **183**
    Warm Green Bean and Bacon Salad, 117–119, **123**

Scalloped Potatoes with Onions, Tomatoes, Anchovies, and Herbs, 219–223, **227–228**

Scallops
    Basic Marinade for, **278**
    Seared, with Cilantro–Mint Pesto, 43–45, **48–49**

Scones, with Crème Fraîche and Jam, 147–149, **153**
Shanghai Beef Short Ribs, 179–181, **184–185**
Shortbread
    Basic, with Variations, **295–296**
    Chocolate–Chocolate, **296–297**
    see also Cookies
Shrimp
    about: deveining and butterflying of, 110
    Basic Marinade for, **278**
    Cioppino, 81–83, **85–86**
    Lemongrass Bisque and, 179–181, **182–183**
    Seafood and Chorizo Salad, 109–110, **111**
    Vietnamese Summer Rolls, 91–93, **94–95**
Snacks, **289–292**
Soft-shell crabs
    about: storing and cleaning of, 157
    Sandwiches with Bacon and Green Goddess Dressing, 155–156, **157–158**
Soufflés
    about: timing and, 221
    Cheese, Garlic, and Herb, 167–170, **174–175**
    Chocolate–Espresso, 219–223, **229–230**
Soups
    about: store-bought bases for, 287
    Cold Yogurt, 43–45, **46**
    Green Pea, Lettuce, and Celery, 219–223, **224**
    Shrimp and Lemongrass Bisque, 179–181, **182–183**
    Tomato–Cumin, 70–73, **74**
Sour cream
    Coffee Cake, **301**
    Rice Casserole, 33–35, **39**
    Tomato–Cumin Soup, 70–73, **74**
Spices, toasting of, 37
Spinach
    Creamed Gratin, 253–257, **262**
    Potato, Veggie, and Garlic Smash, 13–15, **20**
    Wilted Salad, 167–170, **171**
Squid, in Cioppino, 81–83, **85–86**
Stir-Fried Vegetables, **183**
    Shrimp and Lemongrass Bisque with, 179–181, **182–183**
Stocks
    about: making and storing, 74, 285–287
    Basic Chicken, **288**
Strawberries, in Mixed Berry Pavlova, 191–193, **198**

Sugar snap peas
    Green Vegetable Ragout, 13–15, **16**
    Stir-Fried Vegetables, **183**
Sun-dried tomatoes, in Corn Salad with Herbs, 43–45, **51**
Sweet and Spicy Chili Dipping Sauce, **95**
Sweet Mustard–Dill Sauce, **131**
Sweet 'n' Hot Malaysian Chicken, 91–93, **96–97**
Sweet 'n' Spicy Cabbage Salad, 179–181, **187**
Sweet Pie Crust, in Candied Pecan Tart, 235–239, **251**
Sweet Potato–Ginger Gratin, 235–239, **247**
Sweets, **293–304**

T
Tangerine juice, Cranberry– Relish, 235–239, **246**
Tartar Sauce, **275**
Tomatoes, fresh
    –Caper Salsa, **19**
    Cauliflower and Watercress Salad, **111**
    Cioppino, 81–83, **85–86**
    –Cumin Soup, 70–73, **74**
    Gingered Cabbage and Slaw, 155–156, **159**
    Grilled Seafood and Chorizo Salad, 109–110
    Guacamole Salad, 33–35, **36**
    Heirloom Salad, 135–137, **138**
    Scalloped Potatoes, 219–223, **227–228**
    Shrimp and Lemongrass Bisque, 179–181, **182–183**
    Soft-Shell Crab Sandwiches, 155–156, **157–158**
Tomatoes, sun-dried, Fresh Corn Salad with, 43–45, **51**
Tomato Sauce, Quick, **283**
Trail Mix, **289**
Treviso, in Roasted Cauliflower and Watercress Salad, 125–128, **129**
Truffle Butter, **274**
    Mixed Mushroom Risotto, 141–142, **144**
    Pan Gravy variations, **242**
Truffled Almonds, **291**
Truffle Vinaigrette, **280**
Turkey
    about: thawing of, 237
    Chipotle-Citrus Paillards, 33–35, **37**
    Roast, with Pan Gravy, 235–239, **240–242**

V
Vanilla Sugar, **293**
Vegetables
    about: cooking warm, 16; keeping green, 123; roasting of, 30; storing of, 271
    see also specific vegetables
Venetian Polenta Cake with Dried Fruit and Cognac, 141–142, **145**
Vietnamese Summer Rolls with Dipping Sauce, 91–93, **94–95**
Vinaigrettes
    Essential, **279**
    Ginger, **100**
    Lemon–Shallot, **281**
    Marjoram–Balsamic, **138**
    Pomegranate–Hazelnut, **258**
    Truffle, **280**
    Walnut, Hazelnut, or Pecan, **280**

W
Walnuts
    Cauliflower and Watercress Salad with, 125–128, **129**
    Parmesan–Rosemary Coins, **289–290**
    Pesto, **284**
    Salad of Mixed Baby Greens, 59, 61–63, **63**
    Sour Cream Coffee Cake, **301**
Walnut Vinaigrette, **280**
Wasabi Remoulade, Shanghai Beef Short Ribs with, 179–181, **184–185**
Watercress
    Mixed Baby Greens Salad, 59, 61–63, **63**
    Roasted Cauliflower Salad, 125–128, **129**
    Soft-Shell Crab Sandwiches, 155–156, **157–158**

Y
Yams, in Roast of Root Vegetables, 59, 61–63, **67**
Yogurt
    Rice Casserole, 33–35, **39**
    Roast of Root Vegetables and Bell Peppers, 59, 61–63, **67**
    Soup with Fresh Herbs, Cucumber, Cumin, and Feta, 43–45, **46**
    Tomato–Cumin Soup, 70–73, **74**

Z
Zucchini, in Stir-Fried Vegetables, **183**

ABOUT THE AUTHOR

Gail Monaghan is a food writer, editor, and cooking teacher who lives and works in New York City. She writes regular features for the "Off Duty" section of the Wall Street Journal, hosts the *Wall Street Journal* Digital Network web series "Cooking Confidential with Gail Monaghan," and has been a regular guest on ABC's *The Chew*. Monaghan's writing has appeared in *O, The Oprah Magazine, Food and Wine, Martha Stewart Living*, and the *New York Times*, among other places. She has written several cookbooks, including *Perfect Picnics for All Seasons, The Some Like It Hot Cookbook, Lost Desserts*, and *The Entrées*. She has edited others, including James Beard Award–winning chef Jeremiah Tower's cookbook *Jeremiah Tower Cooks* and Lora Zarubin's Julia Child Award–winning *I Am Almost Always Hungry*. Find her at www.gailmonaghan.com.